SCRAP THEORY

SCRAP THEORY

REPRODUCTIVE INJUSTICE IN THE BLACK FEMINIST IMAGINATION

Mali D. Collins

THE OHIO STATE UNIVERSITY PRESS
COLUMBUS

Copyright © 2025 by The Ohio State University.
All rights reserved.

Library of Congress Cataloging-in-Publication Data
Names: Collins, Mali D., author
Title: Scrap theory : reproductive injustice in the Black feminist imagination / Mali D. Collins.
Description: Columbus : The Ohio State University Press, [2025] | Includes bibliographical references and index. | Summary: "Examines works documenting Black mother-child separation, centering them within reproductive and archival justice movements to illustrate how creative work plays a crucial role in processing racial and maternal trauma. Considers the writings of Margaret Walker, Toni Cade Bambara, M. NourbeSe Philip, Gwendolyn Brooks, and Edwidge Danticat, the critical activism of Erica Garner, and visual/material art by Samaria Rice and Elizabeth Catlett"—Provided by publisher.
Identifiers: LCCN 2025007391 | ISBN 9780814215890 hardback | ISBN 0814215890 hardback | ISBN 9780814284162 ebook | ISBN 0814284167 ebook
Subjects: LCSH: African American mothers—Social conditions | African American children—Violence against | Reproductive rights—Social aspects | American literature—African American authors | Haitian American authors—Criticism and interpretation | Women, Black—Political activity—United States | Visual communication in art | Feminist theory
Classification: LCC E185.86 .C5818 2025 | DDC 306.874/308996073—dc23/eng/20250325
LC record available at https://lccn.loc.gov/2025007391

Other identifiers: ISBN 9780814259474 (paperback) | ISBN 0814259472 (paperback)

Cover design by Ashley Muehlbauer
Text composition by Stuart Rodriguez
Type set in Minion Pro

For Sanu, Cuba, and Sania
And all the waterbearers unborn and not yet born

CONTENTS

List of Illustrations		viii
Acknowledgments		ix
Prologue	Ida's Story	xi
INTRODUCTION	Black Maternal Dispossession in the Age of Black Lives Matter	1
CHAPTER 1	The Fictional Archive of Disappearance	28
CHAPTER 2	Margaret Walker, *Jubilee,* and the Fight for Black Feminist Historicity in *Alexander v. Haley*	59
CHAPTER 3	The Corporal Archive of Separation in Contemporary Black Women's Cultural Production	90
CHAPTER 4	Refused Memorials and the Black Feminist Archival Praxis of Samaria Rice	110
CONCLUSION	The Black Maternal Superbody	135
EPILOGUE	The Infinitude of Black Motherhood	147
Bibliography		151
Index		167

ILLUSTRATIONS

FIGURE 1	"Bill of Sale for Charlotte and Her Daughter Kate to John Rouzee"	17
FIGURE 2	*Objects of Care: Material Memorial for Tamir Rice*	114
FIGURE 3	*Objects of Care: Material Memorial for Tamir Rice* plaque	115

ACKNOWLEDGMENTS

Thank you first to all my ancestors and my guides for their unconditional love and support.

Zenzele Isoke: Thank you for honoring me in all that I am. I am indebted to you and pass on your love to the next Black girl who wanders into my office. Jennifer C. Nash worked hard on my behalf when she did not know me. Thank you for believing in me. Tanisha Ford and Tiffany Gill, thank you for your generosity and encouragement. Frank Wilderson for stoking my rebellion. There are editors and writers who encouraged me early on who probably don't even know my name anymore. One of them is Jenée Desmond Harris. Thank you for encouraging me. Tiffany Lethabo King, Alicia Bonaparte, Grace Sanders Johnson, Laura Harris, Kim Price, Christina Carney, and many others supported this work. Thank you for cheering me on.

The American Council of Learned Societies, PAGE/Imagining America, and the National Women's Association made the completion of this work possible. Multiple public libraries of Los Angeles County, especially the Willowbrook Library, contributed to the completion of this book.

I thank Channel McLewis, Jasmin Young, Keitlyn Alcantara, Dillon Sung, Grace Greenlee, Monet Timmons, everyone from AAPHI; Najma Sharif, Simone Austin, Caroline Kent, Lauren Whitehurst, and Uncle J; Erin Whited-Ford, Ryan Frank, Priscilla Leiva, Maleda Belilgne, Robin, and Milton Robinson; and Zakiyah Collier, Jarrett Drake, Erin Glasco, Ego Sohiwe, Aja

Lans, Bergis Jules, Tonia Sutherland, Anne Gilliland, and Kumi James. I thank Kat Cosby, Mohammed Ali, Nahum Chandler, Jessica Millward, Herman Bell, Bridget Cooks, Jared Sexton, and Frank Wilderson for their early kindness and Noah Nash for being a wonderful uncle. I thank Erin Collins, Joshua Aaron-Michael Ross, Kambui Olujimi, Mannya Sharma, Jennifer Evans, Deantre Bryant, Shantay Armstrong (Clinton and Michael), Akilah Nsofor (Olivia and Benny), Akhila Ananth, Anja Akhile, Aisha and Afiya Browne, Chandra Frank, Jasmin Young, Klara Hagymassy, and Jared Leier. I thank Rachel Watson, Emani Lesane, Jana Ross, Nyeneplu, Lacy Johnson, and all of my Howard students as well as Orisanmi Burton, Christina Juhász-Wood, Sybil Roberts, Eileen Findlay, the CRGC, Sara Clarke Kaplan, Kirstie Dorr, Lily Wong, and Onaje Woodbine. Raphael Nelson: you are have been a comrade and thought partner for over ten years. TK Smith—what a comrade. Elizabeth Rule is my favorite work partner. Not moving if you don't. Brenton Brock has been an incredible thought partner and comrade. We ain't never gonna die! This book would not have been created without the expertise, generosity, and humor of Katheryn Lawson. She is the best editor in the world.

To my family: Linette Park has seen me through every phase of this work and my career and our friendship. Kisaye Nyabinyere Jallah is a wonderful soul sibling to have and earn. Kiernan Steiner has been my sister for three decades and has watched every phase of my life while cheering me on. Ashia Bomani Ojore, Menelik and Mansa Ra, Maryann Wills, and Aziza Bomani Ojore: I love you. Zaza Awa-Moon has been a wonderful sibling and elder to my children. Thank you for still walking with me. My loves: Beny and Grandma, there is nothing more to qualify.

Mikal Anderson has given me so much support by always asking me to "say more" about my work, in addition to cheering me on for every little thing—you exemplify what they mean when they say love and care is a practice.

Sanu Mumia, Cuba Nanshe Ramah, and Sania Mali, my beautiful babies, my geniuses and my beauties: Nothing I say here in this language could ever express the gratitude I have for you choosing me.

PROLOGUE

Ida's Story

Shortly after twelve-year-old Tamir Rice was gunned down by a police officer while playing in a park in Ohio, I became pregnant with my own Black son. The expecting, non-Black parents around me counted down the days until their children's arrival, but I wanted to carry mine for as long as possible. Outside me, how short might his life be cut? His first months earth-side were the hardest of my life—I developed crippling postpartum anxiety out of fear that I would not be able to protect him into adulthood. What if, like Samaria Rice, I had only twelve years with my son? At my lowest moment, I pulled a book off my bookshelf, where I met a woman named Ida Hutchinson. Ida appeared to me through Dorothy Roberts's *Killing the Black Body: Race, Reproduction and the Meaning of Liberty* (1994). On the plantation where Ida was kept, in the American South, a few women were allowed to attend to their nurslings throughout the day, but the small cadre of caregivers who were forced to labor shortly after giving birth dug a shallow ditch on the edge of the field so as to nurse when they heard the infants cry.[1] When a thunderous storm came, rain filled the ditch, and all of the infants drowned before their mothers were able to reach them. The loss was a monetary one for the master and an unspeakable one for the mothers. Roberts writes, "Ida understood that the deaths of the babies meant a financial loss to the slave master. . . . But no one recorded

---

1. Roberts, *Killing the Black Body*, 35–36.

the horror their mothers must have felt upon discovering their precious babies floating lifeless in their makeshift cradle."[2] On the plantation, the role of the enslaved mother was overdetermined by the labor she was forced to complete. The intersecting domestic, field, and maternal duties defined what it meant to be captive during one's reproductive life. They enveloped Ida's daily experiences with a unique terror that hinged on the quotidian separation of her from her children as well as from her reproductive choice.[3] The threat of physical, emotional, and emotional harm to her and her children was part of her daily life, in which a child could disappear at any moment from death or sale. The lingering formations of filial dispossession defined her life as a mother and as a captive.

It is within the context of Ida's story that Dorothy E. Roberts attests to the urgency of understanding that "no one *recorded* the horror" enslaved mothers like Ida "must have felt" from losing their babies (emphasis added). We must disavow the tropes—tropes that suggest that Ida did not feel horror or that the monetary loss was more important to document than the fractured relationship—that led to such a lack of recordings in the face of such loss. We may speculate that there are myriad emotions neglected in hand-to-paper documentation. We do not have the records we deserve documenting the babies who cried, like Ida's, and even some "babies [who] never cried" upon being sold, leaving their mothers to grieve their "helplessness" at understanding their social position in infancy.[4] For the babies who cried and those who did not cry, and the mothers and kin who expressed their pain through shown or silent grief, separation was all that marked their relationality. Although the archive might not remember the name of Ida's baby, the ones who succeeded and preceded it, or the stories of those from whom they were separated, it did not forget their separation.[5]

With Ida, as with so many other Black mothers, we are only left to speculate at the site of their dispossession and the subsequent grief of their lives. I imagine her to be a caring and attentive mother, not because all mothers are necessarily caring and attentive but because I also *cannot* imagine the lengths she went to to make sure that she could keep her baby upon its birth and keep it close while she toiled in the field. I *can* imagine that she and her baby were

---

2. Roberts, *Killing the Black Body*, 35–36.
3. Davis, *Women, Race and Class*.
4. Writing of Sis Hetta, a plantation owner's nonconsensual mistress and her own ancestor, Margaret Walker states: "When their children were sold away and some babies never cried she would cry and grieve over their helplessness." M. Walker, *Jubilee*, 14.
5. "We may have forgotten our country, but we haven't forgotten our dispossession" (Hartman, *Lose Your Mother*, 87).

close and that they always stayed close to one another, close enough for Ida to hear a cry or a gurgle. She may have had her baby longer than she thought she would. I can only imagine the grief that overcame her when she found her baby drowned, because I remember the feelings of grief Mamie Till-Mobley expressed when she too found out her child had drowned at the bottom of a river.[6] After her baby died, Ida may have often spoken of the child with anyone who would take a moment to share memories with her. Or maybe she stopped discussing her baby altogether, swearing to herself that she would never have another if she could help it. *If she could help it*—that's all the power she had in her position; she would make sure she would never become pregnant again, even though that's what she was owned to do. Maybe she picked up her rake, returned to work, and never talked about her baby again.

As a parent to Black children in 2025, I am still defined by Ida's lived experience as a mother dispossessed. As Roberts and many historians contend, the reproductive violence perfected during the transatlantic slave trade and chattel slavery in the Americas has institutional, political, and social remnants in our criminal justice and child welfare systems. With the images of these mothers and children vivid in my mind, I fear the abrupt end to my children's lives, or my own. I fear being dispossessed as a mother is an imperative of my experience in America. As you read, I invite you to remember Ida, her baby, and all the children who are at risk of loss of their mothers. With them in mind, I embark on a journey of showing what is further lost when we minimize Black women's interminable ability to magnify their own memories through the imaginative spaces they explore.

---

6. Upon seeing her son's body for the first time, Till-Mobley collapsed and said, "Lord, take my soul." D. Brown, "Emmett Till's Mother."

INTRODUCTION

Black Maternal Dispossession in the Age of Black Lives Matter

Both public discourse on the Movement for Black Lives and scholarship produced on Black women's lives in the disciplines of history, sociology, literature, and Black studies map numerous connections between mothers like me and Ida.[1] Many of these connections are drawn from empirical evidence, animated by the statistics of generations of Black mothers and children subjected to the system of mass incarceration, disproportionate reproductive health disparities, skyrocketing maternal and infant death rates, and the failures of the educational system. The limitations of these discourses are that they do not account for the affective locations of trauma—only the effects of it. The felt experiences of mothers and children live in their DNA and inform their responses to the cycles of terror to which they are routinely subjected. In a political moment of heightened attention to Black families, their legacies of pain remain obscured by the very rhetoric that attempts to publicize the injustices that overdetermine their lives.

At the center of this book is the urgency of Black maternal dispossession. This urgency prefigures American family separation within current contexts of national belonging. It troubles the legacies of racialized enslavement in the United States and the ways that nonwhite families are fractured upon arrival. In recent years, mother–child dispossession has been iterated

---

1. See the prologue, "Ida's Story."

as family separation resulting from cruel immigration policies that have disproportionately torn families from Central America apart. The Movement for Black Lives, #BlackLivesMatter, and its sympathizers have failed to draw clear connections between a state that is complicit in these migrant families' separations and the long history of political and legislative actions that have separated Black families. Slogans like "Families Belong Together" and "Care not Cages" were recently racialized and repoliticized as issues of immigration as well as a core infraction of human rights.[2]

The separation of Black families is so engrained in American culture that only when separation appears in public media in other racialized bodies is it seen as a phenomenon. I investigate this normalization through the lived experiences of Black women, as expressed through the literary, visual, and material texts they produce in the contemporary era. These producers are exemplary documentarians of separation, particularly over the late twentieth century, continually laying bare how families are separated in ways that predate our current immigration crises. Through my engagement with the textual, the literary, and the body politic, this book examines how art depicts family separations over time, genre, and form to challenge the enduring terrors of Black mother–child separation and to plumb the ways it maps onto many other family formations.

In addition to the highly public circulation of Black motherhood in the media, Black motherhood, as a social position, institution, *and* felt experience, poses questions for the theoretical formation of Black maternal subjecthood. Fraught, racialized histories often do not survive institutionally to tell the stories of those victimized. The task of searching for Black mothers in archives of enslavement sparks particular difficulty, not because Black women did not perform the role of caregiver but because the violence of being both woman *and* Black *and* reproductively fertile uniquely conflicts the practice and ethics of documentation by captors and enslavers. A slave ledger or bill of sale often named Black mothers as producers of chattel rather than caregivers, neglectors rather than protectors. Black mothers were born to produce and multiply their master's property; they lived to be divided by the same logic of ownership. This logic overdetermines their archival legacy as well as their lived experiences.

The system of chattel slavery in the United States was a state-sanctioned institution. We thus can see the reproductive violence of maternal dispossession that occurred within it as state sanctioned. Although these dispossessions

---

2. Trivedi, "Family Separation." In November 2020, human rights activists with Families Belong Together placed over 600 teddy bears in and around a cage on the National Mall to illustrate how many children were being held in cages without their families in the United States. See Brehman, "Photos of the Day."

may not have documented the death, sale, or disappearance of a child, Black women writers and artists of the contemporary era tell these stories through creative documentation. Their work supplements these archives with the felt experiences of horror and attests to the transgenerational effects of living with such dispossession. *Scrap Theory* investigates Black mothers' experiences of being dispossessed of their children as radical documentation of their unique lot of dispossession. *How do Black women's creative arts document past and present experiences with motherhood and separation, or Black mother–child dispossession?* And, *How does arts-making historically contextualize maternal dispossession within the archival and creative histories of Black motherhood?* I pose these questions to analyze the emotional lives of Black women's dispossession in a way only a firsthand witness could document.

Scrap Theory is concerned with the revival of creative methods as a means to understand how Black women documented their lives and the lives of their ancestors through creative modalities. To understand this reading practice, I offer a *Black maternal archival praxis* that re-centers Black women's everyday, multimodal memory work as preceding and exceeding institutional conceptions of documentation. While considering the traditional archival and analogue documentation of Black mothers who continue to chronicle their perceived nonhuman status (archives of the transatlantic slave trade, chattel slavery, child welfare, etc.), this book refocuses the documentation of Black mothers as a Black feminist reading practice. It illuminates the many formations of documentation that operate outside the confinements of language and literacy to convey an array of experiences with motherhood. As Toni Cade Bambara writes, "English is a wonderful mercantile language. . . . You can get a lot of trade done with English. But you would find it very difficult to validate the psychic and spiritual existence of your life."[3] Such is the task of leafing through empirical documentation to validate the everyday moments of Black mother–child dispossession.

Theorizing the Black Motherhood: An Introduction to Scrap Theory

There is already a Black feminist tradition of using the arts as historical preservation.[4] A dynamic sampling of contemporary literature and art created by Black women considers the forms of poetry, novel, memoir, book arts, visual arts, and memorial to interrogate Black women's reproductive lives. Such an

---

3. Braxton and McLaughlin, *Wild Women*, 348.
4. Weinbaum, *Afterlife of Reproductive Slavery*, 62.

innovative, yet traditional method of memory-keeping requires a unique method of investigating scraps, or what I articulate as *scrap theory*, to search for traces and fragmentation of Black reproductive life that exist within both artistic and traditional institutional archival documentation. The artists I discuss revive a Black feminist methodology of communing with scraps—what I call scrap theory—to write this story. Radical approaches to what is precious and what is worthless—or appraisal—have always been more than the inversion of that which is useless made priceless, what was originally meant to be ephemeral made timeless. Black feminist approaches to memory work create an intertextual production of memory, time, and space to scale the meaning of scraps as foundational to Black memory work across disciplines: For instance, food studies scholars have traced the predilection for chitterlings through a gastro-genealogy of enslaved people's access to the kitchen scraps.[5] Sneaking the scraps out the back door for their children showed that those working in the enslaver's home gave value and meaning to leftovers for our children.[6] Those who received the "40 acres and a mule" after Reconstruction quickly found that the forty acres were uninhabitable scraps of land that white locals did not want or at least mind consigning to the "ownership" of Black locals. Another dimension of scrap theory calls for the theorization of forced migration of Black Americans who materially haunt the spaces they escaped. Some left small locks of hair that would be enough to remember them by but would remain unfound when a mob came knocking on their door. If someone was caught, and murdered, scraps of their body were circulated as souvenirs and passed down through generations of white families as heirlooms.[7] Historically, Black people also have symbolized scraps: We are who is left for dead or left behind in social and governmental programs, while also being deemed the "excess,"[8] the "too many mouths to feed" and those

---

5. Williams-Forson, *Building Houses*.

6. In 1941 Tom Randall, an informant and "ex-slave" born in Ellicott City, Maryland, told his Works Progress Administration (WPA) interviewer, "Mother was the cook at the Howard House; she was permitted to keep me with her. When I could remember things, I remember eating out of the skillets, pots and pans, after she had fried chicken, game or baked in them, always leaving something for me." "Forgotten History."

7. Woodard, *Delectable Negro*. See also Kerry James Marshall's *Heirlooms and Accessories*, especially within the context of *Non-Fiction*, curated by Noah Davis at the Underground Museum, 2016.

8. Sharpe, *In the Wake*, 30. Sharpe arrives at the term "excess" through C. Riley Snorton ("What More"). We may also consider excess-as-superlative in public rhetoric such as Hillary Rodham Clinton's characterization of young Black men as not just "predators" but "superpredators." Theorizing scraps makes a similar call in undertaking material such as "tending-toward-blackness—a leaning into and caring for," which "animates a range of artistic, social, political, and theoretical practices aimed at establishing an ethical posture toward Black subjects and those related forms of being that have been positioned at the margins of thought and perception yet are necessarily co-constitutive of them." Copeland, "Tending-toward-Blackness," 143.

who leech off the government.[9] Blackness is what is "scrapped" from admissions rosters and course listings—we are the last to be hired and first to be fired. Material scraps are what we must remember each other by, that which we use to construct a semblance of the whole of who our loved ones were and are. Black ancestors are the ones who scrapped pieces of stone and rubble to literally build our statehouses, which hold some of the most prized archival treasures.[10] We conjure scraps and draw community from them to challenge these archival collections.[11] Scraps make up the collage through which our lives are quilted together while at the same time reminding us that fragmentation is our legacy.[12]

I use scraps as a quintessential figuration of what is (un)seen as erasure (dispossession) on top of another erasure (motherhood). I am driven by communing with those whose greatest fear was realized in a social stratum that refused them the categories of mother *or* child.[13] In enacting scrap theory, I situate the process and product of Black women artists' personal papers, archives, and materials which they create on and around themes of dispossession as intermingled and inseparable. I coin scrap theory as an invitation for us to see the ways Black women creatives generationally collect materials and memory of the lost, hidden, and forgotten to tell intrapersonal stories of their own experiences with mother–child dispossession as well as those of their foremothers. I approach fragmented and refused materials that may appear to be otherwise inconsequential or miscellaneous to one's life as scraps. I draw from scraps not to make a semblance of a family that may have been torn apart, and especially not to reassemble a family that I know may have never been reunited. I instead read *with* what is left behind and around separation to observe what contours one's subjecthood without directly constituting it. In a sense, scraps allow us to theorize the silhouette of a mother-dispossessed in its/her/their own right. It does not deny the time spent together between a mother and child as any less significant but poses an opportunity to further explore the unbreakable bond between mother and child. My demands of

---

9. President Ronald Reagan's propagated public rise of the myth of the welfare queen was set in motion in our modern era by Daniel Moynihan's report on the Negro family. US Department of Labor and Office of Policy Planning Research, *Negro Family*.

10. Trouillot, *Silencing the Past*.

11. In Alice Walker's *The Color Purple*, protagonist Miss Celie pieces a quilt together with her family "with her basket full of scraps on the floor" (52). Quilting, an artistic form of memory work centered on scraps, is an activity of which Celie says: "For the first time in my life, I feel just right." See also the quilt work of late twentieth-century artist Faith Ringgold.

12. Hartman, *Lose Your Mother*.

13. Hartman, *Wayward Lives*, 338.

scraps are that they open new formations of visuality and materiality, as well as the affective and medical humanities approaches to yield the haptic consequences of living under the threat of dispossession. A radical approach to the intimate spaces of Black lives invites us to imagine how we document Black mothers' experiences over time, and how their affective and creative lives substantiate the very archive of Black motherhood and its fragmentation. This approach to archival material thus wrestles with a disturbing present in which family dispossession is both normalized and pathologized in the media every single day. In sum, scrap theory best serves this project in underlining the four-hundred-year holocaust that "wrenched" Africans from their "biological mothers as well as their Motherland" and what this "wrenching means, not only then, but now" for Black women creatives and their audiences.[14]

Scrap Theory intervenes in the fields of Black archival studies, motherhood studies and feminist studies, and literary studies by asking how Black women deliberately document their experiences with dispossession through artistic engagement. My transdisciplinary approach of scrap theory and documentation encourages a collapse in disciplinarian discourses on the levels of documentation and practice, making it a much-needed complementary text to move forward the conversations around the status of Black women's documentation under the politics of dispossession. To date, there is a failure across fields to fully discuss Black women's artistic work as a form of archival labor.[15] Yet, contemporary arts practice is an archive rife with the experiential evidence of mother-ancestors' experiences with dispossession. I drive this interdisciplinary conversation forward by asking what forms of radical documentation—animated by theorizing with scraps—must be considered so we might contend with maternal dispossession in all its discursive forms (for example, mother tongue, motherland) for a more capacious image of dispossession itself.[16]

In total, I define Black motherhood as the social location of African diasporic femmes or women or self-identified mothers who care for, protect, and prepare children for adulthood through the conditions of dispossession. African diasporic people's contentious history with these formations of motherhood create specters of separation as reproductive injustice. Literary, visual,

---

14. Christian, "Fixing Methodologies."
15. Powell, "This [Black] Woman's Work."
16. This anxiety is evidenced in the booming of Ancestry.com and the passion to take DNA tests to locate one's African ancestry on the level of tribal location. One such website, AfricanAncestry.com, claims to locate lineages based on region to a present location in Africa. Such businesses now capitalize on international phenomena made popular by pan-African cries such as "Wakanda Forever!" made popular by Marvel's *Black Panther* (2018).

and performative art of the African diaspora iterates separation as a literal separation of the bodies of mothers and children. I also undertake maternal dispossession as the separation from motherlands (lands of origin) and the figurative separation from mother tongue (language of origin). An all-encompassing definition of maternal dispossession scales the degrees to which Black mothers are victimized by the enduring projects of capitalism and colonialism. Thus, a capacious undertaking of maternal separation includes an analysis of the high maternal and infant death rates of Black people and the child welfare system that disproportionately affects Black mothers' potential to raise Black children safely without state-sanctioned permanent and/or semi-permanent dispossession. My intention in undertaking such a capacious view of Black maternal separation is not to find new ways to highlight the wounds of Black mothers. I am also not interested in naming these violences so that I can save them from the violences that caused these wounds. This definition of Black maternal dispossession simply aims to examine the many ways that Black motherhood is obscured and rendered an archival impossibility for research in my attempt to define it. This impossibility invites us to reimagine and revive cultural production as a site to theorize the many experiences of Black motherhood. Such an invitation also creates the opportunity for us to revel in the ingenious ways Black mothers antagonize our nationalized notions of belonging and remembrance in their arts making.

I also expand the notion of motherhood so as to mobilize Black motherhood beyond gendered and racialized forms of embodiment. At many points, this project investigates mothers who are men or nongendered, but who care for other Black people, especially in the pursuit of liberation from oppression. Framing Black motherhood outside the gender binary, we are disabused of categories of similarity through which we assume a homologous "Black community" experienced enslavement.[17] This approach locates Black mothers as queer in their historical relationship *to* the diaspora and the history it will not or cannot keep, as well as *within* their intramural relationships to members of the diaspora.[18] I qualify the term "queer" in Omise'eke Natasha Tinsley's

---

17. Walcott, "Outside in Black Studies," 91–92.
18. Richardson, *Queer Limit*, 15. Richardson writes, "Reimagining is the process of taking something that has already been conceived of and recreating it with new elements, thereby infusing the past with difference." I think of reimagining Black motherhood through a Black maternal archival praxis as infusing the theoretical and literal history of Black motherhood with difference to further intensify the constitutive singularity that structures the grammar of Black suffering. See also Cohen, "Punks, Bulldaggers, and Welfare Queens." This essay radically altered conversations about queerness and the Black matriarchal-led household. Cohen's essay imbues meaning and potential to every sentence of this project, even when not cited directly on the page.

offering of "*queer* in the sense of marking disruption to the violence of normative order and powerfully so: connecting in ways that commodified flesh was never supposed to, loving your own kind when your kind was supposed to cease to exist, forging interpersonal connections that counteract imperial desires for Africans' living deaths."[19] Thus, the cisgendered body and heterosexuality are a dynamic instead of a foundation to our conceptions of Black motherhood. The definition of Black motherhood is an expansive one when drawn from the creative archive of Black feminist thinkers.

Black Maternal Dispossession in Theory and Experience

Black maternal dispossession returns Black motherhood to the fore of Black studies scholars' many undertakings of the possession and dispossession binary. Black motherhood is an often neglected space for theorization even within social death and Afropessimist critiques. In sum, Black motherhood ushers in new theorizations of notions of freedom and unfreedom.[20] Dispossession is the organizing framework through which I conceptualize the separation of mothers and children in the anti-Black *afterlife* of slavery both in terms of mother–child separation and their position within the archive that occludes them.[21] This book fashions dispossession in relation to motherhood as the state's interference with the *possibility* of a Black woman's relationality with biological or fictive kin, their language, and homeland, or the foreclosure on a sustained relationship after filial (fictive or biological) relation is established.[22] Throughout the book, I use the term "dispossession" interchangeably with "Black maternal dispossession," "maternal dispossession," and when applicable, "filial dispossession" to depict the forced, institutional, and transgenerational deprivation of motherland, mother tongue, and kin toward a project of alienation from heritage and cultural thriving. These terms all fail to encompass the infinite technologies of separation, loss, and paradigmatic violence against Black mothers. But my various versions of the term expand upon the condition of natal alienation, as described in Orlando Patterson's

---

19. Tinsley, "Black Atlantic," 199.
20. See Bradley, "Vestiges of Motherhood," for more on the intersections of the Black maternal and social death.
21. A similar framework of dispossession is also explored in M. Fuentes, *Dispossessed Lives*. The relationship between enslaved women and power articulates itself in many forms: within their relationship to other enslaved or free women of color, their white contemporaries, capitalism, and the archive itself.
22. Morgan, "Partus Sequitur Ventrem."

work as an essential to the program of shaping slave subjectivity.[23] Natal alienation brings out an itinerary of ownership that thwarts the slave's choice of blood ties or kinship to form a sense of belonging to anyone other than the slave's owner, thus creating a legacy of alienation through the dispossession of "birth and both ascending and descending generations."[24] I navigate the implicit semantics that place dispossession and possession on a binary to suggest the stark bifurcation as a dangerous terrain that reproduces rhetorics of ownership and enslavement, but it has a place in current debates regarding intersectionality and Black feminism.[25] For Black feminist M. Jacqui Alexander, navigating the arena of "self-possession" is one of empowerment and an elision of one's potential to be owned.[26] Self-possession is an act of recovery in which a process of internal decolonization still signals containment.

Like Black motherhood, Black feminist artists and culture workers transform the meanings of freedom and dispossession. As such, my investigation of Black motherhood in the contemporary space could not occur without mention of Toni Morrison's *Beloved* (1987). Morrison's novel combines nonfictional historical evidence with a ghost story of a young girl who returns to her mother after her mother has killed her in order to free her from a slave patrolman. Morrison's words parallel with Alexander's when she writes through her main character, Sethe: "Freeing yourself is one thing, claiming ownership of that freed self is another."[27] Dispossession is expressed as multifaceted and works as one who is dispossessed through the practice of ownership *and* the existence within the liminal space Sethe outlines. To be sure, this liminal space is also bondage. Sethe's words replicate the redemptive view of self-possession but are troublesome when thinking of Black motherhood. The redemptive view of possession is represented through Black women's ability to claim ownership of kin, replicating the same dynamics of ownership the enslaved owners wielded. To be free is to be impervious to containment: Sethe is propositioning us with a sense of unfreedom that accompanies the social death of Black mothers. To *belong* to our Black mothers may mean something else entirely, a something else that we are afraid to admit we have never felt. Mothers like Sethe confuse the semantics of dispossession in their care for kin. Black mothers are depicted as mothers who either emphasize the possession

---

23. Patterson, *Slavery and Social Death*, 7.
24. Patterson, *Slavery and Social Death*, 7.
25. See Nash, *Black Feminism Reimagined*, 76–80. Nash outlines a tension between intersectional coalition building and Black feminists, linking Ange-Marie Hancock Alfaro's idea of "careful stewardship" rather than what Nash calls "pernicious possessiveness" when it comes to allowing intersectionality to challenge conditions of Black feminist theory-making.
26. Alexander, *Pedagogies of Crossing*, 271–75, 282.
27. Morrison, *Beloved*, 124.

of their kin through the cold, overprotective parenting of the Black Mammy stereotype, or through the restorative justice model that reunites Black mothers with kin against oppressive conditions. However, Sethe's mothering leads us to ask another question: Does dispossession exist only within the context of once being owned by an "owner"? How do Black mothers replicate this violence themselves? Is this violence contingent on a Black mother's present agency or the conditions of inheritance that impact her reproductive viability for kinship?

The schema of Black maternal dispossession is an entry point for much larger discussions about what is scrapped from history when we create presentist, redemptive narratives about those living at the intersections of gendered and racialized subjecthood. I investigate maternal dispossession in creative works fully aware of the foreclosures of Black women's maternal status and the denial of Black children's nonage on a symbolic and figurative level in public discourse as well as creative and institutional archives. These foreclosures may have been made at the hands of institutional actors. But these choices make up the overall logic that rendered Black motherhood unsanctimonious, and therefore unworthy of protection. On a very technical level, it produced archival lacunae that said *because Black mothers do not exist, the loss of a child cannot occur.* It would seem that motherhood is an unavailable social position to Black women. This could account for no one "recording" the "unspeakable" loss of losing a child. Perennial experiences with structural anti-Blackness, combined with a transgenerational haunting that is both embodied and creatively expressed, contribute to the demand for a framework of a Black maternal archival praxis that explicates the history and present of dispossession as one of violence that is both thought and unthought.[28] In turn, scholarship that locates contemporary Black maternal activism as the redemptive antidote to the ongoing violence caused by such early technologies of separation is not foregrounded, despite its remarkable contributions.[29] My method of analysis complicates such activism within the context of enduring archival, physical, and spiritual estrangement evidenced by contemporary artistic work.

Historicizing Black Motherhood: Framing Dispossession as a Reproductive Justice Violation

Contemporary reproductive justice scholarship has expanded the notions of reproductive in/justice far beyond direct applications to cisgendered women's

---

28. Marriott, *Haunted Life,* 4.

29. Visualization and the politics of representation are explored in D. Fuentes, "Visible Black Motherhood"; and Story, *Patricia Hill Collins.*

relationships with having children.[30] In succinct terms, a critical analysis of Black motherhood and Black women's reproductive lives expands the definitions of such violations as "the right to parent children in safe and healthy environments."[31] It is under this tenet that we can see the specific intersections of gender- and sex-based violence against Black women and their reproductive lives as violations of their own person as well as those of their children, partners, and family. Conversely, violations against Black women are a reproductive rights violation of their children, partners, family, and community members. My operating use of dispossession thus argues for the physical and legal urgency of identifying dispossession as having roots in the constructions of race, gender, and sexuality formed during the early years of enslavement of Black women in particular. Of course, we must also consider the ways that these horrors were (un)documented, whereby the attempted rhetorical violences made in the archive (for example, ungendering Black mothers, the opacity of kinship in archival material through naming) made clear other forms of insurrection. Even still, without the clear substance of mothering, the documentation of a mother's loss cannot be done.[32]

Black women experienced filial dispossession from an array of social situations and extralegal violences committed against their families during colonization of the early Americas. In the nineteenth and early twentieth centuries, the conditions of chattel slavery that separated families and the legacies of imprisonment, such as convict leasing, sent members unrightfully incarcerated miles from home.[33] Sharecropping kept families toiling on barren land for little to no pay, domestic indentured servitude deprived Black mothers from holding their children six days a week,[34] and many people were left behind to raise families after their partners and fathers were lynched. Fear of lynching led families to disperse and disappear as part of the more nuanced experience of the Great Migration, when many families were intimidated into leaving their hometowns for fear of retribution.[35] Bussing children into hostile communities, the forced displacement due to gentrification that occurred as urban and rural city planning codified geographic racism, and the institutionalized forms of surveillance of Black women's reproduction are all violations of Black women's right to have healthy families and stable lives. These forms

---

30. In recent years, the National Women's Law Center has released numerous white papers that connect environmental racism and control to reproductive injustice.
31. Ross and Solinger, *Reproductive Justice*, 169.
32. This is putting aside some critical Black studies schools of thought that displace motherhood as an impossibility in the scheme of racial capitalism. In this context, Black mothers are mere "producers." See Hartman, *Scenes of Subjection*; and Wilderson, *Incognegro*.
33. Haley, *No Mercy Here*; and Hartman, *Wayward Lives*.
34. Hartman, "Belly of the World."
35. Griffin, *"Who Set You Flowin'?"*

of state-sanctioned violence encompass the violation of reproductive rights even though the institution of slavery allotted no human rights to African-descended people whatsoever. As its legacy lives on, so does the infringement on reproductive rights.

The racialized historical project of dispossession aimed to disabuse Black mothers of their status as mothers, therefore rendering them incapable of suffering separation. The fashioning of enslaved Black women's statuses during chattel slavery as mothers was a visual, cultural, social, and economic project, a project that worked to violently inscribe and reinscribe what we would understand as Black womanhood.[36] This formulation shored up the relational dynamics of plantation life in the early formations of the Americas and the transatlantic slave trade from which it profited. Jennifer Morgan and Sasha Turner proffer that gendered violence initiated the fashioning of African women's identities as caregivers, breeders, and mothers in the Americas.[37] Morgan's *Laboring Women* confronts how Black motherhood has always been subject to a number of "historically contingent actors," including the insistent comparison to European and Indigenous women's subjecthood.[38] Sharla M. Fett, Deirdre Cooper Owens, and Marie Jenkins Schwartz similarly argue how the Black parturiency concretized depictions of Black women's savagery.[39] Corporal violation during parturiency is not the sole index of reproductive violence, however. Iterations of reproductive violence span sexual contact, the inability to choose a sex partner, rape, wet nursing, and anything that violated a woman's autonomy over her reproductive choices at any stage of life. As Black women's reproduction meant different things (like producer, breeder, liability) to the institution of slavery as well as their captors, their potential to provide care for kin was determined at the will of the enslaver. The precarity of Black motherhood throughout chattel slavery in the United States is marked by these visual and rhetorical scenes. The denial of Black women's humanness produced bodies to be categorized by their potential to be caretakers, mammies, and other domestic workers to white children. These tasks required Black mothers to forfeit time with their own children.[40] The lack of agency over these choices was fundamental to the development of the

---

36. Spillers, "Mama's Baby, Papa's Maybe," 65.
37. Morgan, *Laboring Women*; and Turner, *Contested Bodies*.
38. Morgan, *Laboring Women*, 201.
39. Fett, *Working Cures*; Cooper Owens, *Medical Bondage*; and Schwartz, *Birthing a Slave*. Bonaparte discusses the organization of Black women health practitioners, healers, and midwives who attended to reproductive health during parturiency to mitigate the risk associated with such depictions, which often meant convening with white doctors or trained veterinarians who acted on their perceptions of Black women as subhuman. Bonaparte, "Satisfactory Midwife Bag."
40. Hartman, "Belly of the World."

social and cultural mores that vilified Black mothers as unworthy and unable to mother children. They codified cultural and social stereotypes that labeled Black women incapable of making safe and healthy choices for their reproductive futurity.

My historicization of Black mothers contends with a robust definition of Black women as categorically defined by tropes of neglect and incompetency. This definition justified violations of their bodies and their ability to care for their children. In the early twentieth century, prominent Black women activists aligned themselves with political milestones that refused to include them in a womanhood characterized by whiteness. Despite Ida B. Wells's advocacy for the white suffragette and the bullying by the much celebrated Susan B. Anthony, Black women were not allowed to vote after the passing of the Twenty-First Amendment.[41] Contemporary Anna Julia Cooper asserted that only "the Black woman can determine when and where I enter in the quiet, undisputed dignity of my womanhood" that was not civically or politically acknowledged.[42] Yet and still, Black women were denied the category of womanhood.[43]

Prominent scholarship produced during this time drew flawed conclusions that situated morality on a binary and rendered Black women as pathological to neoliberal middle-class mores that were never meant to include women like Anna Julia Cooper in the first place. Sociologist E. Franklin Frazier's early works positioned poor Black women as unfit mothers and as anathema to American dreams of morality and piety. Frazier's early work laid the ground for governmental justifications to place Black mothers under unique scrutiny in consideration of welfare programs.[44] Roughly fifty years later, such depictions of Black mothers became legislative fodder in state-sanctioned studies such as the infamous 1965 "The Negro Family: The Case for National Action," more often referred to as the "Moynihan Report," published by then secretary of state Daniel Moynihan. Moynihan's report came during the era of the civil rights fights, which hinged on tropes of respectability and nonviolent civility for the right to vote. Instead, Moynihan's conclusions concretized the theory of Black women–led households as a driver of the erosion of Black family formation. This report developed the racist origins of the welfare system

---

41. Ida B. Wells-Barnett traveled the lecture circuit with her still-nursing children. Susan B. Anthony remarked that she seemed "distracted" because of her children. Dennison, "African-American History."

42. "Black Women."

43. Black women have historically appealed to (white) womanhood as an entry point for respectability or recognition as free and/or human status. For more, see Collins-White, "Rethinking the Human."

44. E. Frazier, *Free Negro Family*; and E. Frazier, *Negro in the United States*. See Roberts, *Killing the Black Body*, 204, for more.

and reified national discourses that saw Black motherhood as an antagonism to patriarchal, middle-class visions of assimilation. This report drew greatly from Frazier's findings and used intramural misogyny to evidence its claims of Black mothers as unfit mothers. Despite the institutional and political project to vilify Black mothers, Frazier and Moynihan formulated Black mothers' strength to raise children alone with little to no emphasis on legal cohabitation (in other words, marriage) with partners. Such perceived deviancy was labeled a structural antagonism to the American family.[45]

There are other ways Black motherhood appears as perpendicular to gendered notions of family. Black feminist and queer theory deconstruct traditional notions of the mother as solely feminine, embodied, and/or antagonisms to the state. I thus decentralize motherhood as essentially feminine or biological to "Othermothering," "activist mothering," and "community othermothering," queer formations of mothering that Black mothers have mobilized through the fragmentation of biological genealogy despite the characterizations of bad motherhood.[46] This terminology, like the Black women who lived it, suggests an alternative logic to the rise of neoliberalist America that depended on demonization of Black single mothers for political and social strategies that decimated Black communities.[47] Such formations of Black motherhood are queer in their orientation to the standardization of the nuclear family in the United States, asserting a formation of the Black family that has never been legible under the tenets of American domesticity. At the center of these formations, however, is the exacerbation of dispossession itself, or a subject definition that is mobilized by an original separation, the kind that forced us to make new ties because the old ones seemed to evaporate.[48]

Toward a Reproductive Justice Analysis of Black Women's Activism

Reproductive justice activists Loretta Ross and Rickie Solinger define the tenets of the reproductive justice agenda as tripartite: (1) the human right to have a child, (2) the human right to not have a child, and (3) the human right

---

45. These tropes are interrogated throughout the twentieth century. See Cohen, "Punks, Bulldaggers, and Welfare Queens."

46. Hill Collins, *Black Feminist Thought*, 183–94. Alexis Pauline Gumbs's dissertation (chapter 5) also delves into the mother–daughter relationship between June Jordan and Fannie Lou Hamer and the ways that Black women formed fictive kinship bonds of mothering. Gumbs, "We Can Learn."

47. Gumbs, "We Can Learn," 195.

48. Hartman writes, "Fictive kinship was too close to the heart of slavery's violence for my comfort." Hartman, *Lose Your Mother*, 199.

to parent children in healthy and safe environments.[49] The last tenet intersects directly with the Black Lives Matter movement's expressed platform, which states that all Black people have the right to parent without fear of violence from individuals and the state.[50] Reproductive analysis highlights how the third tenet of the reproductive justice platform, the ability to raise children without the fear of violence from individuals and the state, is broadly applied to threaten Black children's and their parents' ability to live and age into an anti-racist society. A reproductive justice analysis emphasizes the ways that *all* forms of contemporary Black women's activism implicitly and explicitly engage with reproductive justice. Reproductive justice agendas have long been implicitly entwined with Black feminist political agendas and continue to shape the rhetoric around contemporary Black women's activism, especially in the Movement for Black Lives.

Black feminist scholarship, which engages with marginality as a site of knowledge production, creates a sticky but productive inquiry into Black women's role in addressing the reproductive injustices of their communities. Indeed, Black women continue to be important political actors, whether or not they explicitly engage with the Movement for Black Lives. Ultimately, I use a reproductive justice analysis to approach the issue of Black women activists' experiences with bodily trauma to show how the aptitude for Black women's deeply affective political organizing exposes the dark underbelly of their brilliant actions against violence. For one, Loretta Ross became involved in reproductive justice because of her own life-threatening experience with an early form of birth control, called the Dalkon Shield. Due to an infection caused by the Dalkon Shield, Ross was forcibly sterilized via a hysterectomy in 1976.[51] She was one of the first women of color who won a lawsuit against its manufacturer, A. H. Robins, and has been a pillar in reproductive justice movements since, serving as a director of national organizations, an instructor at major institutions, and a public speaker and advocate. To this day, Ross's work combines myriad reproductive health struggles that reflect her own experience, such as housing rights justice, food justice, and domestic violence. A reproductive justice analysis presents a real and present engagement with the world of reproductive politics that produces new forms of knowledge and different understandings of history.[52]

It is within a political project of Black motherhood, wherein sex, gender, and race are displaced and codified all at once, that we are paradoxically

---

49. Ross and Solinger, *Reproductive Justice*, 168.
50. Ross and Solinger, *Reproductive Justice*, 194. Also found in Cullors and bandele, *When They Call*, 233.
51. Ross, "Loretta J. Ross."
52. Ross and Solinger, *Reproductive Justice*, 5.

unable to fully recall the moments of Black mother–child dispossession. Because the archive makes it difficult to glean Black mothers as mothers who *have* children, we are required to register Black mothers who *lose* their children on a different note. How might Black motherhood be recorded? How does Black motherhood change the formations of documentation altogether?

Cultural production serves as both a document and a means for documentation. We may then engage Black mothers' experiences as archival subjects that move beyond the deniability formulated in binaries of silenced/unsilenced to constitute a Black maternal archival praxis. In such a praxis, dispossession documented itself through the silence and the wail of grief. We can read what is scrapped from notions of Black motherhood—the queer, the woman, the affectual nature—to speculate upon the "horrors" of dispossession they encountered upon losing a child. I return to Ida again to engage in a similar speculation of her status as a mother and as a "mother-dispossessed" of a reproductive life that determines its own survivability.[53]

Naming That Which Cannot Be Silenced: Black Maternal Dispossession in Institutional Documentation

The unspeakable cannot be accounted for in the discourses of "silence" and "voice" to which Black archives are often subjected.[54] Yet, unspeakability is the language of the archive of Black motherhood. We can see the unspeakability in the "special fear" Black mothers like Ida may have felt in the everyday encounters of sale and purchase during plantation life in nineteenth-century Virginia. There were many like her. In 1805 an enslaved woman named Charlotte and a young girl named Kate were sold together to a man named John Rouzee of Virginia for 185 pounds (figure 1). Though I name them mother and daughter here, this is not how their relationship was characterized in the bill of sale that documented the transaction that reduced them to commodity. Written by their profiteer, J. Muscoe G. Hunter, the bill states that "a negroe woman called Charlotte with her child Kate" were sold.[55] This relationship is stated differently in its clerical description. The description in the digital archive of the National Museum of African American History and Culture (NMAAHC)

---

53. Hartman, *Wayward Lives*, 67.
54. For works that operate on the scale of silence/unsilencing, see Falzetti, "Archival Absence"; and Dadzie, "Searching." Trouillot, *Silencing the Past* invests in silencing too, as the title of his monograph demonstrates, although his work is not as invested in "giving voice" to the silenced history of Haiti.
55. Smithsonian Institution, "Bill of Sale."

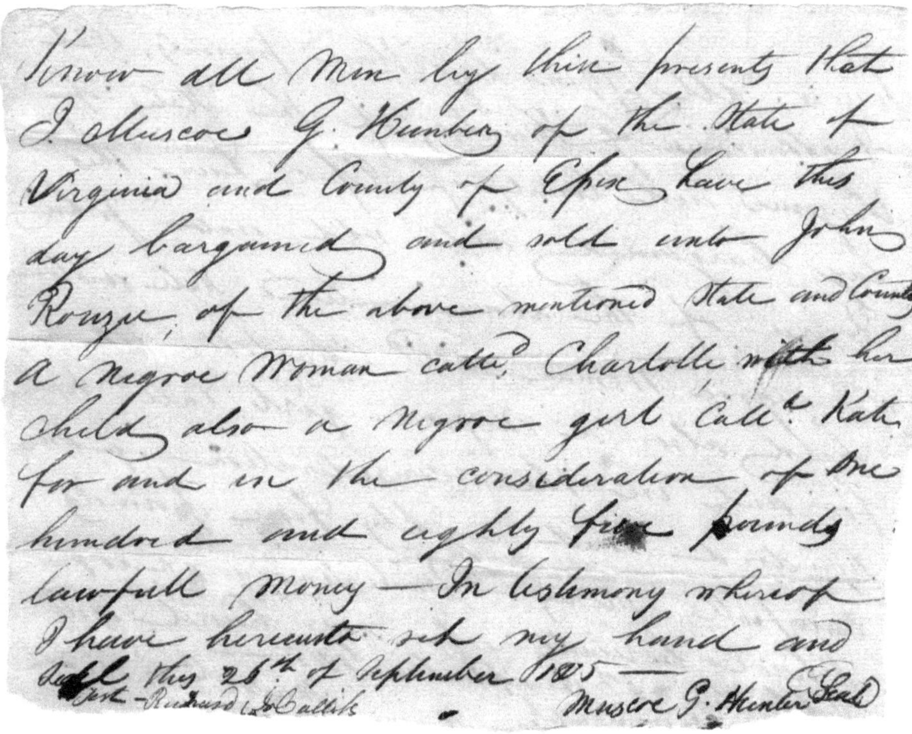

FIGURE 1. "Bill of Sale for Charlotte and Her Daughter Kate to John Rouzee."
National Museum of African American History and Culture Archives (1805).

is "Bill of Sale for Charlotte and her daughter Kate to John Rouzee." This is one of the examples in which technical language attempts to recuperate the mother–child relationship, to reestablish the kinship broken by separation.

"Daughter" is used nowhere in the bill of sale, although it is implied by the use of "her child." Kinship is a relationality often restored by archivists, giving breath to the love and fear of staying together as mother and daughter, kin and kin, auntie and niece. The NMAAHC's database redressed the relationship that the pair were denied in the bill despite its gesture that children simply *accompanied* women in the institution of slavery. Charlotte and Kate remained together for that sale. But if they were to be sold separately, it would not have been documented as a separation. Even in tales of unification, Black women are not the mothers of their children. Black maternal dispossession was a lived atrocity as well as one that all but defined the archival documentation Black mothers inhabit. Dispossession predates and encompasses all physical separation, emotional estrangement, and alienation. Maternal dispossession cannot be documented if Black motherhood too is undocumented. Charlotte and Kate may not have been separated from that sale, but the question of whether or not they belonged to one another can be answered in the negative by the institution of slavery that held them captive. Documentation of belonging remains presumed rather than evidential.

There is an eagerness in recuperating a memory of kinship between these two people. But we might actually fortify the raw violence of dispossession in doing so. (Re)naming the two could commit its own injury in that it blurs the rebellious act of self-fashioning during enslavement. Rouzee's bill of sale denotes that the "negroe woman," Charlotte, is merely "called" Charlotte, rather than named as such. Perhaps Charlotte was named by kin and her captor called her Charlotte. Perhaps Charlotte did not want us to know that she mothered Kate, nor to know that Kate was important to her. Black women's "rebellious acts" of asserting names other than those given to them along with a branding iron are widely proven and conjectured.[56] The common use of community names created double names for some of the enslaved. Charlotte and Kate's enslaver may have given them these names, or they may have chosen these names minutes before the bill of sale was written. The auctioneer also may have changed the names of the enslaved so that they would be hard to track down by kin later. The auctioneer may have also misheard the names, prompting him to change the names while they stood vulnerable to purchasers. Perhaps they could use their true names one day, on their own terms, or on the terms of their mothers, who valued them for something other than their labor. To be "called" Charlotte and Kate portends a future in which their subjecthood would be flexible to any owner's whim of "calling" or hailing someone, including by a derogatory epithet. One day, they are called Charlotte and Kate; another day they could be called by another name, something else by another master.

Like a hot branding iron, the "proprietary rights and entitlements" of naming a child born into slavery is equally important to foreclosing on relationality between the enslaved, transforming them into "instantiations" of the institution of slavery itself rather than of their family.[57] Thus, we must not only account for the dispossession of family, kinship, and sociality as a categoric violation of one's humanness done in the past. It could be further compounded by our own impulses to redress the harms done to them in the present. We often do this rather than accepting the truth: We cannot know every affinity of Charlotte and Kate's relationship beyond that they were sold together.

---

56. Turner, *Contested Bodies*, 185.
57. Lawrance, *Amistad's Orphans*, 12–13.

Searching for Charlotte's motherhood could be like looking for what we think was there or *could* be there. For some, it may look like searching for a relationality that is structurally impossible to appear. The traditional archival evidence of Black motherhood appears to us through that which is denied. How might their subject position as Black mothers be animated in the nontextual document or artifact if they could not even name themselves? For Black mothers, the textual document is the artifact of enslavement itself, not of their lives after and during their reproductive violations. Artistic archives ask us to imagine history as an entanglement of the future rather than a construction of the past.[58] They ask us to investigate Charlotte on Black feminist terms that privilege her existence as an archival paradigm in itself rather than a problem for the so-called archives that cannot contain her in the first place.

The Kate and Charlotte that appear to us in this document were not named but "called" into the institution of enslavement as property. They were "invented," like the millions of other women and girls who survived and did not survive their enslavement. Scholars have named this invention the "Venus"—a girl who appears in one incarnation as the "*dead girl*" and in so many others who survive;[59] Venus is "variously named" and "found everywhere in the Atlantic world."[60] It is hard to resist who and what we cannot name when we live in a moment that embraces writing injustices by first acknowledging them on the symbolic order of naming.

Today, naming resurfaces in political actions such as #SayHerName chants and online campaigns to name the babies who are separated from their mothers. We call on each other to "name" our feelings, the #MeToo movement empowers us to "name" our assailants, and activists demand us to "name" our social ailments and the hurt caused from trauma. Our mothers continue to "call it like it is!" Dispossession hinges in a language of speaking "truth to power" and calling out our traumatizers and yet it fails to fully speak to the broken bonds between mothers and their children.

---

58. This is similar to what Tina Campt argues for as a "Black feminist grammar of listening." Campt writes that this grammar "is a performance of a future that hasn't yet happened but must. It is an attachment to a belief in what should be true, which impels us to realize that aspiration. It's the power to imagine beyond current fact and to envision that which is not, but must be. It's a politics of prefiguration that involves living the future *now*—as imperative rather than subjunctive—as a striving for the future you want to see, right now, in the present." Indeed, Black feminist futurity as a grammar of looking, and looking as a reading practice of the visual, is not to be isolated to the optical sense. Campt, *Listening to Images*, 17.
59. Scholars of feminism, cultural history, and historical methods, including Janell Hobson (*Venus in the Dark*), Saidiya Hartman (*Lose Your Mother* and "Venus in Two Acts"), and Sasha Turner (*Contested Bodies*), all discuss a similar "unnamed" girl as a metonym for the many women and girls who go unnamed and whose lives go untheorized because they experienced similar archival misrepresentation.
60. Hartman, "Venus in Two Acts," 1.

Engaging the Nonrecord

When Lucille Clifton writes that she makes people "mad" just by "remembering" her own "memories," she is writing about the emotional labor or work one must also bear when practicing creative archiving.[61] Documenting one's history does not always have to be the deliberate undertaking of a written, oral, or aural process that results in a produced, external record. It is not just the arduous task of designating physical space to preserve artifacts, or even bearing a wave of emotion that comes when one is reminded of a childhood memory of their parents growing up in Jim Crow. These are all forms of archival labor associated with keeping a people's memory alive. Black women artists complement those who do this daily work in and out of institutionalized settings while also taking on the burden of "remembering mine."[62] Their work uses expressive modalities to offer their perseverance in the face of opposition and anger. The creative practice of memory-keeping undermines the assumed truth or fact within the historical, political, social, and interpersonal contexts from which they are created. Clifton and her contemporaries pose theoretical and conceptual questions to archival preservation, particularly at the sites of race, gender, colonialism, and queerness as they express in their own lives. Their work is part of a long tradition that exists inside and outside a bona fide technical archival practice.

Black women writers and artists participate in the production of a "*Black feminist philosophy of history*,"[63] what Alys Eve Weinbaum aptly names as the retrieval of the experiences of mothers and their children's lives overdetermined by the reproductive violences of chattel slavery through their production of consistent documentation that is not part of the "official" record.[64] My treatments are to be conceptualized within Weinbaum's formulation and as treatments of documents, not dissimilar from the *nonrecord*, according to the Society of American Archivists: "Information or data fixed in some media, but which is not part of the official record; a nonrecord."[65] These works question Black personal and communal memory and the personal ramifications of living as a descendent of a "lost" history in a number of late twentieth- and

---

61. Clifton, "Why Some People Be Mad," 20.
62. Clifton, "Why Some People Be Mad," 20.
63. Weinbaum, *Afterlife of Reproductive Slavery*, 62.
64. The Society of American Archivists defines "document" as "any written or printed work; a writing," "information or data fixed in some media," "information or data fixed in some media, but which is not part of the official record; a nonrecord," or "a written or printed work of a legal or official nature that may be used as evidence or proof; a record."
65. Society of American Archivists, "Document."

twenty-first-century works. For example, although not explicitly analyzed in the book, I draw extensively from Octavia Butler's *Kindred* (1979), in which the protagonist is literally thrown from the 1970s into the antebellum South. At first blush, Butler's book presents a juxtaposition between her protagonist's life in Los Angeles with her white husband and the antebellum South, where she is subjugated to the subhuman treatment of enslavement. But upon closer analysis, we find that Butler is warning us of the similarities between the present day and the antebellum era, especially in terms of the violent interpersonal treatment of Black women and white men. Butler subtly revives themes of anti-Blackness and gender-based violence as physical wounds that Dana carries once she returns to her own time continuum. As Dana loses an arm to her antebellum South, her ancestral history keeps a scrap of her body while she bears the evidence that it was scrapped from her. She lives on not as one who was "built" from a violent ancestry, but rather as one who gave a part of her present self so that her past could survive. Dana's physical sacrifice shows that her sudden placement into the historical past was not the actual disruption in memory. It was the violence she experienced that altered her genealogy. In other words, Black women's reproductive lives do not present a crisis for historicity. Yet their play with the nonrecord perfectly combines the "historical and presentist preoccupation with a slave woman's insurgent past" to confuse and madden audiences from any era.[66]

Visual and written texts like *Kindred* exalt the expressed, felt experience and relay the stakes of filial dispossession as a crisis of documentation as well as reproductive rights. However, abstraction more aptly names the exploration of "the power and limitations of communication" through the written word.[67] I apply Rudolph Arnheim's canonical understanding of abstraction to realize modern forms of abstract Black motherhood that are not opposed to concrete examples of Black motherhood treated in this book and in our lives, but exist alongside them to make very material understandings of Black motherhood that are otherwise thought to be *unbelievable* or ungrounded. Again, Arnheim removes the abstract from a dichotomy between the "concrete," stating that it is actually "an organization of the mind that passes beyond the concrete

---

66. Buter's *Parable* series has significant resonance with our experiences of the COVID-19 pandemic and the Trump era. Scholars find this series frustrating, albeit delightfully so, in that "Octavia tried to tell us" of the ills of political demagoguery, fundamentalist religion in the public sphere, and xenophobic philosophies of governance. See Coleman, "Octavia Tried to Tell Us."

67. Caroline Kent (b. 1975) is a mother and abstract painter living in Chicago. Her abstract painting has gained popularity in the past ten years. She creates worlds on large black canvases and only black canvases to "evoke cosmic unknowns." Pelly, "Artist."

and has freed itself from it."[68] "Freeing" us from concreteness and myopic views of Black mothers disavows material "evidence" and even artistic renderings against the violences of representation. Abstraction has many registers and can at times create distance (like historical distance) from the people or objects through which we read Black motherhood. It does, however, offer many theoretical encounters through which we can see Black motherhood both everywhere and nowhere, its pain legible and illegible to its audiences. It reproduces itself everywhere and in everything.

Conversely, abstraction works to understand the particle nature of Black motherhood often used to create its own language of memory and experience. We must account for the many ways culture, society, and history have confused Black motherhood with a set of anti-Black relations. It offers a complex singularity that is enveloped in various figures, modes, expressions, and experiences. This means staying grounded in the structural properties of Black motherhood rather than an overextraction of certain traits that are contingent on social-political rhetorics that accompany it.[69] An approach of abstraction rather than representation broadens the conversation around figurative Black motherhood and the literal occlusion of Black women's labors in normative American histories. Where Catlett's series is exacting in its elevating of specific heroines, it problematically emphasizes the collective anxiety to redeem "the mother" herself, ancestors, the motherland, and the archive-as-mother as a site of origin.

Abstraction centers Margaret Walker's coined "black belief," which "cannot be killed by "the lynchers' rope nor the bayonet": constructing and deconstructing, expanding and collapsing Black motherhood to understand the treatments I give it in this book, a modicum of the many samples through which Black folks understand motherhood in their lives, diasporas, and histories. Shifting abstractions also allow for Black mother–child dispossession in the many forms in this book and move toward expanding rather than retracting Black mother–child dispossession, while announcing through terms beyond the relations from which it is known.

Extant examples of Black women's cultural production paradoxically expand the documentations of Black mother–child dispossession under the conditions of "erasure," noting that the fear of forgetting our foremothers is not necessarily assuaged but rather revived in different forms. The rejoinder of "erasure" does not necessarily signal a "recovery" in which subjects can or must be saved from their meeting with violence.[70] What's more, some

---

68. Arnheim, *Visual Thinking*, 154–56.
69. Arnheim, *Visual Thinking*, 174.
70. Collins-White et al., "Disruptions in Respectability."

memories belong to those who experienced them and are not bound to be reproduced. Nevertheless, a more pervasive, paradigmatic approach to violence and the archive contorts the ways the Blackness becomes (im)material for readers engaging with racially fraught histories and how repertoires of archival material survives or remains lost in the afterlife of slavery.[71] Rather than suggesting an alternative archive or the imagined archive, I am more interested in making clear the relationship between Black mothers as impacted archival agents whose archival lives mirror the violence they experienced firsthand, thus codifying Black motherhood as an institution of separation and institutional archives as complicit in this formation. Rigid notions of what constitutes evidence, data, or artifact rely on a universal language that reproduces Black motherhood in such a discordant archive. The nature of this discordant archive sounds as neither silent nor roaring, only serving as an aural contour to the rhetorical violences enacted upon Black mothers in description and classification. These are the resonances that overdetermine their intimate relationships with their children in the archive. The archives that deny their actors motherhood and care are archives of Black maternal dispossession. The felt effects of this dispossession appear in culture work to complicate such archival material while creating its own archive of possibility and reverence.

There are multiple examples that mirror the varying definitions of motherhood taking place in other cultural discourses. Late twentieth-century Black feminist and womanist discourses in the United States sought to define Black motherhood as separate and distinct from the institution of white motherhood through an entire body of creative work focused on Black motherhood. Novelist Alice Walker's expectations that motherhood means "handing down the creative spark" of the "seed of the flower they never hoped to see" in particular resonates with Elizabeth Catlett's multidecade *Mother and Child* series (1956–95?), which features the undeniable embrace and protection of a mother's arm.[72] And, like Barbara Christian, who writes that in contemporary fiction, motherhood is still the "context for the slave woman's most felt conflicts," Catlett's use of the Black maternal allows us to position the confrontation of feelings like separation and grief alongside joy and beauty within the lives of Black mothers.[73] In this sense, Catlett's imaginary evokes the long range of responses to the responsibility of caring for children under the strain of dispossession.

Black women artists create *with* written discourses to construct that which *can be* and that which might never *have been*. The arts are important to the

---

71. Hartman, *Lose Your Mother*, 6.
72. A. Walker, *In Search*.
73. Christian, "Fixing Methodologies."

creative origins of Black motherhood as well as its theoretical applications, if only to pierce through theoretical debates concerned with motherhood in our present moment. Functioning as archival practitioners, we wrestle with what it means to continually create Black motherhood from archives that render them invisible. Arts production asserts questions of method, time, place, and space while also imagining moments of motherhood even as they are dispossessed of that title themselves.

My generous approach to contemporary visual and written art is predicated on the fact Black women have historically given birth to and raised Black subjects within conditions of unfreedom despite being socially positioned as "free" Black subjects themselves.[74] Black women's artistry explores these complexities through felt experience at length, even when recent theoretical debates argue against the symbolic potential for Black motherhood to exist at all.[75]

Scrap Theory embraces questions about Black women's creative memory work and its usurpation of the limitations of traditional documentation of Black reproductive life. Because creative contributions are often overlooked as documentation, I consider a close reading of other refused materials and methods that offer new paths for making memory, reading memory, preserving memory, and acknowledging the emotional labor of enduring the ire that doing so provokes.

The above-mentioned artists further urge a new direction of a Black feminist philosophy of history that focuses on smaller, unexplored formations of documentation that are often cast aside for the focus of the product of the document. These include a deeper analysis of emotional response and labor as well as an inverted notion of history where we are not just made up of pieces from our history, but our history is also made up of small pieces of our present selves. The remnants left from such a production gesture toward other overlooked senses, like the optical and the haptic. I also believe these modalities are ripe for treatment to engage Black women's activism and the bodies that

---

74. Morgan, "Partus Sequitur Ventrem."

75. Wilderson relies on the ungendering of slave subjects as a key argument, for, in quoting Spillers, "motherhood, fatherhood, and gender differentiations can only be sustained through the taxonomy of subjects." Thus, the origins of Black motherhood are not the affective impulses of care but of the production of a continued set of relations. Such kinship is made only to mirror the relationship between the asymmetrical power structure of the master–slave schema. Structurally, the state continues to blot out the opportunity of kinship, often referring to children as "dependent" on parents, and if in state custody by way of foster care, they are then a "ward of the state." The state, and the archive formed around it, renders Black motherhood an impossibility. For Spillers and for Wilderson, "motherhood" seems to only exist through "birthing" "the reproduction of the relations of production." Wilderson, *Red, White and Black*, 137.

contain their spirits, as a text for understanding Black maternal dispossession. Laid bare in these, my chosen objects, are the tensions of violence that foresee a Black longevity in which shared intramural visions of possibility and impossibility are conjured.[76] The visions this book offers are a dialectic of violence and durability that situates Black motherhood as a site of knowledge that can course the emotional interior of Black maternal dispossession as a polyvocal, multiphonic, and multidimensional text. I position the novel, the body, the material, and the emotional scrap heap as both the document and the non-record to be interpreted and theorized against the backdrop of contemporary crises of Black infant and maternal mortality, police violence, #BlackLivesMatter, mass incarceration, and the deportation of immigrants and refugees.

I begin the book with a novel exemplar of the time-bending and Black feminist meaning-making praxis central to their own documentations of dispossession. "The Fictional Archive of Disappearance" probes Toni Cade Bambara's text as a turn-of-the-century posthumously published behemoth of a novel that chronicles the two years in which a mother searches for her disappeared Black son. Published in 2000 but written during and about Atlanta's Missing and Murdered Children crisis (1979–81), Bambara's novel brushes against a contemporary institutional archive's documentation of the same events. I start here to mark the clear juxtaposition between what we may believe to be a binary of facts preserved in institutional archives versus fiction produced by novels. I position the novel as one of creative nonfiction, where the roughly twenty years of political activism and volunteering for groups dedicated to finding the killer(s) of the missing and murdered in Atlanta is documented. I read Bambara's novel with and against local urban histories told by the Mayor Maynard Jackson Administrative Papers collection at the Atlanta University Research Center and Bambara's personal archival papers located at the Spelman College Archives to foreground the life of her protagonist, mother Marzala Spencer, as the prism through which dispossession via gentrification, poverty, and the local fallout from Black Power politics expands meanings of maternal dispossession in the urban space.

Black women writers and activists fight maternal dispossession of all forms. In chapter 2, I take up poet, novelist, and educator Margaret Walker's struggle to complete her novel *Jubilee* (1967). Where this chapter focuses on her fight against Alex Haley and his alleged copyright infringement of her first and only novel, Dr. Walker Alexander's journey to write the some 600-odd pages was a venture in memory-keeping of her great-grandmother's

---

76. Visual artist Adler Guerrier's 2018 exhibition *Conditions and Forms for blck Longevity* defines the Black imaginary as a "shared space for visions of possibility."

life story. Drawing from her Southern and artistic background, Walker spent around twenty-five years writing the novel, all the while having four children of her own while reckoning with what it meant to write the first Civil War and Reconstruction narrative told from the perspective of a Black woman. Where many read Walker's novel as a turning point in American history, Haley's *Roots* rose to the level of cultural moment for African American culture and quickly eclipsed the legacy of her work, despite being published nearly ten years later. The interconnections between cultural production and reproductive labor span the contemporary conditions Black maternal people and Black mothers undergo to preserve the memories of their ancestors. This chapter also asks about the state's culpability in discarding Black women's cultural production and memory-keeping, and the ways other institutions, such as literary communities and academic institutions, work to cleave their memory-keeping, all while upholding laws, practices, and cultural mores antithetical to the cultural projects of Black literature and Black feminism.

I begin my third chapter, "The Corporal Archive of Separation in Contemporary Black Women's Cultural Production," with the work of Black women authors who problematize the "figurative realm of an imaged past" by also throwing an "existent territory with objective coordinates" into crisis through an exploration of mother/country or motherland, the foreclosure of which subsumes a rhetoric of dispossession. In this chapter, I examine the body in relation to its potential to separate and be separated from motherland and mothers, and how the body collapses as metonym and metaphor in the work of Haitian American novelist Edwidge Danticat. Just as the body assumes its own archive, we might imagine how mothers' bodies store their own information, and how mothers learn this information from ancestors of all gender expressions, including the uncles and fathers who mother them.[77] The multigenerational filial body creates a feedback loop for its own descendants to consume the trauma of being separated from motherland as their mother kin experienced. In my treatment of the work of Danticat, poet and novelist Dionne Brand, and visual artists Firelei Báez and La Vaughn Belle, I disruptively explore the gendered and racialized constructions of the (maternal) reproductive body as a geographic space made of the scraps of dispossessed bodies. These texts feature themes of illness of the lungs and the womb and cultivate myriad meanings for lineage and futurity of Black filial relationships.

---

77. Scholarship of Black queerness animates how these *individual* experiences may be irretrievable, but their opacity demands a deeper theorization. The lacunae of the canons from which we retrieve Black queer lives show that the "limits" of memory are not constituted by blackness but the unwillingness to understand history as categorically subjective. Richardson, *Queer Limit*.

Themes of Black maternity and morbidity are central to all of the aforementioned texts, but their emphasis on the fragmentation of biological genealogy in colonial islands of Antigua, Haiti, and the continental United States explore maternal dispossession as a spatial disruption. In the efforts to naturalize identities of colonized African women, these texts show how the landscapes they inhabit are "both haunted *and* developed by old and new hierarchies of humanness" and how these landscapes have become interchangeable with their bodies.[78]

Chapter 4, "Refused Memorials and the Black Feminist Archival Praxis of Samaria Rice," continues to ask questions of space, place, and scraps material after Black children have been disappeared. It specifically addresses the memorial of Tamir Rice, saved from demolition and then installed by Tamir Rice's mother, Samaria Rice, and artist Theaster Gates. Designated by Gates as *"not* a piece of art," this chapter discusses the methods through which the materials for Tamir Rice's memorial were saved from demolition. It analyzes Samaria Rice as an archival practitioner who privileges grief as an analytic of creative production.[79] Also, it considers the long through line of Black mothers as practitioners of Black maternal grief or the specters of grief and the repurposing of refused materials. This chapter perhaps most clearly addresses my demand to consider the multiple material modalities of archival documentation Black mothers explore to document their children's deaths in our digital age.

I conclude the book as a call to action around the visibility of gendered and racialized trauma against Black mothers who are fighting for their reproductive lives, and to offer a reproductive analysis as one tool to understand state violence as a reproductive justice issue. I embrace the life of Erica Garner's activism as an exemplar of the capacious meanings of sacrifice and dispossession, and how maternal dispossession is often eclipsed by the tendencies of patriarchal-leaning framings of anti-Black, state-sanctioned violence. Taken together, I offer these chapters to engage a meta-discourse of Black maternal dispossession writ large, asking how the plunder of state, community, and one's individual memory rely on the disenfranchisement of Black mothers and their children while attempting to move toward an increasingly fleeting notion of liberation for all families, both past and present. This book is an invitation for all of us to remember the children who refuse to be forgotten, and the mothers who keep them present through scraps.

---

78. McKittrick, *Demonic Grounds*, xvii.
79. Williams, "Black Maternal Grief," 29.

CHAPTER 1

The Fictional Archive of Disappearance

At first, it was called *Ground Cover*. In 1989 the *Atlanta Journal-Constitution* published an interview with Toni Cade Bambara in which she mentions she's writing a new novel to follow the acclaimed *Salt Eaters* (1980). Near the end of the interview, as a near aside, she mentions that *Ground Cover* is something she's been working on, slowly, for ten years. The novel would be about her new adopted home of Atlanta, Georgia, and its struggles with a string of kidnappings that occurred earlier in the decade. Writing on such a weighty topic was taking a toll on her mental health: "The novel contains the most difficult writing [I've] ever done."[1] Displayed in the middle of the article is an up-close image of Bambara looking off to the right of the camera and off the newspaper page, as if to gesture to readers that the new book is on her mind, calling her away from the interview. She wears the "difficulty" of writing on her face. She looks concerned; she looks distracted.

After starting the book in 1979 as a series of journal entries and then changing it into a series of investigative journalism essays, Bambara concluded that she finally would turn her stories into fiction because it was "the best vehicle to tell the community's story."[2] Although not explicitly detailed, "the community's story" later became her posthumously published novel *Those*

---

1. Boyd, "'Osage Avenue' Docu Shoots," Toni Cade Bambara papers, part 1, box 10.
2. Boyd, "'Osage Avenue' Docu Shoots," Toni Cade Bambara papers, part 1, box 10.

Bones Are Not My Child (1999), which amounted to a pseudofictional account of a mother's search for her disappeared son. A self-described "community scribe" living in southeast Atlanta, Bambara was uniquely poised to commiserate with a fragmented community surviving state-sanctioned violence. She was compelled to take up the task of writing with them instead of for them.

Community tragedy shaped the modern history of Atlanta, for which Bambara was present. The generations-long economic, social, and political inequities Black Atlantans experienced were brought to an apex when a string of violences against Black children and adults occurred in quick succession. Between the years of 1979 and 1981, the city experienced the bombing of an all-Black day care center and the vanishing of at least twenty-eight Black children and adults.[3] The media depicted this concentration of missing and murdered people as the "Missing and Murdered Children" and sometimes the "Atlanta Child Murders." In Bambara's *Those Bones Are Not My Child*, Black people disappear spatially, physically, and filially. Over a span of 365 days, Bambara tells the story of Zala Spencer, a Black working-class/poor mother in Atlanta trying to find her missing preteen son, Sonny. The novel takes place in twenty-four journal entries, and through Zala we experience the Atlanta Child Murders and the terror produced from trying to find her son—either living or dead. Just as those missing were affectively wiped from their neighborhoods, the oscillation between appearing and disappearing creates new space for theorizing the other forms of terror discussed in the book, such as police brutality, maternal health precarity, and deportation. *Those Bones*, then, presents a framework of disappearance that articulates multiple formations of maternal dispossession. What is considered "senseless" or "unexplained" in missing-person cases crystalizes how the ontological statues of Black children in Atlanta were constructed and deconstructed by the governing body of the city and its administration. Analyzing the disappearance of people, and especially children, yields an ugly promise that in American cities, Black folks do not disappear into or out of thin air, but rather that social, circumstantial, and legal conditions make them prone to do so. Disappearance is one way, in what feels like a series of no-ways, to make sense of the senseless distinctions that render Black folks invisible to the state, even when they are physically manifested. This chapter analyzes disappearance on these terms so as to plumb the intimate encounters of loss and grief between those who disappear and their kin. Through an investigation of fictionalized and nonfictional characters, disappearance presents as a material and mystical formation of family separation.

---

3. I say "at least" because there were other disappearances of Black people during this time, but they were not included in the roster of Atlanta's "Missing and Murdered" because of dissimilar circumstances of their deaths.

In other words, these characters make clear that people can be disappeared but still boldly exist to portend the repercussions of loved ones being erased from our streets, institutional archives, and lives.

The disappearance of Bambara's community members literally shifted the pavement beneath their feet, thus in part racializing the space- and place-making of a modern Atlanta. These events occurred when Atlanta was rapidly gentrifying, attempting to portray itself to the world as the safe, major cultural hub of the American South. This was one of the primary goals of Mayor Maynard Jackson: alleviate the city's racial and economic inequities. The Atlanta Child Murders distracted the city from this plan. "The City Too Busy to Hate" underwent several cultural shifts during the era of the Atlanta Child Murders, not least of which included the election of its first Black mayor—Jackson—in 1973. For the next eight years, Jackson's efforts of urban renewal and Black economic revitalization cowed to the retrograde race relations and poor infrastructure pummeling Atlanta's working-class/poor and poor neighborhoods. The new city Jackson imagined came to fruition at the expense of displacing hundreds of Black folks for the debut of the new international terminal of the Hartsfield Airport and its burgeoning business district.[4] Many of the folks affected by this gentrification were Atlanta's Black, poor, and working-class/poor neighborhoods, which spanned across the city's southwest and northeast and neighborhoods. Disappearance was not something that simply occurred to another person. It shifted the ground beneath Atlantans' feet while they were simultaneously reaped from the same streets.

"Disappearance" is a term often associated with phenomenal circumstances. I may seem to contribute to the clichéd application of this word when, by definition, we know that the disappearance of Black women in particular is not phenomenal, but common, and occurs at alarming and disproportionate rates.[5] An interrogation of the verb in its transitive and intra-transitive forms, however, wrestles the nuances of its applications in Bambara's novel. The novel is both fiction *and* artifact that serves as a "vehicle" for readers to account for the quotidian nature of spectacular circumstances of Black death. *Those Bones Are Not My Child* breaks open the creative uses of the verb "to disappear" defined in the chapter's epigraph, while reimagining the state as an actor (and perhaps *the* actor) of the disappearance of Black life. Bambara then explores the effects of disappearance through the intimate relationships Black mothers and women share with their loved ones. *Those Bones* anchors these relationships without sacrificing her political impulses, which

---

4. This happened elsewhere. For instance, Black Miamians were displaced to build I-95. See Connolly, *World More Concrete*.

5. Moss, "Forgotten Victims," 737.

position disappearance as state-sanctioned and therefore subject to community resistance and reproach. Bambara layers disappearance in both abstract and concrete, representational and literal, ways. She also positions it as verb of extraction and one of multitude, proffering a series of questions that ask to whom or to what Black mothers and children are reaped. Her Black poetic espouses a grammar of curiosity as it relates to her own subject position as a Black mother, empathizing with Zala's obsession with finding her son and the many other horrors of dispossession that rapidly compound as she is unable to cope with the pace at which the trauma accrues.[6]

Bambara's choice to write the story as fiction is significant because of Mayor Jackson's vehement suspicion of writers and writers who might privilege an exploration of "truths" rather than "clues."[7] Archival material preserved in the Missing and Murdered Children files of the Mayor Maynard Jackson administrative papers, located at the Robert W. Woodruff Library Archives in Atlanta, Georgia, underscores the urgency of interrogating "disappearance" within a story of Black mothers and their children. The mayor's administrative records reveal a concerted effort to preserve the community and global responses to these victims' missing and murdered statuses. The meeting records, memos, and correspondence with media groups in the archive also seem to suggest that the city was both complicit and ill-equipped to infrastructurally grapple with the disappearance of Black life in high concentration. The city's responses then disallowed residents from remembering other formations of violence, thus connecting these disappearances to structural violences. For instance, a large amount of the materials are mailed-in monetary donations from concerned global citizens (both incarcerated and enfranchised) put toward the investigations and citizens arrests of suspects, along with handmade memorials for the victims. Some materials suggest these donations were used for high-profile benefit concerts, surveillance of community programs, and flyers that blamed parents for the disappearance of their children.[8] It also features multiple correspondences between Mayor Jackson's office and various media outlets that sought to produce films, books, or specials about the tragedies.[9]

---

6. I recognize here that Bambara was notably not interested in labels of "feminist" and identified as quintessentially "Black." However, I would argue her method is a Black feminist one because of the ways she positions her maternal character as a reliable, authoritative voice within the story.

7. Derrick Bell, in his foreword to the book's 1995 edition, writes that the project "eschews a search for clues and, instead, undertakes an exploration for truths." Quoted in Baldwin, *Evidence*, vii.

8. "Atlanta Child Murders," series B, Maynard Jackson mayoral administrative records.

9. "Letter from Mayor's office to CBS," box 143, Maynard Jackson mayoral administrative records.

One letter directly relates the mayor's skepticism in "opposing" one film's "avaricious exploitation" of the city, which was "still in mourning."[10] Despite Jackson's apparent distaste for the film, documentation reveals that the mayoral office welcomed high-profile benefit concerts that sometimes raised more than $6 million and attracted celebrities such as Michael Jackson and Stevie Wonder. Also present were media articles or press releases of specials or articles being written about the missing and murdered children. Because Atlanta's major opposed creative explorations of these disappearances—which might pull funds and attention from his own programs—this chapter analyzes the function of Bambara's fictional reckoning. Rather than overlook the personal affordances of fiction, I interrogate Bambara's choice to tell this specific story of Black struggle without drawing on this significant trove of institutional archival documentation.[11]

Where the direct correlation between Bambara's choice of fiction could only be drawn by the author herself, *Those Bones* indicates that fiction is the best way to emphasize the spectacular and extralegal forms of disappearance the author experienced firsthand while in Atlanta. Toward that end, Bambara's own experiences with community organizations such as S.T.O.P. (Save Them or Perish) find their way into the book, making it an "imagined record" of community responses to the disappearance of these children.[12] Her work challenges the popular media's impulse to document these kidnappings only as criminal investigative work. Her capacious treatment of disappearance to include kidnapping, arrests, imprisonment, death, spatial displacement, gentrification, and poverty critiques the novel's political aptitude as a literary form. *Those Bones* asserts disappearance as the primary killer of Black people, both real and symbolic—a perennial matter of Black life and death.[13]

On Disappearing

The disappearance of Black life is a structural project of racism. Literature makes clear disappearance's affects and effects, challenging the genre of historical fiction, memoir, and storytelling. LaMonda Horton-Stallings, in considering

---

10. In a letter to CBS's inquiry about filming a movie about the missing and murdered children, his office responded: "I oppose it: rotten timing, profoundly bad taste and rank, avaricious exploitation. The door of my administration is shut to this project and to anyone peddling it. I respectfully urge you to reconsider your plans. Our city, still in mourning, needs no added burden." "Letter to CBS Television," box 135, Maynard Jackson mayoral administrative records.
11. This archive was assembled in the early 2000s, after Bambara's death.
12. Gilliland and Caswell, "Records and Their Imaginaries."
13. Patterson, *Slavery and Social Death*. Some of these cases remained "unsolved," although Wayne Williams was charged with killing the two adults.

the tension between Black imaginative lives and power, articulates a generative crux when reading and writing disappearance:

> Imagination remains the major force that individuals can rely on to thwart or subvert power, but it is not solely an ocular force of the human mind as it has been defined. *Imagination precedes, and proceeds from, power, power-knowledge, and power plays.* Yet, the materiality of both creativity and imagination, outside of products produced by them and controlled by power, cannot be made evident as material within our current order of knowledge and its systems of discourse.[14]

Disappearance is caught within one such "power play" in that it struggles to express itself outside the violence from which it is born, even when it is creatively pursued. An author's efforts to write humanity into someone who is only authored through the specter of violence is a quandary that resonates throughout this chapter. With this in mind, how might a seemingly sudden and fantastical act—the disappearance of a child, for instance—converge with the centuries-long state and global project of anti-Black racism? Disappearance is both the long and short of the physical erasure of Black folks' lives and bodies. Fictionalized storytelling's tradition of truth-saying makes these layered erasures legible. Literary arts, as embodied in Bambara's *Those Bones*, experiment with lived experience *as* documentation, while acknowledging that they cannot evade documentation entirely.

Enslaved people carried stories of kin disappeared by captors through the Middle Passage. On ships, many were disappeared by disease, violence, and then themselves if they decided the ocean floor was better than that of a cursed ship. M. NourbeSe Philip re-creates the disappeareds' testimonies of being held captive aboard the eighteenth-century ship *Zong*.[15] Those who lived to reach the shores of Jamaica were disappeared by their captors when they were drowned for insurance monies. Philip reappears the spirits and experiences through the language of *Gregson v. Gilbert* (1783), the legal case argued by the murderous captors to collect what they believe they were owed when their "property" was murdered. Philip reorganizes the words from the court case into a book of postmodern poetry told by the drowned enslaved. The bottom margins of the pages list an assortment of West African names—Abioye, Bomani, Ra, and many others—as a nod to those disappeared by their captors and racial slavery as a whole. In addition, she reappears those enslaved as an amalgamated coauthor, Setaey Adamu Boateng, who initially "told" the story

---

14. Horton-Stallings, *Funk the Erotic*, 8; emphasis added.
15. Philip and Shockley, *Zong!*

to Philip—a technique noted on the cover. Not nearly enough of those who are disappeared are reappeared in any form. We often never hear from those who get away: Runaways who escaped enslavement in the middle of the night, those who jumped from slave ships, those who flew away at night to return to their motherland, and those who escaped incarceration continue to erase themselves from the captors that reduced their existence to cargo, slave, and social antagonist.

At the same time, disappearance has, for some Black folks, been a tool to reclaim the structure of their lives in the face of social death. Disappearance is not an act of trading one existence for another, nor is it trading an existence for the lack of one. Under the wide view of state-sanctioned disappearance deployed in Bambara's book, nearly all Black novels whose characters encounter state violence could be considered texts of disappearance. But specific works describe disappearance as a coercive tool by the state, compelling Black folk to disappear and remerge different people. In the years following chattel slavery in the Americas, literature depicted literal and figurative disappearance as an opportunity for Black characters who sought to abandon social and filial expectations that burdened their ability to autonomously fashion their own racial and gendered identities. Both Nella Larsen's novel *Passing* (1929) and Langston Hughes's short story of the same name (1932) situate racial passing as a disappearing act, where one abandons their previous Black life and emerges as white. The protagonist in Richard Wright's *The Outsider* (1953) takes advantage of a train car accident in Chicago to switch identities with a dead man, exploring his new life through mid-century communist and anti-racist organizing. *The Outsider* joined a genre of Great Migration stories, which were published during and after the mass Black exodus north occurring the 1930s and 1940s. These migratory texts also instrumentalize disappearance for those that sought to outrun state-sanctioned violence. Passing approaches one of many forms of oppression: that anti-Blackness can be evaded and outrun. In this sense, disappearance is ensconced in the mythic as well as the real. These cases suggest that a person can disappear into a less oppressive environment than the one they fled—or, in other words, where they had previously appeared. The "new" start of African Americans who disappeared in the night for fear of lynchings in the American South during the early and mid-twentieth century was national terrorism. In this sense, disappearance becomes both a freedom act for the individual and a successful disappearance from the racist South.[16]

---

16. Jacob Lawrence visually reappears those who left the South in the Great Migration in his series "The Migration Series." To view all sixty panels, see the Phillips Collection online, "Jacob Lawrence: The Migration Series," https://lawrencemigration.phillipscollection.org/.

In the myriad ways African American literature plays with and offers up the concept of disappearance, figures are not defined by the circumstances of their reappearance. In other words, Black life is not necessarily made legible through imagined resurrection, either creative or structural, institutional or interpersonal. Just because someone reappears physically does not mean they were only disappeared physically, nor does it mean that they are "back." Anti-Black violence does not always leave material residue, but the dead haunt us as reminders of the power relations that disappeared them. Structural dispossession produces silence, opacity, and disconnection. Avery Gordon conceptualizes haunting as "real only when it is apparitional," a definition that falls short of the complexity of Black disappearance.[17] She notes, "Making contact with the disappeared means encountering the specter of what the state has tried to repress, means encountering it in the affective mode in which haunting traffics."[18] This confrontation with disappearance does not approach the footprint of Black disappearance altogether. Rather than an event, the set of relations that produce Black disappearance is an ongoing project with spatial and spiritual implications. The affective modes of apparition might be obsolete when trying to "make contact" with the disappeared. The haunting lives on to disappear others. But how and when do we account for lives that were never legible to the state beyond their capital? And how can someone be gone only when the scene of their disappearance is subsumed by the violence that replaces it? Does that mean that person was not there at all? Saidiya Hartman's use of *fungibility* may better frame the formations of Black disappearance. Fungibility renders Black subjects beyond their subjecthood or cultural identity, making their absence the bedrock of contemporary urban spaces.[19] In my readings of *Those Bones*, "repression" does not fully describe the methods of Black dispossession it animates, as Gordon suggests. Those who are disappeared cannot be haunted, resurrected, or restored; nor can they haunt, because they form the foundation of capital and life that attempts to interchange them in civil society. Yet, the set of power relations remains.

Writing on the Periphery, Disappearing with Scraps

Bambara rejects such an *apophasis* of Black life through explicit naming of state-sanctioned violence and the state's gains in disappearing Black people. Bambara reimagines Black life in 3D form, embodying an archival practice

---

17. Gordon, *Ghostly Matters*, 126.
18. Gordon, *Ghostly Matters*, 127.
19. Hartman, *Scenes of Subjection*.

that is animated by a similar, Black-centered praxis of reading the periphery and establishing a preconceived life beyond the characters' existences on the page. The author blurs the lines of mothering and mother-author, novel and notes, within her own personal documentation. A mother and artist of the time, Bambara's personal archives pull the scraps from the community and her own home to construct her novel. Take, for example, a note written on a used paper plate. It is quite literally the plane of documentation, the artifact of inquiry and of upheaval.

When I encountered a paper plate described as a "Research Note" in Toni Cade Bambara's papers, I immediately reattuned my orientation toward archival research to encompass the author's lived experiences as a working mother.[20] As a working mother, Bambara may not have had notebooks or legal pads handy. In addition, she could have left her legal pads at home, because taking notes on one might signal her outsider status at a community meeting. The compulsion to write Zala's story may have struck her after taking her daughter to school. The notepad she may have reached for was the plate that she was using at the very same moment. It would have been convenient and disposable. She may not have had time to wash dishes on a regular basis and might have habitually written on paper plates because there were so many strewn about the house, left over from a community picnic.

The paper plate contradicts its own longevity as an ephemeral item that is used to record a research note that may be needed for years to come. The writing in the center of the plate is a draft of an excerpt from the story. On the top far right-hand corner she writes, "Sonny, born Aug, con'd [conceived] Dec." The plate asks us to decenter the plot for a moment and consider a detail as part of the larger story. This detail foregrounds intimate details about her character's lives and her own. Her note about the conception time of her disappeared character demonstrates how intimately entwined she was with her characters and how she cocreated these children with her mother-characters. These characters both precede and exceed the novel itself, and not just by virtue of living in an archive. Bambara's scrap of story helps the plate transcend standard notions of "ephemera," thereby shifting its intended disposability

---

20. I performed this archival research during the summer of 2019 while six months pregnant, extremely hot from the Georgia heat, and disoriented by my one-year-old son, who sat next to me in the umbrella stroller at the Spelman College Archives. I recorded most of my notes on the margins of a receipt I had in my bag because I forgot my notebook for the day. The paper plate struck me because of a similar lived experience. Most of what I write begins on similar materials, like this plate.

and usage.²¹ The placement of Bambara's note about Sonny's conception gestures toward the peripheral writing of research notes, whereby that which constructs the narrative (the prose in the middle of the plate) is elevated, on the ridged lines. This imagery evokes a Black feminist theory of (de-)marginalization, especially understood with bell hooks's call to theorize Black women within feminist theory "from margin to center."²² Bambara answers these calls to literally write on the periphery, creating layers of complexity to her character's stories as she midwifes them along with their mothers. Bambara repurposes the paper plate as a research notepad to organize her thoughts around narrative, form, and character formation.

The paper plate demands that we consider scraps, or that which is seen as disposable, as documentation of one's daily life. Bambara's papers are rife with materials that cannot be processed within traditional schemas of archival metadata and description, such as food stains, dust, hair, hair ties, lint, and other fragments from one's lived existence. They are present in the base of the provided document boxes containing Bambara's papers. Although these are not included in the collection guide, their existence indicates that her materials were not "cleaned" or scrubbed of any previous use before processing. The surprising scraps brighten the properly processed materials. One such example is a one-hundred-page military uniform catalog addressed to Bambara's Philadelphia residence.²³ Earmarked and torn pages render a thirty-year-old, sun-stained document's contents nearly indecipherable, but the catalog itself is not what provides the information. Rather, a small Post-It scribbled with the note "these are the type of boots Sonny would have worn" opens a window onto how Bambara communed with repurposed materials in her small Atlanta apartment. Her mundane activities—such as eating or perusing a catalog—were defined by the characters who spoke to her. The paper plate, the Post-It, and the catalog demand a Black feminist orientation toward preservation and research that encompasses her lived experience. Black women's archives demand care.²⁴ Caring for them alters the institutional processes that quell the power of ephemeral materials. This process allows readers and researchers

---

21. Toni Cade Bambara Collection, 1939–1996, Spelman College Archives. Appadurai's *The Social Life of Things* also discusses tensions around commodity, use, and its ephemeral lives.

22. hooks reestablishes a feminist theory based on the centralization of Black women's lives instead of an accompaniment to a larger, white-dominated theoretical community and conceptualization of feminism. hooks, *Feminist Theory*.

23. Bambara lived in Philadelphia before and after her stint in Atlanta and would eventually spend the last ten years of her life there.

24. The university archivist who processed this original collection was the late Taronda Spencer and a Spelman student assistant, Spelman alumnae Malika Redmond.

to make room for the many focal points of a story that illuminate the many dimensions of her characters and their preconceptualized (material and metaphysical) lives. Her archives grow an ecosystem of writing, documenting, and constructing, while also fashioning other forms of reality that extend into the spatial conception of the city she writes in written form.

The Making of Bambara's Mid-Century Atlanta

Black people, and the vanishment of their bodies that renders them disappeared, alter the physical construction of the spaces they (once) inhabit(ed). There is a politics that attends Black bodies' disappearance, as it is inhabited by Zala and her son. These politics affect the spatial formation of Atlanta. The long history of Atlanta's social, geographic, and economic space-making is beyond the scope of this project. But Bambara uses Zala to draw the map of Atlanta while exposing what she perceived to be the nefarious political motives of Mayor Maynard Jackson's first and second terms. The co-constructing, antithetical projects—in this case, working well within the binary of disappearance and appearance—manifests in the physical body of Zala and the mothers she represents, as well as the land they stand on. Many attributed Atlanta's prolific period of urban renewal (in its physical manifestation) to the city's self-described "youngest, fattest, Blackest, Mayor in America" and his investments in Atlanta's capitalist industry sect.[25] Even still, those who were attempted to be disappeared cast a shadow on the mayor's efforts, making the Atlanta he aimed to grow an allegory for the one the Atlantan citizens physically experienced. He aimed to grow a city that held disappearance and appearance in one hand, while holding the attempts to survive material conditions of urban life that invested in buildings, instead of quality of life, in the other.

Histories of the late twentieth-century American South depict a region fraught with racial and economic unrest, despite the mayor's attempts to literally build it otherwise. The social confrontations that defined the precarity of Southern civil society did not taper off after the passage of federal civil rights legislation in 1964. Alabama, Mississippi, Missouri, and Georgia entered a new phase of rebellion after the failures and successes of the civil rights movement's attention to voting rights. The city had its own unique responses to the civil rights era and the Black Power movement that included sit-ins, business boycotts, and rebellion that sparked images of idyllic coalition politics.[26]

---

25. W. King, "Black Commissioner of Police."
26. Kruse, *White Flight*, 180.

Atlanta's image emerged out of this time as a progressive one, despite the fact that controversial issues like school choice and land development shored up subtler forms of social conservatism.[27] Decades of land grabbing in the city's most desirable downtown and northwest areas, the building of the Interstate 285 perimeter, and excessive school zoning rules came into fruition. Gentrification efforts secured the white, upper-middle and rich ruling class within the north city limits of Atlanta, while the city's slow relegation of Black residents to the south and southeast began to populate its outskirts.[28] Maynard Jackson shone as a jewel in the crown of its *representational* veneer, and the city's business developments brought to bear even more attention to the new mayor's savvy. He would be heralded for developing Atlanta into a national and global destination for business and leisure in the decades to come, redefining Atlanta's post–civil rights legacy.

Jackson scored a large political backwind when 95 percent of Black Atlantans across the socioeconomic spectrum elected him. At the same time, his in-office decisions continued to alienate his meager white electorate.[29] In 1974 he fired Atlanta's white police chief, John Inman, after calls for his removal on the basis of racial insensitivity to the Black community. Many saw Atlanta's deep-seated racial issues as systemic, especially when Jackson appointed a close friend with little experience as the public safety commissioner.[30] This scandal revealed a status quo corruption agenda to some Black Atlantans.[31] Symbolic moves like these cosmetically aligned with his campaign promises to Black Atlantans, but had little political payoff for larger public opinion.[32] It appeared that Jackson used cronyism to achieve success in the white sectors of business and finance, despite the uproar among white citizens over the

---

27. Jackson's campaign seized the rise of Atlanta's return to Black organizational prowess. Energetic and young, the vice mayor entered the city's highest office just in time to quell the fever for Black political representation, as well as infrastructural issues such as the crime and high unemployment rate. His campaign won an empowered Black Atlanta—both in the political and cultural sense—with a business and financial acumen that staved off the complete alienation of white voters. Behind closed doors—which most working-class/poor Black folks were not privy to—Jackson's administration ushered in a series of gentrification efforts in what later became an era of business development and urban separatism.

28. Former opponent Sam Massel described him in his obituary as "a thorn" in the side of white people in Atlanta: "But I think most [people] respected the role he pursued and the strength he demonstrated with his success." Suggs, "From 2003."

29. Kruse, *White Flight*, 240; based on the 1970 census of Atlanta. Gibson and Jung, "Historical Census Statistics."

30. W. King, "Black Commissioner of Police."

31. Eaves was fired by Jackson in 1978 for admitting to selling copies of the police service exam to a select few, and then exposed by the FBI for selling his vote on two rezoning projects. "Eaves Convicted"; and Ayres, "Atlanta Mayor."

32. Firestone, "Census Shows Growth."

firing of the former chief. The pocketbooks of white Atlantans swelled despite their distaste for a man 83 percent of them had voted against.[33] The totality of Black Atlanta was not reflected in the city's newfound prosperity, despite their representation in the mayor's office.

The Black people who felt left behind grappled with supporting their new mayor while experiencing the displacement of their neighborhoods and small businesses. Working-class unrest flared in a 1977 strike of Black sanitation workers, concretizing the separation between Atlanta's "Black political class and the Black working class it governed."[34] To the sanitation workers and their sympathizers, Jackson's "word was garbage," as they protested for better wages and health protections for those who served the city in one of Atlanta's worst cold snaps.[35] Mayor Jackson successfully increased the number of contracts to minority-owned businesses from around 1 percent to a whopping 35 percent during his time in office, during his first and second terms, which went into the early '80s.[36] Minority business owners were specifically instrumental in the construction of the new international terminal at Hartsfield Airport—which was completed "ahead of schedule and under budget" in 1980—but histories rarely mention their workers.[37] The airport's completion signified that the divisions of Atlanta once drawn to demarcate race were now shored up by those of class. Bambara's characters play out these divisions in a conversation between Zala, an affluent business owner, and a reverend. Their interplay determines that the "Black Mecca of the South" was growing "too big, too fast" for *all* its citizens: "We're always so busy patting ourselves on the back about our achievements, we totally ignore those who can't get ahead."[38] Also, the "demographic changes" caused by the developments did not go unnoticed by Bambara's characters, who observe a connection between a "series of fires set in the West End area, the proposed school closings there, the proposed reapportionment schemes, and the aggressive offers real-estate dealers were making to the old-time residents of the neighborhood to get out."[39] The "take

---

33. Both white and Black business development boomed during the mayor's tenure. This does not mean that white business owners or Atlantans were happy, however. Many were spooked by the perception of scarcity evoked by Black prosperity. Some characterized it as "an unfriendly business climate and rising crime." Michan Andrew Connor points out that these are both racialized constructs. Connor, "Metropolitan Secession," 445.

34. Prescod, "Black Political Class."

35. During a televised Atlanta Braves game people in the stands held up a banner that read, "Maynard's Word is Garbage." Prescod, "Black Political Class."

36. Ortega, "Black *Flâneuse*."

37. Some reports put this as high as 42 percent. B. Rice, "Maynard Jackson"; and Connor, "Metropolitan Secession."

38. Bambara, *Those Bones*, 81.

39. Bambara, *Those Bones*, 226.

over schemes of the seventies" were well documented by Bambara and the community members she portrays.[40] Jackson relied on the airport as a key success on which he ran and won his second term in office. The downtown area was set to develop the same way: "The downtown area [Zala] mastered at five . . . was a confusion of sawhorse barriers, open ditches, plank sidewalks, and sandy pathways for yellow Caterpillars carrying boulders in their maws."[41] Despite intraracial class tensions, the mayor hoped his ability to grow Black business would characterize him in his second term as a firm but fair Black mayor for all its residents.

Although he failed to avoid some scandals, Jackson appeared to be headed toward a strong finish of his two-term mayoral tenure until the missing and murdered children's cases.[42] The mayoral administrative records contain roughly 160 folders of materials from his campaign and first (1974–77), second (1978–82), and third (1990–94) mayoral terms. The Atlanta Child Murders materials are archived in the first and second mayoral term series, along the lines of his terms. Contracts, media, and correspondence from his first and second terms comprise these boxes, while laudatory media over his successes is overrepresented. His collection also delineates a clear "before" and "after" the missing and murdered children—success before, scandal during, and then a scandal-less glide into retirement. *Those Bones Are Not My Child* textures the mayor's archival legacy by collapsing other forms of disappearance occurring during and around the mayor's administrative years. Despite Bambara's unapologetic centering of the missing and murdered children, she manages to interweave the voices of everyday Black people dealing with the totality of Jackson's administrative actions. Her narrative undoes the perceived linearity of the mayor's boxes. She paradoxically fills the gaps in the collection guide by presenting disappearance as void—the archival narrative that a three-term organization fails to tell the mayor's story, warts and all.

Clear in the organization is that the mayor, rather than the city he served, was the protagonist of his own administration.[43] Bambara tells the story of Jackson's Atlanta from the perspective of a range of modern Atlantan characters, instead of the mayor who attempted to embody it. To give voice to its many speakers and their chorus, Bambara evokes Zala Spencer as a type of flaneuse through whom readers experience a survey of different groups of people with varying political and social orientations. The urban streetwalker's story of an administration is especially successful in intervening on Jackson's mayoral

---

40. Bambara, *Those Bones*, 82.
41. Bambara, *Those Bones*, 85.
42. Jackson was reelected as mayor in 1990 and served until 1994.
43. This mirrors the organization of his own materials.

memory by positioning his administration as a key factor in concretizing the mechanisms that made the disappearance of so many children possible rather than circumstantial. This creates a novel in which our narrator vocalizes an entire city for us through the gesture of noticing. This treatment allows the audience to co-observe the reeling that occurred before and after the scandal was "over," much like in Gwendolyn Brooks's *In the Mecca* (1968). Brooks, an expert reader of "Blackness and region and space," and master of the urban realism motif, depicts the South Side of Chicago in the aftermath of the civil rights era, during which many of its leaders were assassinated. Atlanta's popular "Black Mecca of the South" nomenclature is part of a long tradition of evoking Meccas like the one depicted in Brooks's work. Much like varying references to Mecca throughout the country (Harlem, New York, and Oakland, California) and its original geographic space (hajj), it represents "deliverance from Western oppression but also a site of many deaths."[44] Bambara explores the trope in her novel,[45] clearly relaying the proscription of its vibrancy as the nuance of its geographic texture.[46]

Those Bones is a continuation of Brooks's literary location of the "Mecca," which more accurately represents a decentralized network of urbanity rife with its own beautiful disarray. Figuring Atlanta as Mecca, a building/space where people could mingle, mix, and find refuge, Bambara figured Atlanta as a Mecca that was active but not too "busy" to be hardened to the political factors that continued to define its spatial confines.[47] Bambara's protagonist continues the tradition of Brooks's late-twentieth-century poetics to ground the "Mecca" folklore in a celebration of the heterogeneity of Blackness. Both Brooks and Bambara also challenge readers to configure a Black cartography defined by the intramural sociality of its citizens, rather than a physical map. Bambara takes up the work of many Black women artists of the time who produced work impervious to the focus on mainstream politics of place. The literary map drawn of the holy-but-bustling city was defined by the vernacular of its own community, rather than by a garish politician.

Those Bones also organizes its version of Atlanta around the lived experiences of the disappeared. As such, readers are privy to the inner thoughts of characters who are socially located in different parts of the appearance-disappearance-reappearance schema. Bambara is especially successful in

---

44. Clarke, "After Mecca," 3.
45. Bambara, *Those Bones*, 81.
46. Jackson, *Harlem World*.
47. It is arguable that since the civil rights movement, Black and white Atlanta politicians evoked the "Mecca" in their slogan of "the city too busy to hate." The phrase was popularized in the mid-1960s by its then mayor Ivan Allen's testimony before Congress in favor of the Equal Accommodations Act.

exploring Vietnam War veterans' struggle to integrate into civilian life upon their return to the United States. Spencer, Zala's estranged husband and Sonny's father, occupies most of his literary space by grappling with the traumas of serving as a Black infantryman. As Atlanta searches for kids who have disappeared, Spence wrestles with the guilt of reappearing as a veteran. His emotional vacancy gestures toward post-traumatic stress syndrome, which characterizes most accounts of those returning from any war. His affect was heightened by the fact that Atlantans were essentially "out of primary society during its biggest growth of change" of civil rights and racial turmoil, thus arriving in a new social terrain.[48] We witness the woeful integration of veterans in a despondent Spencer, who struggles to find community and understanding even in his best friends. He even materializes an imaginary comrade who also served in Vietnam, and this "front-line buddy" "would be able to see with Spence's eyes—'Nam, Bowen Homes, the look of the woods during those search weekends."[49] Spence's experience relates, for instance, the explosion of the Bowen Homes day care not only as a community tragedy but also as one that was felt intimately by those who lived through literal war and the warlike conditions of living amid criminalized survival strategies. The novel positions panic as a communal ethos across unique communities of Black folks who were already living with multiple threats of disappearance, struggling with and for those they wanted to reappear.

Disappearance was a quotidian violence that attended the late twentieth-century Black residents of Atlanta. First the men disappeared to Vietnam. Then the city to big money. Then the children. On July 21, 1979, Edward "Teddy" Smith disappeared walking home from the Greenbriar Skating Rink in southwest Atlanta. Four days later, Alfred "Q" Adams disappeared after being dropped off at a bus stop. Their disappearances marked a string of around twenty missing and murdered children and two adults who died in similar circumstances. By the summer of 1981, roughly twenty-seven children and two adults had gone missing. Some were found dead, and some were never found.[50] Most of the murders remain unsolved today. Wayne Williams, named the "Atlanta Monster," was charged and convicted of the two murders

---

48. Jones goes on to discuss how he was overseas during most of the civil rights era, so when he returned in 1968, he couldn't fit the new social fabric of the country "into his head." Jones et al., "Oral History Interview."

49. Bambara, *Those Bones*, 349.

50. One of the few linkages of the victims' deaths was that many of them were strangled by putting clothes or plastic in their mouths. Of course, DNA analysis was not yet widely used or available, so detectives linked the victims by similar circumstances of abrupt disappearance, the age and race of the victims, and then similar circumstances of found bodies. It's also notable that two adults were incorporated into the list, which is widely used to dispute the assumption that Wayne Williams was behind all the crimes. For more, see Lindsey, *Atlanta Monster*.

of the adults. Most of the remaining unsolved murders remain attributed to him, but with inconclusive evidence. Many saw Williams's arrest as a quixotic response to the desire to quell fears and unrest. Mayor Jackson struggled in the final years of his second term (1978–82), as he worked hard to balance the mounting cases and his efforts to tout his reputation of crime reform and business growth.[51] Many agreed that the federal government needed to be involved—either as a flex of the mayor's connections to federal officials or to take over an unsuccessful investigation. The mayor's tenure was supposed to symbolize a new Atlanta for everyone, but Black Atlanta was no monolith. Jackson's primary electorate paid the price of Atlanta's renewed city.

The Missing and Murdered Children cases did not stain the otherwise untarnished celebrity of Maynard Jackson. Most public administrations are rife with controversy, and Black administrations pique particular scrutiny.[52] His legacy, however, should be understood as deeply entwined with the racialized socioeconomic luxation of Atlanta's eroding Black working class. Jackson's administration espoused the "geographic margins" Black Atlantans came to symbolically and physically occupy, creating the untenable space through which they were disappeared.[53] Bambara's fiction spotlights these lives, centering the community instead of the public administrator—thus giving voice to a few boxes of his administrative papers. She also exorcises the tragedies within the global geographies of anti-Blackness and spatial exclusion that thrived on demonizing the victim's mothers. *Those Bones* describes in detail how the children were wrenched from and fought for by their community. Bambara continues the Black feminist poetic of the community voice fighting for these children and, like Brooks, evokes its audience to demand its leaders "sit where the light corrupts your face" in demand of state accountability, both present and past.[54]

Lighting the Way

> We are the light
> we are robbed of
> each time one of us
> is lost.[55]

---

51. Halbfinger, "Maynard H. Jackson Jr."
52. Musgrove, *Rumor, Repression, and Racial Politics*.
53. Perry, *Black Women*, 90.
54. Brooks, *In the Mecca*.
55. Bambara, *Those Bones*, i.

This four-line poem is the epigraph of the published edition of *Those Bones*. Bambara typed these words on the dedication page, writing "'Dedication' page (four-liner against map of Atlanta)," as archived in Bambara's collection of papers at Spelman College. Behind the typeface is a hand-drawn map of the continental United States. The book was dedicated to the children whose "lights" we were robbed of, as well as the community left to persevere without them. This four-liner serves as the initial departure point for Bambara's oscillation between appearing and disappearing, where even though the "light" is robbed of us, she evokes a "we," in which every person is interrelated. In the novel, Bambara oscillates between Zala Spencer's experience and the communal terror experienced as a result of the kidnappings. At times, Zala's is metonymic for the communal terror. It is in this way that Bambara continues to play along the lines of the universal and the individual. While zooming in and out of Zala Spencer's experience over a year's time, the author explores the larger social issues of the time, such as gentrification and global anti-Blackness. Much like the four lines atop the map of the United States, the disappearance (kidnapping, runaway, death) and appearance (living, staying home, coming home) of Black children spatialize Atlanta's Black geography. As a narrator, Bambara deploys light to map the "robbing" of children's life onto Atlanta. It considers this map from different voices, characters, and frameworks to analyze how the Black maternal pronounces these contours in both universal and individual terms. Bambara plays with a blurred notion of disappearance, where those who disappear continue to reappear by memory. I plumb her use of light, a term she uses to produce the metaphor for missing and murdered children, as a flashpoint in a larger struggle against the systematic erasure of Black people from their geographical and urban habitations. This erasure was systemized by the growing white urban class's displacement of Black people's homes and lives. Bambara's deployment of light hails her audience to bear witness to the emotional expense of the mother and that of the entire community. Bambara plays on this epigraph for the duration of the novel in macro-, micro-, and metaphorical terms. Using it as our guide to understand her narrative form, we are able to see a community's unfoldment of resistance to the full "fading" of any one of its members' light.

The author deploys a series of "lights," symbolizing the need to widen our scope of atrocities beyond just the Atlanta Child Murders. She makes visible the global implications of anti-Blackness and the locals' sensibilities to attune them to other tragedies. We encounter a griot-like character, who is described as a "dark-skinned, bumpy faced brother" who first jolts Zala at an arts festival with a braying, "Wake up, Africans!"[56] The man goes on to index modern

---

56. Bambara, *Those Bones*, 167.

white supremacy's atrocities, including the US involvement in Grenada and Panama—much to the chagrin of the folks at the park, who are dismissive of him.[57] The character's ramblings mirror the expressed collective frustration of other characters who found connections between the reorganization of Atlanta's social, cultural, and systemic institutions and the missing and murdered cases possible.

The griot in the park speaks as the voice from the archive. Several folders in the Mayor Maynard Jackson Administrative Records, for instance, house cards, letters, and art pieces made in solidarity with the families of the victims. This includes things from university chapters of NAACP (like at Dillard University),[58] local organizations from all fifty states, children's classrooms,[59] and locally incarcerated people who donated their commissary monies.[60] Many concerned citizens, including those of the local Socialist Worker's Party of Atlanta, sent a letter directly connecting the United States' deployment of funds for global coups with the perceived lack of resources available to search for kids: "The fact that the Reagan administration has just sent $5 million in military aid to the murderous junta in El Salvador while refusing to forward a penny to aid the investigations in Atlanta *amounts to criminal neglect*."[61] Using both local and global politics to draw attention to the missing and murdered children, local Atlanta citizens also wrote to mayoral and federal administrations demanding that funds be allocated in search of the children. For one, the aggregate of predominantly Black Universal Fellowship of Metropolitan Community Churches in Atlanta demanded of the Reagan administration:

> You have at your disposal tremendous resources of *all* the people of this Republic. Our concern is that you use *those* resources. This terror *must* stop!

---

57. A Black former government agent appears on pages 434–46 on a reel of footage that members of S.T.O.P. view in order to glean information on federal involvement in the investigations. His interview with Zala and another mother, which occurs over twelve pages, details COINTELPRO, the destruction of the Black Panther Party, and the imprisonment of Angela Davis.

58. "Letter from Dillard University's NAACP Chapter to Mayor of Atlanta," April 14, 1981, box 143, Maynard Jackson mayoral administrative records.

59. "Letter from ten-year-old class in Houston, TX to the Mayor of Atlanta" and "University's NAACP Chapter to Mayor of Atlanta," box 135, Maynard Jackson mayoral administrative records.

60. These monies totaled about $423 and were donated in sums of up to $25 and as little as $1. "Funds donated by prisoners," 1981, box 143, Maynard Jackson mayoral administrative records.

61. "Letter from Economic Opportunity Atlanta (EOA) to Mayor of Atlanta," box 143, Maynard Jackson mayoral administrative records; and "Letter from Atlanta Teamsters to Mayor of Atlanta," June 1, 1981, box 143, Maynard Jackson mayoral administrative records.

It is now of longer duration than the Iranian hostage situation. We plead with you and implore you to express more than compassion. We recognize that you and the Congress have sent money—but more is needed to rebuild the morale of those people.[62]

The money referred to here is the $1.5 million that Reagan reallocated from the Department of Housing and Urban Development budget to the city of Atlanta to aid in the search for the then nearly twenty children who had gone missing. A specific folder of the collection is dedicated to the press releases published by the mayor's office. One release stated that the money would be put toward local "community development" of the "lower income areas of the City," where most of the kidnapped children lived.[63] Local, national, and global sympathizers had no difficulty connecting what they saw as another mode of injustice done to a predominantly working-class/poor Black neighborhood.

Bambara's griot gives ripe context to pluralized sentiments of the time, thus challenging readers to draw their own connections between them. Bambara plays the griot's declarations off the mundane nature of Zala's daily life without her son, expressed via detailed prose. Zala pushes against her own deployed universality when, throughout the novel, she hails the audience with her boldly placed "you"s. "You" begins the prologue: "You're on the porch with the broom sweeping the same spot, getting the same sound—dry straw against dry leaf caught in the loose-dirt crevice of the cement tiles."[64] And "you" begins the epilogue: "You're at the keyboard trying to answer a letter."[65] This use of the second person brings readers into the novel when time, distance, or belief is suspended. The beginning "you're" throws us into a scene with a mundane activity that sparks the dull nature of shock. We are sweeping "the same spot, getting the same sound," a nod to the slow-moving, monotonous behemoth of a novel that is about to play out for us in daily activities marked by twenty-four journal entries (twenty-four hours) that span over a year. Several other times we hear "you," sometimes directed at the readers, and not other characters. Again, the man in the park ends his diatribe with an emphatic, "Can you hear me?" and when Zala is punitively questioned by a

---

62. Universal Fellowship of Metropolitan Community Churches, "Letter to President Ronald Reagan," March 29, 1981, box 143, Maynard Jackson mayoral administrative records. The italicized terms were originally underlined in the document.
63. "Press Release on funds from the United States Department of Housing and Urban Development," June 1, 1981, box 143, Maynard Jackson mayoral administrative records.
64. Bambara, *Those Bones*, 3.
65. Bambara, *Those Bones*, 665.

detective, we too are asked, "Did you kill your son . . . ?"[66] Readers are folded into the scene to question their inherent culpability as passive spectators.

"Wake up, Africans!" Zala reads one morning on the cover of a local newspaper.[67] Like the man in the park, Bambara invites both the audience and Zala to "wake up" to the issues that the concerned citizens raised to their local government. Like a lighthouse whose light blindingly flashes one moment and then brings darkness the next, we are guided through a singular story that leads to a much larger one. The projection of guilt, fear, anxiety, and terror is shone in Zala Spencer's daily affect, and we with her by the aforementioned provocations. In this sense, Bambara's novel centers maternal trauma as the method and means to articulate the emotional scene of disappearance. It also addresses our own culpability in the disappearance of the Atlanta children, and our role in the global manifestations of anti-Blackness within it.

Dimming the Light: Bad Black Mothers

We are given the precession and succession to darkness, spotlighting the missing and murdered children in one moment and illuminating another social crisis the next. In the novel's early drafts, Bambara pitched the manuscript as a story about "what it was like to live under siege" in the three years of the highest rate of kidnapping.[68] The siege she depicts in the novel, however, is a result of the slow, methodical violence against the mothers of the Atlanta's working-class/poor neighborhoods. Siege plays an important role in Bambara's attempts to convey the sustained maternal terror and the long-standing resistance to it, rather than the sudden terror inflicted on an entire community. GerShun Avilez analyzes *Those Bones Are Not My Child* through the lens of "terror" to suggest that scenes of mundanity fix the novel in a "language of emergency and siege."[69] Avilez's treatment aligns with the imagery of the book's original title of *Ground Cover*, where the small, unorganized communities of Atlanta spread to protect their children from kidnappers.[70] Avilez arrives at the lens of terror through James Baldwin's book-length work on the

---

66. Bambara, *Those Bones*, 188.
67. Bambara, *Those Bones*, 428.
68. Boyd, "'Osage Avenue' Docu Shoots," Toni Cade Bambara papers, part 1, box 10.
69. Avilez, "Aesthetics of Terror," 18.
70. According to Encyclopedia.com, ground covers are "low-growing, spreading plants that help to stop weeds from growing." This title is fitting because of the many forms of resistance deployed by the community, extending from "bat patrols" of men night-patrolling their own blocks with baseball bats, to the people incarcerated who sent their commissary money to funds to help find the kids.

Atlanta Child Murders, *The Evidence of Things Not Seen* (1985), which tells the story of the murders by investigating the case of Wayne Williams, who was eventually convicted of two of the murders associated with the case. Baldwin's sizeable nonfiction work takes on the tropes of terror, siege, and "state of emergency" to surmise Atlanta's making of a man like Wayne Williams. The trope of "siege" is notable here, but Avilez a missed an opportunity to delve deeper into the maternal politics of the book, especially since the editor of *Those Bones* once likened the process to writing-while-mothering.[71] The tropes of siege and terror could be interrogated further by investigating the extensions of Zala's maternal status and the specific trauma of being located within the condition of Black mothering itself. Bambara lays out these connections clearly.[72]

A barrage of kidnappings, explosions, and other forms of slow violence punctuated the conditions of siege for Black Atlanta mothers circa 1980.[73] In 1980 the Bowen Homes day care center exploded, killing four children and one teacher in a low-income area of northwest Atlanta. The explosion rocked the community, and many maintained that it was a bombing rather than an accidental explosion caused by a gas leak.[74] This event joined the kidnappings in ongoing conversations about the direct assault against Black mothers and children. The mothers in Bambara's version of these intertwined events resist the unsolved murders of their children, which were regarded by larger society and the mayor's office as coincidental.[75] This exceeded the written page into

---

71. Toni Morrison once said in an interview: "There was never a place I worked, or a time I worked, that my children did not interrupt me, not matter how trivial—because it was never trivial to them. The writing could never take precedence over them. Which is why I had to write under duress, and in a state of siege and with a lot of compulsion. I couldn't count on any sustained period of free time to write. I couldn't write the way writers write, I had to write the way a woman with children writes. That means that you have to have immense powers of concentration. I would never tell a child, 'Leave me alone, I'm writing.' That doesn't mean anything to a child. What they deserve and need, in-house, is a mother. They do not need and cannot use a writer." Morrison and Taylor-Guthrie, *Conversations*, 238.

72. Rankine, "Condition of Black Life."

73. Rob Nixon describes "slow violence" as gradual violence that appears out of sight in the context of environmental inhabitability and disaster. See Nixon, *Slow Violence*. My definition is shaped by Christen Smith's use of the term to discuss Black mothers and the violence they experience by extension of police violence. I would also suggest that there is a cultural production component to slow violence, one that frames its victims as ignorant of the assaults they endure, and thus deserving of them. This helps frame violence that ruins lives as something they "did to themselves." C. Smith, "Slow Death."

74. Bambara, *Those Bones*, 276.

75. The explosion was chalked up to a gas leak, but many citizens thought it was a racialized attack reminiscent of the bombing of the Birmingham Church that killed four small girls during the civil rights movement. Bambara, *Those Bones*, 382.

reality—many mothers of the victims formed their own search parties and hold vigils to this day.[76] By working with private investigators, police (past and present officers), and other community members, the mothers of Atlanta refused to be depicted as the "Renaissance pietas"[77] they believed the media attempted to portray them as. Bambara's characters saw the weeping Virgin Mary imagery as part of a project of pacifying mothers and discouraging them from finding their children.[78] The mothers digested this portrayal as a suggestion of them being ignorant and negligent. They were not victims. They were fighters. In other words, by depicting the mothers as engulfed by grief, they could impose a culpability or guilt from being bad and "unconcerned" mothers.[79] Archival records reveal an advertisement for a community group called Save Them or Perish, or S.T.O.P., which encouraged Atlantans to wear green ribbons in solidarity with the families of those who went missing and stressed that society was both "the victim and the victimizer." The ad continues, "Perhaps this is a time in history when we *must* signal one another that we want LIFE. Drugs, including alcohol, lack of decent moral codes, erosion of the family, perversions against people of the world . . . indicate the NOW [sic] is the time for people to act with love."[80] S.T.O.P. is depicted as S.A.F.E. in the novel, and many of the scenes most likely derived from Bambara's personal interactions with the mothers of the victims at the time.[81] She illustrates the frantic mothers' perceived anguish and the culmination of a slow cultural project to depict mothers as the reasons their children disappeared.

Bambara places the theme of culpability strategically throughout the novel to test the audience's own tendencies toward vilifying Zala as a negligent parent. Zala's inner battle with her status as a mother incenses her anguish to find Sonny. After Sonny is disappeared, Zala's choices, hobbies, and actions are scrutinized by the media, city, and country. Mayoral recordkeeping reveals the city pushed parental responsibility as an actionable agenda item. A city staffer's notes from a meeting with the Department of Justice in 1981 literally

---

76. Suggs, "From 2005."
77. Bambara, *Those Bones*, 428.
78. Georgia State University professor and journalist Lemoin DeLeaver Pierce has a large repertoire of Black Madonna figures in the Atlanta University Research Center Archives as well.
79. Bambara, *Those Bones*, 40.
80. S.T.O.P. flyer, 1981, box 147, Maynard Jackson mayoral administrative records. "'Save them or Perish' (S.T.O.P.) Want to build a monument for the children 'that is more than a tomb stone.' . . . Many people are wearing Green Ribbons in mourning for our children." Italicized words were originally underlined in the text.
81. Bambara said that the novel originally began as journal entries, then essays, then a piece of investigative journalism before it turned into a novel. Boyd, "'Osage Avenue' Docu Shoots," Toni Cade Bambara papers, part 1, box 10.

underscored the words "stress parental responsibility."[82] Bambara reveals the role of detrimental intracommunal rhetoric. Gossip intensifies Zala's personal experience of terror. Media and government portrayals of Black mothers accompany the politics of self-policing of Black mothers as "respectable" citizen subjects. Where examples of external negative portrayal are represented in administrative and activist documentation, it is most poignantly revealed in Zala's perception of herself. She often attributes her status as a primary caregiver/single mother,[83] her working-class/poor status,[84] and her unkempt appearance[85] as contributing factors to Sonny's disappearance. Zala unjustly corroborates her insecurities with the circumstances of most of the children's kidnappings. Last witnesses saw most of the children being lured by the promise of doing odd jobs of making money, or bagging groceries for a few cents a bag. These are all offers she feels her son would have been intrigued to take because of her inability to care for him.[86] At one point, she even resigns to the fact that Sonny has run away because of her bad mothering.[87] The mothers' paranoia, which Bambara personally encountered as an activist, attunes with Zala's paranoia of being seen as a bad mother, or one that would be apathetic to her son's well-being. With little state accountability, mothers like Zala blamed themselves for their children's disappearance.

Zala's various social locations—single mother, working-class/poor person, Black woman—all converge under a long social and cultural project of determining Black mothers as "unfettered" to their status of respectable womanhood.[88] Under these constraints, Zala resists the idyllic Black Madonna portrayals that determine her to be unwieldy because of her statuses. Still, she spends time arguing and proving her care for her children. Zala's acts push against the ideas of early Black sociologists, who were surprised that an "unmarried mother" could be "as sensitive as the legally married mother"—implying that her marital status may void her of "normal" feelings in search of her son.[89] Zala balances her discouragement in looking for her son herself with trying to prove that she was indeed a good mother to the media and

---

82. Staff notes, Mayor Maynard Jackson, January 30, 1981, box 147, Maynard Jackson mayoral administrative records. "Missing and Murdered Children," "discussion agenda for meeting with department of justice officials," underscores "massive volunteer program," "don't use the word crisis," "parental responsibility."
83. Bambara, *Those Bones*, 51.
84. Bambara, *Those Bones*, 314–35.
85. Bambara, *Those Bones*, 215.
86. Bambara, *Those Bones*, 200; and Lindsey, *Atlanta Monster*.
87. Bambara, *Those Bones*, 104.
88. Frazier and Platt, *Negro Family*, 114–15.
89. Bambara, *Those Bones*, 103, 156.

government: "They'd gone through packets and packets of pictures looking for a suitable one [for flyers], a photo in which Sonny wasn't squinting, making a face, or looking sloppy and uncared for."[90] The probing of Zala's personal choices and relationships signals a larger phenomenon of scrutiny over Black mothers' parenting choices that cropped up with the 1965 Moynihan Report and the introduction of state welfare. Black mothers without men living in the home were seen as a threat to the American institution of family.[91] Social digestions of respectability kept Black women from being recognized as heads of households and—crucial to this study—as people who were givers of love and worthy of secure intimacy.[92] Black motherhood serves as a prism through which the novel reflects all dimensions of public anxiety about Black sociality: the social and governmental pressure to end the kidnappings of Black children, the paranoia of mothers and community members regarding the state and each other, and the pressure for Atlanta's first Black mayor to end the crises while enduring skepticism from both Black and white communities.

Ultimately, Bambara's light coaxes us away from images previously brought to bear that might visibilize redress for maternal mourning. Black mothers in activist groups mourned while they searched. Although the police stopped looking, the mothers did not, and readers are forced to wait, impatiently. The novel gestures toward our inability to leave the scene of maternal mourning and disappearance. The prologue is written by Zala in 1981—after the Atlanta Child Murders were "over"—showing that the "light" of which we were once robbed does not necessarily come back when a child returns. Rather, the trauma of disappearance lingers. Interpolating the audience into Zala's subject position fails, however, for in the bulk of the proper novel, Bambara takes a "me vs. the world" trope with Zala, and the mothers of the disappeared, who took to "cracking the investigation" themselves,[93] forcing readers to grapple with their own passivity. This passivity becomes palpable as more children are found dead and the novel approaches four hundred, five hundred, and then six hundred pages. Sonny eventually returns after taking a "trip," and Zala's suspicions of his "escape" from her are confirmed. But there is no relief after a tight-lipped Sonny exhibits a number of odd behaviors that send Zala into a desperate mission to understand what her son endured for the last 365 days. The mourning is sustained.

---

90. Bambara, *Those Bones*, 108.
91. Cohen, "Punks, Bulldaggers, and Welfare Queens."
92. I've written further on "anti-respectability as methodology." See Collins-White, "Rethinking the Human."
93. Bambara, *Those Bones*, 371.

Finding the Light

Those Bones Are Not My Child shows that kidnapping does gesture toward mystery but yields a more pronounced memory than any "resolved" crime possibly could. Bambara's use of the light is an inverse one. As she undertakes the cases of the missing and murdered children, she actually emphasizes the social and cultural issues that were made hidden by the widespread attention to the children. It is here that we can see one of the major correctives *Those Bones* provides to the mayor's records of the disappearances. In his attempts to rebuild Atlanta, the mayor foreclosed upon the missing and murdered children's investigations as part and parcel of the intermingled tragedy of gentrification. The children were disappeared by their environment, rather than the spontaneous social actors who took them from their families. Bambara's culture work re-centers the missing and murdered children and their primary injured affiliates: the Black mothers who were left behind to grieve their loss. In this sense, Bambara moves past some diasporic aesthetic practices invested in visibility and representation, creating instead a "shared space of visibility," or the apex of the multiple political and social crises in these three fraught years.[94] Her multiple applications of light were grounded in the petering Black Arts Movement's Black aesthetic and literary practice. As a key player in the movement, Bambara replicated its hypervigilant cognition, which speaks to the ways whiteness had previously colonized light and its many forms, in order to show us how the light of these children was commandeered before they even went missing.[95]

The full range of visibility that Bambara leverages in the novel does not just "shine" on one person, social issue, or thing, but invites a deeper consideration of how *Black life* is also *"Black light,"* or an interminable ability to allow "for heightened visibility of whiteness and of other elements that would otherwise be rendered visible in the dark."[96] Bambara's work directly challenges Mayor Maynard Jackson's inability to harness public attention away from the disappearances. We may then align Mayor Jackson's recorded suspicion of filmic and textual representation with his inability to create a shared space of visibility of Black light / Black life, for Black life cannot flourish if Black light is simultaneously being "robbed." The mayoral office chose to capitalize on media attention in matters concerning celebrities and to demonize "bad press" that did not paint them in a more favorable light. Letters to the

---

94. Thompson, *Shine*, 46.
95. Thompson, *Shine*, 257.
96. Thompson, *Shine*, 245.

mayor's office also communicated their abhorrence that the Atlanta's Children Foundation—started to benefit the families of the disappeared—was placed within the office itself. One letter, written by Economic Opportunity Atlanta, accused the office of mishandling the funds and contributing to the vitriolic "bad press," which "sensationally abled the problems of inadequate family structure and poverty as contributing to our children's deaths. . . . We must respect the parent-child relationship and then examine what influences it."[97] Still, an avid media corps held the mayor accountable for the kidnappings and murders, and Economic Opportunity Atlanta took over all donations and finances related to the missing and murdered children shortly after this letter, in 1980. The mayor was also held accountable post facto by writers like Bambara, whose characters shouted, "Tell the truth, Maynard!" and demanded transparency.[98] The mayoral administration may have captured global attention with highly public events, fundraisers, and business development, but the local community reeled. They demanded answers for the whereabouts of their children *and* a fixed city.

Investigating disappearance and Bambara's expert interlays between state institutions, public officials, and community experience invites a consideration of the subjects impacted by these disappearances and the ways their knowledge affectively produces space. Most poignantly, Bambara embraces Zala and her maternal social location to expand meanings of disappearance beyond the circumstantial. These contributions complement a sustained cultural obsession with the Missing and Murdered Children: As of 2020, it is still the focus of HBO miniseries, special broadcasts, and podcasts.[99] *Those Bones* thrives as an indispensable record of the events, although it is rarely cited or considered in the tragedy's larger repertoire. The novel surreptitiously thrives among this public interest, especially when compared to modern investigations of the murders and kidnappings. It pans out far enough not to lose focus of the missing and murdered children's families, articulating the tensions between institutional failure and families' daily grief, searches, and mourning.

Returning to Zala Spencer's social location to understand the criminal, business, and cultural project of disappearing Black Atlantan children articulates the Black maternal position, as it challenges and constitutes the geographic spaces it inhabits. The dispossession of subjects that need care is also a geographic crisis. This crisis renders Black mothers "disposable subjects"

---

97. Economic Opportunity Atlanta, "Letter to Mayor Maynard Jackson," box 143, Maynard Jackson mayoral administrative records.

98. Bambara, *Those Bones*, 295.

99. This preoccupation is in part because of Atlanta Mayor Keisha Lance-Bottoms's reopening of the cases in 2019.

because they are not able to move or escape their environments of harm.[100] This tradition of spatial oppression defines city planning as contingent on the various ways that Black people are disappeared by the city and how their disappearance makes the city possible. Engaging in an urban realism to change the map of an urban space brings out the social panic of daily acts of exclusion. When Atlanta was made an unsafe space for Black children, Black people responded to the new strategies of mapping. This mapping was never without racial implications. In the 1950s, then mayor William B. Hartsfield (the other half of the namesake to the Hartsfield-Jackson Airport, also named after Maynard Jackson in 2003)[101] began to plan the building of the I-20, the east–west interstate that would become "a boundary between the white and Negro communities."[102] Years before, a blockade called the "Atlanta Wall," and later dubbed by activists "Atlanta's Berlin Wall," stood for seventy-two days to separate the Black and white sections of the Cascade Heights neighborhood.[103] Of course, such racialized "mapping" can occur onto bodies, an exercise in interpreting particular social questions as they affect the physical embodiment of specific peoples. In a sense, the local politics and business ventures of Atlanta could be "mapped onto" Black bodies of Atlanta during the time, and its constant changing geography required Black folks to learn and relearn their homeplace; their refusal to do so meant explicit urban planning demonstrations.[104]

Such a literal use of mapping may position Bambara as someone who testifies to the resistance of said mapping. Resistance is urgent and essential. But the novel does not save her characters from their disappearance. She asks us to consider how maternal experience is also an operative of spatial exclusion, and how this terror is manipulated, engendered, and exploited by the state. Much like the drawing of her own map of Atlanta on her dedication page, Bambara reminds us that mapping is a geographic conquest that permanently changes the physical experience of space and its subjects. Like the sudden switch between a satellite map and the grid on a GPS, the Black folk of Atlanta become immediately legible and illegible in the natural elements of the city.

---

100. McKittrick and Woods, *Black Geographies*, 3.
101. Hartsfield-Jackson Atlanta International Airport, "History of ATL."
102. R. Singh, "Atlanta Streets."
103. Carlisle, "Atlanta's Berlin Wall."
104. I'm referring here to the demonstrations against the Atlanta Wall in the 1962 and those who also protested until 2021 to get certain road names changed away from "Confederate," thus literally signposting, or at the very least virtue signaling, a progressive renaming of the city. Bentley, "Atlanta Mayor Signs Bill."

Atlanta is essentially a city built amidst a rainforest.[105] The myth of the cattle paths that form the winding roads of Marietta, Peachtree, and Piedmont Avenues reminds residents that the winding terrain is difficult to see from right to left. The topography illuminated in a satellite vision of the city reveals a watercolor of elevation ranging from 1,188 feet to approximately 800 feet, creating hills and elevation in the city center and its downtown area. Its lowest elevation occurs in the southeast and southwest, shoring up the vision of the "City on a Hill" post–civil rights nomenclature afforded to Northern cities. It could be argued that Atlanta did aspire to the meteoric rise of industry and popularity of Northern urban centers made possible by the boon of Black migrants during the Great Migration as well. Atlanta was invested in a "rise" of some sort, albeit a middle-class one, and one that at times outright excluded working-class/poor folks from the image of "the Mecca." Again, Jackson secured 95 percent of Black Atlantans' vote. The ongoing evaporation of economic resources from Black poor and working-class/poor people positioned them as vulnerable to the more violent forms of taking. As a culture worker, Bambara weighs in on spatial construction to define Atlanta's many issues within global and local contexts. The lives and lights of the children continue to haunt this period of Atlanta's history, casting a shadow over the city in its failure to find their killer(s). The Missing and Murdered Children cases predated the postracial neoliberalist discourse of the "disavowal and hypervisibility" of Blackness in order to usher in a "diverse" Atlanta.[106]

The Material, the Memorial

A fifth-grade class from Houston, Texas, reanimated Black light / Black life as they embarked on their own material memory work, one of the only indications of children's responses to the disappearances left within the mayor's records. A collage was made by a small class and sent to the mayor's office to show solidarity with the children of Atlanta. In the center of Mayor Maynard Jackson's papers stares Eric Middlebrooks. This object asks in what ways the physical container and its protagonist deny and dictate the documentations of his life and death. Community stories, those fictional, those material and practiced, emphasize the need for Black feminist approaches that commune with unconventional practices of memory. Mining the unconventional forms of

---

105. This was colloquially detailed to me by conversations with TK Smith and alludes to its well-known nickname, "the city in a forest." I add "rain" to stay true to the original quote from TK Smith and add a once-resident's sentiment to my definition.

106. Summers, *"La Douleur Exquise,"* 154.

memory, whereby a memorial of Eric can sit just inches from a mention of the mayoral administration's negligence, preserves his material memory by other means. This collage also marks the resistance to materialize him after death.

I feel called to highlight Eric's particular story because of the circumstances of his afterlife. Eric Middlebrooks was the fourth victim in the Missing and Murdered Children cases, murdered at the age of fourteen. His electric gaze pierces through to us in the collage as if he lives now in the pasture behind him. Eric stares at us in the top left corner of the page, at the top of a fecund, snow-capped mountain. Foregrounded in the collage is a clipping of what looks like the climbing flowers often used in weddings, proms, and other life events: creeping baby's breath. Unlike in the class's angelic representation, Eric was laid to rest in an unmarked grave after his funeral. Most of the victims' funerals were paid for by donations to the city. It is unclear if Eric's was as well. But records do indicate that Eric's foster father became very ill and could not afford a headstone for his gravesite. Only centimeters away from this 2D memorial of Eric in this folder are two folded notices from Kennedy Memorial Gardens in Decatur, Georgia, to City Hall, asking the mayor's administration to cover the remaining "$113 balance so he can have a marked grave."[107] That balance was never paid. Eric's unmarked grave indicates the importance of understanding the material memorialization of this work, and how fictionalization is another form of memorial and archiving. Bambara's novel memorializes those who go unmarked and unnamed in the archive, like Eric. Her contributions pose questions to the other notes in the administrative papers that are not governed by one viewer's witnessing of events. These questions are only answered by the material neglect. Maynard Jackson's professed skepticism for cultural production around this time can be taken as an earnest attempt to control the hysteria about the brutal murder of someone like Eric. But the administration's suspicions and the actions born from them replicates the same violence that neglected to pay for Eric's headstone. The denial of a material memorial—a headstone—and the phobia around imaginative text are both formations of state-sanctioned archival denial. Bambara's book and these collages do not recover these children or save them. Instead, they supplement the scant cultural and historical archive around children's disappearances due to anti-Black violence, asking us, all with the potential to do our own memory work, how we can preserve their memories through a radical unmaking.

The novel aids in this unmaking of the disappeared institutional archive's creation by texturing the stark juxtapositions of the mayor's own archival

---

107. At the time of writing, Eric has a digital gravesite available for public viewing. There are over thirteen pages of digital GIFs, flowers, and notes on *Find a Grave*. Southworth, "Memorial Page."

legacy. *Those Bones* models the kaleidoscope effect of focusing on one mother to illuminate the broader social and political issues of the time, without losing the interior image of Zala's plight. This kaleidoscope then distorts portions of its intersecting patterns as we turn to other aspects of the disappearances and search for new meaning in what was a saga with few answers. In being drawn inward and then outward depending on Bambara's kaleidoscope turns, we are given the full picture without being denied the novel's full capacity to tell what would appear to be a different version of events, or what may also be the whole of it. The author's invitation to her audience is not that we ignore other parts of the story, but rather that we take notice of how they are constitutive of each other and how we as people are constitutive of one another. Each one of our lights is as imbricated in the other, and these lights do not fade or go out, but exist in another form, time, and place to shine a broader truth on disappearance.

The potential for the novel to produce spatial and literary memory, rather than intervene on it, offers reformations in the archival practice altogether. Maynard Jackson, in denying cultural production, sought to control the memory of the tragedies. The novel produces memory altogether to show how it cannot be explicated from the political and spatial forms of exclusion, thus undermining the ability for history to be institutionalized archivally at all. The fictionalized account continues to document the lived horror of searching for a missing child rather than turning the disappearances into a sole question of crime. Far from recovering the children, or finding them, Bambara explores the sustained grief of dispossession and the ongoing project of removing Black life, which continues to texture the fabric of urban renewal.

CHAPTER 2

Margaret Walker, *Jubilee,* and the Fight for Black Feminist Historicity in *Alexander v. Haley*

This chapter scales the politics and injustices done to Black women's reproductive systems by asking us to consider literary production as reproductive labor.¹ Far from minimizing reproductive labor in this abstraction, the reproduction of Black feminist memory argues for the rights of Black women creatives and their right to preserve their stories and tell them in the ways they wish. In so doing, this book challenges the idea that Black women's reproductive labor is fashioned only in domestic settings, and only with children. Rarely is it contested that reproducing people are made despite challenges, and that the children produced present challenges to writing. There is an art to folding one's reproductive labor for children into one's reproductive labor of family. In this sense, as Alys Eve Weinbaum quotes Donna Haraway, "It's high time we thought more about making kin than about making babies and population."² In this vein, I look toward the full life and accomplishments of Margaret Walker and her only novel, *Jubilee* (1967), her matrilineal impulses to preserve her family's orally transmitted stories, and her attempt to protect

---

1. Series I, Margaret Walker Alexander Personal Papers, Margaret Walker Center, Jackson State University. In this letter from Nikki Giovanni to Margaret Walker, Giovanni said, "They will love both of us when we are dead. People will write wonderful books. Folk will get tenure deciphering our poetry. It's the living author they don't much care for and that seems to be the burden we bear: We're Nobody's Baby."
2. Sirvent, "BAR Book Forum."

their stories against copyright infringement—all via an archival praxis carried out in prose, dairies, and scrapbooks. By weighing out the theft of Walker's (and others') lives and creativity, we encounter yet another manifestation of the afterlives of dispossession: of children *and* family, including ancestors. Her life and work remain painfully relevant, laying bare the very real threat of the erasure of memory.

This chapter investigates the extent to which Black maternal memory-making antagonizes cultural memory-making, and how and where the two run parallel. While this project's other case studies ask how Black mothers document the deaths of their children (and how these documentations help us understand reproductive injustice), this chapter asks how Black maternal archival praxis takes shape in documenting the loss of ancestors and other children, and to what extent these documents challenge the Black patriarchal undertones of "African American history."[3] In so doing, it commits to a philosophy of history that runs through this entire book: Black women are *believed,* and these beliefs form the foundations of Black ancestry. Circumventing the assumed patriarchal and male-dominated themes of history that feature mostly men is not enough, however. We must also investigate where patriarchal tropes manifest—in this case, Walker's struggle to retain control over her family's lives and labors. The (heteropatriarchal) state continues to antagonize Black women's creative reproductions and falls flat in responding to the sanctity and, more pointedly, legal authority to tell their stories about their families.

In this chapter, scraps are literal. Walker fashioned scrapbooks in her commitment to documenting both her family's history and the theft of her labor. She began writing what became *Jubilee* at fifteen and saw it as her life's work. Despite identifying as a poet, she felt that her novel would make her a major writer of her time. One's oeuvre is just that—a self-contained canon and a testimony to permanency. But Walker wanted it to be spherical and well-rounded. The story of her great-great-grandmother Elvira (Vyry) did not start with Walker or her grandmother, the daughter of Elvira. It started hundreds of years before, and she was determined to write the epic with the few details she had. Walker's investment in maintaining her written legacy is a product of the reproductive labor gone into preserving family memories and stories, an unaccounted-for—often maternal—labor of reproducing not just family memories, but *family* itself. *Jubilee* was not only her life's work; it also culminated the compounded, multigenerational histories of her family.

Margaret Walker's journey of writing her novel pulls on the authority of Black women's history. In 1979 she waged a copyright infringement legal case

---

3. Hull, Bell-Scott, and Smith, *All the Women*.

and media campaign against Alex Haley and his publisher, Doubleday, for his acclaimed book *Roots: The Saga of an American Family,* published originally in 1976. The baked-in patriarchal logics in the legal proceedings, along with Walker's unsuccessful bid for the lawsuit, prompt a deeper consideration of the appropriation of Black feminist history-making, documentation, and reproductive labor. Walker preserved her life's memories in decades of detailed journals and correspondences. Her robust archive, located at Jackson State University, is over 110 linear feet. The collection comprises primarily journals, framed pictures, newspaper clippings, and other notes pertaining to her lawsuit. The materials cover nearly her entire life, with journals spanning from 1929 to 1998. Walker's scrapbook and journals in particular reflect her resentment, disdain, and what would appear as a full-fledged media campaign to raise awareness over what she believed to be a federal crime.[4] Her documentary creations question the stakes of a culture (both individual and by corporate enterprise) to wield history-making and the legal program that protects these rights.

This chapter breaks into parts Walker's reproductive labors at home, in life, and in her writing community. It asks questions about her role in forming other Black male writers' inspiration, craft, and publishing, and her struggles to marry her positions in the writing and academic worlds. These worlds were unmade by Black women like Walker, who, like other contemporaries and those before her, dared to do artistry differently, who chose to parent and survive and refuse to end their careers after bearing children. In sum, this chapter traces her journey to create *Jubilee*—a physical document in prose that manifested what had been lived and recounted as an oral tradition for generations—and the subsequent denial of its gravity as beyond the implications of the publishing world. It forms an institutional antagonism to the cultural memory-making of Black history during the civil rights and Black Power eras, uprooting male tellings of Black history. It is here that the genius of Margaret Walker's praxis of scraps is what a nation's history makes. Scrap theory is a Black feminist theory. A Black maternal theory. A world-making praxis.

Overlooking Walker's Literary Importance

For Walker, Nikki Giovanni's aphorism was true: The world didn't seem to have much use for a living author—especially one that was a Black woman. Despite coming from an upper-middle-class, well-established family of preachers in New Orleans, Walker's craft was always *work,* and that work,

---

4. Walker submitted multiple articles to local and national print media outlets.

especially her important place in the Chicago literary renaissance, was never fully recognized. The manifestations of her genius were never taken as seriously as she wanted. Born in 1915, she spent her younger years writing at her father's encouragement, reciting Greek poetry and learning literary histories from around the world. She read and she listened. Her literary history involved nightly stories while her parents socialized with other established New Orleans families. She would sit at the foot of her grandmother's bed and listen to the matriarch's stories. Walker, both skilled and insatiable, was taught and believed in her craft. She knew she would be a writer first and not a wife or mother. In her late teens, Walker was discovered by Richard Wright, one of the greatest Black authors of all time, setting her up for a career of literary prestige, though not without its costs. After high school she received a scholarship to Northwestern University in Evanston, Illinois, to study English literature. There, she began to feel the simultaneous weight of institutional racism and the gift of developing her craft at an elite school. It was also in Chicago that she joined what was later understood as the Chicago literary renaissance, forming relationships with not only her mentor Richard Wright but also Arna Bontemps, Elizabeth Catlett, and Jacob Lawrence.

Before stepping foot in Chicago, Walker began the six-hundred-plus-page novel that she spent a quarter of her life writing. Born to a privileged, educated family who lived with her maternal grandmother, Margaret and her siblings were often left in the care of her grandmother when her parents attended evening social events. At night, she writes, her father often returned home to find Margaret on the floor listening to her grandmother tell another story about her own mother, Elvira, a woman born a slave in Alabama. Although he ushered her off to bed, Walker often wrote the stories down before going to sleep, putting her recitation skills to practice. Her grandmother's sayings later became the titles of chapters, and her hymns became the epigraphs. "My grandmothers are full of memories, smelling of soap and onions and wet clay, they have many clean words to say, my grandmothers were strong," she later writes in poem form. The task of honoring her people, and specifically the trials of being a mother, was primary and perennial.

Reproductive violence foregrounds *Jubilee*. The first twenty pages open with a scene in which Sis Hetta (Walker's great-great-great-grandmother) is a young woman of twenty-nine years. Sis Hetta lies hemorrhaging from a tragic birth experience. After spiking an infection from the retained placenta of a stillborn child, the young woman lies in despair. As Sis Hetta perishes, the novel introduces us to a young Vyry, one of Sis Hetta's fifteen children by their plantation owner's son, with whom she was forced into a sexual relationship as a young girl. As a dying wish she calls for young Vyry, not more than four years old, living on an adjacent plantation, to witness her mother's death.

It is in these opening scenes that the originary wound of her family's story is toned as reproduction, rape, and medical violence.[5] The beginning of the novel parses two histories: one where Vyry becomes the only known descendant of her mother and therefore her maternal legacy, much like Walker felt as she wrote the novel. The stillborn child is also a gesture toward her uselessness to John Dutton, her enslaver, and the plantation itself. Dutton treated Sis Hetta as merely an object for sexual gratification that happened to produce commodities.

Importantly, Walker could not let that be the end of her elder nor the lost child. If she had, there simply would be no history to tell—when in fact, there were many. Sis Hetta did not die in vain. She was the catalyst for a family's history, told from her birth-death bed. The story was reproduced over and over in her family's nightly story time, and Margaret's labor was writing the book, telling the story, and fighting for its veracity for the rest of her life.

Reproductive Labor and Maternal Connection

Although Richard Wright is credited with Walker's "discovery," she arrived on Northwestern's campus a fully formed writer with arms full of her grandmother's literary creations. Before Wright, Margaret's literary mentor was her grandmother and the mothers who came before her. For Walker, writing both remade the kin that had passed and helped her navigate the kin that she had or sought to maintain while she was having children. Self-doubt sewed its way into her dreams of living a writer's life, as she feared the external world would not know how to accommodate or support a writer, married woman, and mother concerned with making kin *and* making babies. These fears were validated throughout her life, as writing proved to be unsustainable for her family, financially and emotionally. Before she married her husband toward the end of the Second World War, Walker had navigated interpersonal relationships that presented themselves at odds with a young Black writer's life. Instead of taking these as omens to end her career, however, she used them to inflame her passion to write.

---

5. It is remarked upon in these introductory pages that Sis Hetta's retained placenta could have been avoided if her midwife had more support from a physician. Where the novel clearly does not condemn the granny midwife's involvement, it is the physician who decided to take "nearly two days" before he arrived. The doctor scolded the midwife for using her "tricks" instead of calling the doctor sooner. These "tricks" would have included contraction-inducing herbs to get the placenta to dispel or having Sis Hetta suck on a portion of the placenta that was already dispelled to prevent the hemorrhage. Both of these methods are still used today. M. Walker, *Jubilee*.

The young author engaged in multiple forms of reproduction at once, with kids, family, and her own writing of her family's history. Where her writing was interrupted by these obligations, family and lineage were the entire bedrock of what compelled her to write fastidiously and with urgency. Although she wrestled with the notion of family, she was highly devoted to it even before her children came into the family picture. During the war, she began quietly dating an American soldier named Firnist "Alex" Alexander. While home on active duty, Alex was supportive but married, estranged from his wife. His later deployment worried her but also gave her solace and space to write, not to mention discretion. A fairly private person, she liaised with her small cadre of artist friends in the Chicago literary renaissance, Lawrence, Bontemps, and her mentor and rumored ex-lover Richard Wright.[6] After finishing the tour for her poetry collection *This Is My Century* in April 1944, Walker's attention in her diligent journaling practice became consumed by her health status, and soon after, she accepted that she was pregnant. Not even divulging Alex's name in her journal, she reported that "the baby's father" was set to be away on active duty on the due date. In spite of her small frame, she was able to hide almost her entire pregnancy. At first, she told no one but her close friend and confidant Elizabeth Catlett. In one entry from Monday, May 22, 1944, Walker writes, "First, I was too emotionally upset to think clearly. I was so desperate and unsettled and though none of my situation has yet resolved itself I am calmer and better able to think."[7] "My situation" included the pregnancy *and* the emotional weight of hiding it. She hid it, which "sometimes" led her to feel "depressed and morbid—rather moody especially considering my marital status, but I try not to worry too much and think too much of what my family's reaction will be."[8] Walker wrestled with shame about the pregnancy, given her devoutly Christian parents and upbringing, as well as the reaction of her writing community and the world around it. Her insecurities were later confirmed on both fronts.

As Walker tracked the growth of her baby without much prenatal support, she lived with Catlett, who provided her stability while she was too ashamed to visit other family or friends. In turn, Walker stayed home cooking her cravings of New Orleans and Southern comfort foods like homemade potato salad, fried chicken, cornbread, and mashed rutabaga. Together, they enthusiastically

---

6. Walker has maintained publicly that she and Wright had a platonic relationship, but biographer Graham and others have intimated that their relationship was romantic, if not intimate, at times, and that the conception of the child overlapped with time she spent with Wright. Graham does not question this, and neither did Walker. The paternity of her first daughter is clear. But to her friends, speculation ensued.

7. Journals 1943–48, box 4, series II, Margaret Walker Alexander Personal Papers.

8. Journals 1943–48, box 4, series II, Margaret Walker Alexander Personal Papers.

anticipated Walker's baby and dreamed of spending their first year in Mexico.[9] Catlett became her protector in awkward social situations. Catlett was an early "other mother" of Walker's not-yet-born baby and Walker herself. The artist's esteemed cadre—Lawrence, Bontemps, and Wright or "DW"[10]—indeed disapproved of her pregnancy, and it affected her emotional health: "They thought it highly necessary that I have an abortion. I would not have it. . . . I have begun making elaborate preparations for my child. I know fully what this means—what the implications are, and repercussions will be—already I catch the wind of idle evil sorrys and the staring disapproval of my so-called friends. I know what reaction I need to expect from my parents and family."[11] Remembering Arna Bontemps's strong reaction to her pregnancy after a reading—a look of surprise—protector Catlett asked pointedly, "Why!?" He warned her solemnly: "Every child you have is a book you didn't write." Bontemps's sexist comment stoked and projected Walker's fears of losing her identity as a writer back onto her, at a time when she hadn't yet told her family. All this and more contributed to her perinatal depression, and still she was even more determined to finish her book. Vastly underestimating her writing time, she aimed to do so within the first year of her daughter's life.

As archives to her maternal and writing labors, Walker's journals were a constant sounding board to every wayward thought, entwining her writing with the logistics of life. They show her tallying up anticipated costs to live in Mexico or abroad while her daughter nursed and she wrote.[12] The mix of ordinary and dream were formulated in the very first journal entry after her daughter was born, the addition and subtraction of childcare costs and plane tickets in the margins of her daughter's birth story. The time it took to write would be interrupted by pockets of child rearing and teaching, but writing her ancestors' story never left her focus. Although some of the writing was "ten years old" and there were "150 pages of ideas," Walker was prepared to write the novel speedily, and hopefully in Mexico with her new child.[13] Doodles, grocery lists, and stick figures were the typical marginalia. But the backs of

---

9. Catlett went on to spend most of her life in Mexico and became a dual citizen after marrying artist Francisco Mora and raising three sons in Cuernavaca, located just south of Mexico City.
10. Early journals also suggested that the group was stunned because the paternity of the child was not initially disclosed.
11. Journals 1943–48, box 4, series II, Margaret Walker Alexander Personal Papers.
12. Journals 1943–48, box 4, series II, Margaret Walker Alexander Personal Papers.
13. Journals 1943–48, box 4, series II, Margaret Walker Alexander Personal Papers. This time frame would have corresponded with the time that Catlett was awarded a fellowship that allowed her to work with the Taller de Gráfica Popular. It's possible Catlett had connections to Mexico beforehand, of course, and part of Walker's plan to go to Mexico with her young daughter would have been so Catlett could help her co-parent.

the notebooks were devoted to constant reminders of her place in the universe, that she was in the world and not of it. There is an undercurrent in Walker's decision-making that oscillates between remembering who and what she came from and planning diligently for the future.

Accompanying her more logistical planning notes were religious passages, made holistic by the spiritual practice of astrology. Astrology was her "hobby," and it helped her make sense of her world. It also reproduced a cosmic connection with her maternal ancestors.[14] It was how she calculated her mother's mood in order to determine when to tell her mother about her pregnancy. Her journals reveal her mother's and grandmother's natal birth charts. The circles divided into twelve wedges (for the twelve houses) were hand drawn with careful haste: "Grandmother's chart" was written in ink and with only one error, which seemed only a misplacement of a word. Astrology to Walker was quite accurate: She reveled in the consistency of the charts during uncertain times like unplanned pregnancies and publishing timelines. The planet ephemeris would tell her where she should orient. These orientations gave clear direction for favorable time frames but spoke little to the social and cultural conditions that led her mother to pressure her to give up the baby once it was born. Balancing astrological favor and free will produced an emotionally conflicted pregnancy experience. She ultimately respected her mother but knew that the disappointment of having a child out of wedlock was more disappointing than any choice she could consequently make. Her parents presented her with three options: giving the child up for adoption, giving her parents the child to raise, or getting married and ending her career. The conclusion spoke volumes in her personal choice to name her daughter Marion, after her mother. Young Marion, born in July 1943, inspired Walker to continue writing her novel. Mother Marion struggled to accept the strong-willed writer who wanted to live her life as a writer *and* be a wife and mother, when the time came for both.[15]

---

14. Walker performed natal chart interpretations for people while in college and, at the time of her pregnancy, was going through her own Saturn return, a once-in-twenty-nine-year transit in which Saturn returns to its original sign in which she was born. One's first Saturn return symbolizes the effective end of one's own childhood and the beginning of one's adulthood. Weighty adult decisions, like telling her mother about her pregnancy, would need to wait until the transit finished, Walker had decided. Journals 1943–48, box 4, series II, Margaret Walker Alexander Personal Papers.

15. Marion's middle name is Elizabeth, after Elizabeth Catlett, with whom Walker lived with while she was pregnant. Catlett was Walker's main caregiver while she was pregnant and has written and spoken about the various negotiations of time and resources required to be an artist and a mother herself.

Margaret knew she was at a spiritual precipice in her life. Young Marion's birthdate fell auspiciously close to that of Walker's grandmother, Elvira Dozier, suggesting that Margaret would give birth to an ancestrally sanctioned child. Still, Walker struggled with preserving her maternal legacy, which she equated with strength, pride, and achievement despite the odds of being a notable Black woman poet. "Lineage," published in *For My People* (1942), attests: "My grandmothers were strong. / Why am I not as they?" She saw her domestic and interpersonal problems—she and Alex married once they were able—as relatively small compared to her ancestors' problems but wondered why it was so emotionally taxing for her to be creative how and when she wanted to be. After the birth of young Marion, she journaled, "I do [not] let anything short of sickness or death separate me from my baby. She needs me and I need her. Whatever arrangements I make, we must be together. . . . She will not be abandoned or adopted unless it is over my dead body."[16] Walker's reinvention of matrilineal legacy was cosmic and material. By the time her fourth child was born in 1954, she felt the call to continue her writing. Youngest daughter Margaret Elvira was named for Walker herself and the grandmother who brought the story to her. Like the burst of writing energy Walker experienced in birthing her first child, in little Margaret she saw the end of her childbearing years and the birth of the second part of her career. As biographer Maryemma Graham writes, "*Jubilee* became an act of creative birthing in the same way," and that birth lasted longer than anticipated: the first seven years of Margaret Elvira's life.[17]

The reproductive lives of both *Jubilee* and Walker were naturally concomitant. Her writing and mothering lives were at times fitful, braided, and at odds. There was no separation between Walker and her writing, or her children. She struggled with stability, childcare, and other domestic issues, including disagreements over disciplining her children. While writing *Jubilee*, Walker's health and "nerves and general debility" worried her, and she grappled with the idea that she "may have to leave them with someone else who may rear them." Suddenly, these moments of having her children leave her for long periods of time seemed like the only viable option for her to survive. She believed at times the children would be better raised by someone else.[18] With her struggles of having and raising children, Walker felt like she would never

---

16. Journals 1943–48, box 4, series II, Margaret Walker Alexander Personal Papers.

17. Graham, *House Where My Soul Lives*, 295. Elizabeth Catlett also took seven years off from her art practice after her middle son was born. She decided that it would be less effort than working between naps. She couldn't give justice to her practice by simply working between nap times. Herzog and Catlett, *Elizabeth Catlett*.

18. Journals 1943–48, box 4, series II, Margaret Walker Alexander Personal Papers.

be able to devote what she could to her craft like others, and her confidence in it wavered.[19] Unlike the "invisible" labor of maternal reproductive laborers—invisible due to lack of financial compensation—her labor was invisible because she carried it out in times of exhaustion and excess. Much of her writing came when it was too late, after being on bedrest for exhaustion, when she felt down from her depression, or while the children napped. Walker's labor on the story cannot be quantified, especially in the years of emotional work she put into writing *Jubilee*, the traumatic toll it took on her ancestors to live it, and the many others who made her work possible, like archivists, librarians, children, babysitters, mentors, and her husband.

Walker, a Black Feminist Philosophy of History

Amid these layers of production, reproduction, and struggle, Walker (re)constructed matrilineal history in a time both ripe for and in direct conflict with the story she had to tell. She worked to write and publish her history in the Black Power era, when the predominant politics of the civil rights movement were quickly going out of style. This moment ushered in the establishment of new Black studies programs in colleges and universities, new publishing houses, clinics, and much more—all with the goal of reclaiming their history and making sure that institutions that produced knowledge about Black history reflected the perspectives of Black people. Though Walker's work and philosophy fit well with this push for Black literary reclamation, *Jubilee* joined the throng just a handful of years too late.

Jubilee is a novel that encompasses the lifetime of a Black woman over critical decades in Black American history, the Civil War era through Reconstruction, and beyond. Its publishing date *should* have been the perfect time for Black culture to rally around such a novel. In 1968 both Robert F. Kennedy and Martin Luther King Jr. were assassinated, followed by Malcolm X one year later. The year 1968 also marked the beginning of the burgeoning Black Power era, with groups such as the Student Nonviolent Coordinating Committee and the Black Panthers emerging in US cities and rural centers alike. It also came into a Black literary ecosystem made up of diverse Black feminist texts such as Alice Walker's *Meridian* (1976), Toni Morrison's *Song of Solomon* (1977), and Octavia Butler's *Kindred* (1979). Although some of its authors may have cited Margaret Walker as a legendary literary figure and influence, *Jubilee*

---

19. "Sometimes I accidentally write a good poem, but that is becoming more and more infrequent." This was written shortly after her daughter was born in the summer of 1944. Journals 1943–48, box 4, series II, Margaret Walker Alexander Personal Papers.

wasn't necessarily an urtext to this milieu.[20] After all, Walker either explicitly or implicitly impacted these writers, having been part of the WPA interviews throughout the 1930s, working with Zora Neale Hurston, and, of course, being the protégé of Richard Wright and a good friend and mentor of Nikki Giovanni. The novel was the narrative with a Black woman protagonist that spanned the late nineteenth into the twentieth century. Where many of these writers, namely Alice Walker, cite Walker as a catalyst in their development, her more conservative views did fit into the construction of the plantation critique that Angela Davis set forth in *Women, Race and Class* (1981), or even the large-scale mythology that formed around "Black feminist" figures—in other words, Black women aligned with the Black Power movement, implicitly the Black Panthers, like Elaine Brown or Assata Shakur.

What we now call Black feminism emerged within diverse notions and concepts that were explicitly liberatory. Perhaps this is where Walker's "womanism" nuances conversations of feminism. But Walker presented a different feminism that did not apologize for Vyry's presentist ideas about race, gender, and liberation. Vyry is very much an inconvenient hero that many Black mothers saw as liberating, but whose children found entirely antithetical to liberation. By the time that Walker's lawsuit against Haley came to public view, it wasn't so much that her personal beliefs prohibited people from supporting her lawsuit, nor its success because of her social and political beliefs. Instead, it's important to frame these beliefs, and the release of *Jubilee*, within a national carving out of publicly available Black feminism and feminist emergence in contradistinction to what may have been viewed as a traditional slave narrative. And although Vyry is the protagonist, she is not necessarily a feminist hero, representing instead a more race-woman archetype, rooted in Christian belief. There are multiple times in the novel where Vyry takes a more conservative approach to her relations with her white enslavers to say the least, letting herself be led in her Christian faith and fearing the choice to seek revenge on those who owned her and did her wrong. Walker's ancestor was a realistic character nonetheless, but Vyry would hardly have been the heroic character that would have been exalted in the late 1960s, in a time when

---

20. "Urtext" is a term borrowed from music, defined as an "original" score that is closest to the composer's autograph manuscript (in the composer's hand), with little editorial intervention, or with editorial markings and decisions stripped or reversed. Introduced and popularized around the 1950s, urtexts were treated as authorities, but often, multiple complications in composition, performance, and publication make an urtext impossible. A body of work in musicology has been devoted to the complexities of urtexts, music editing, and music publishing. I thank Katheryn Lawson for sharing this background with me.

people were captivated by activists like Fannie Lou Hamer, the women of the Black Panthers, or even Betty Shabazz and Coretta Scott King.[21]

The Black feminist imagines freedoms that are not comfortable for everyone to read. Black feminists are an affirmation of the "historical reality of Afro-American women's continuous life-and-death struggle for survival and liberation."[22] Black feminists situate themselves as a screen through which freedom can be differently realized, sometimes in step with other Black feminists' visions of freedom and sometimes not. Black feminists remember the cycle of life and death, recognizing that their lives would not exist without the death of their ancestors. Walker, in life and writing, exemplifies this discomfort. But Vyry as a character locates the lack of range afforded plantation women to resist: Resistance was daily for some, but it was not always conceptualized as such. Vyry was very much informed by (1) a nonliberatory worship of Christianity and (2) the constraints of Black women with children. At one point during the novel, Vyry is supposed to leave alone to escape. She is to meet her children's father and told that they will return for her children at a later, unknown time once they make it due north. As Vyry begins to walk out the door, her son wakes up and asks where she is going. She solemnly replies, "Nowhere," and abandons her efforts to escape.[23]

This was the reality of many enslaved women: to choose children, freedom, or themselves. Just as religion played a role in Vyry's enslavement, her reproduction tethered her to the plantation. The need to hang on to the two children she was allowed to raise herself was unthinkable as a woman with countless siblings "who would never be slaves" or sold into unthinkable futures.[24]

The construction of Vyry's character could perhaps be tied to the novel's quelled appreciation in Black feminist literary history. The year 1966 was only two years after the passing of the Civil Rights Act. Groups such as the Black

---

21. There were other characters and moments that would have registered in national consciousness and have been named. The iconic discussion about what Du Bois would call "the Negro problem," between Vyry's two husbands, Innis Brown and Randall Ware, at the end of the book very much represents the perceived ideological differences between Martin Luther King Jr. and Malcolm X at the time. Many people think this was Walker's presentist meditation on the ideologies, but arguably she was more showing how ideological splits in freedom-seeking have been a persistent issue in Black families and communities for centuries. In addition, many forget that she was very close friends with Medgar Evers and a next-door neighbor at the time of his assassination; she was very much an advocate of *all* of his work.

22. Combahee River Collective, "Combahee River Collective Statement."

23. M. Walker, *Jubilee*, 164. She did later try to escape with the oldest child but was later caught. She was beaten so harshly that "she could remember deep waves and complete inundation in the dark waters that threatened to take her under. She could not remember her own children and when they were brought to her she did not know them."

24. M. Walker, *Jubilee*, 152.

Panther Party were steadying for their impending worldwide attention to the battle for Black Americans' human rights. A novel with a female protagonist would have been welcomed by a culture enlivened by a newfound identity in Black Power, and Black women's power at that, but Vyry was certainly not inciting some of the threads of revolution that excited budding anti-institution revolutionaries. Where it is, of course, not "enough" for a book to simply have a Black woman protagonist for it to be labeled "Black feminist literature," we do know that Walker's work personally and professionally impacted two of the most lauded Black feminist writers of all time, Nikki Giovanni and Alice Walker. And because the Black Arts Movement was deeply communal, it is hard to imagine her craft was not influential to the movement.

The lack of popular attention to *Jubilee* in Black feminist knowledge-making into the twenty-first century results in a largely binaried understanding of Black feminist ways, meaning the complexities of reproductive labor often bury Black maternal people as "passive" in the archive of human rights–seeking. Revolutionary activities were not just enacted by those who took part in more public-facing activities. The truth about Black women's revolutionary activities is that they do not erupt in sudden transitions of power or large-scale events. Our progress is made up of *years* of calculated action. Where Vyry's actions of patience were at times rife with the disturbing lauding of her enslaver and the institution of slavery, she and *Jubilee* are no less a realistic depiction of the radical orientation to choice Black mothers must have in order to survive.

Alexander v. Haley and Patriarchal Thefts of Women's Work

plagiarize: to steal and pass off (the ideas or words of another) as one's own:
    use (another's production) without crediting the source
    : to commit literary theft: present as new and original an idea or product derived from an existing source.[25]

Ten years later, Alex Haley published a work of what he termed "historical nonfiction" that gained critical and popular acclaim, written on the back of Walker's decades of painstaking archival and ethnographic work. The issue of plagiarism is not just one of the likeness of one story being taken as one's own.

---

25. *Merriam-Webster*, "plagiarize," last updated January 10, 2025, https://www.merriam-webster.com/dictionary/plagiarize.

In the case of *Alexander v. Haley*, it was an issue of replicating the reproductive labor that went into constructing a griot's story, revealing her subjugation to the patriarchal legal system. Walker, under her legal married name of Margaret Walker Alexander, filed the lawsuit in 1978 against Haley and Doubleday in the US District Court of Southern New York on copying *Jubilee* for several passages of *Roots*. The court decided that the passages cited fell under nonactionable similarities, and the case was dismissed.[26] Walker's scrapbook and notebooks outline this in delicate yet exacting means. I am mobilized by Walker's essays "A Literary History in Plagiarism"[27] and "State of the Black Women in America."[28] Walker conceptualized the alleged plagiarism as a condition of her state of being "Black, Free, and Female" in America, even though she polarized the conception of freedom. Her journal also reveals her thought in organizing this book/journal entry to key questions:

What is freedom?
Versus bondage?
World of necessity—?[29]

The last inquiry is a philosophical one, and one that demands a philosophical, but aspirational answer. What is a world of necessity? What is a world that necessitates bondage and freedom? The external world is one in which Walker grapples with her own freedom as a descendant of slaves. Just as Morrison engages in the praxis of "becoming," Walker struggles with her existence as a born-free Black woman still experiencing professional and institutional restraints. The cyclical relationship—between the maternal ancestors of great-great-grandmother Elvira, grandmother Vyry, mother Marion, and then Margaret Walker and her children—offers Walker's work as a reproduction of family and story. That necessity mirrors the necessity of the freed person–master dialectic that supersedes the slave–master relationship. By this I mean the relationships between Walker, the world in which her great-great-grandmother was born, and the reproductions of the story through generations are always in debt to the histories that deny the story's nuance. The popular and frustratingly persistent histories born from patriarchal storytellings like *Roots* framed the twenty-first-century master–slave

---

26. Walker Alexander v Alex Haley, Doubleday & Company, Inc., and Doubleday Publishing Company (460 F. Supp. 40) (N.Y. 1978).
27. M. Walker, *On Being Female*, 10.
28. M. Walker, *On Being Female*, 11.
29. Scrapbook, box 3, series X, Margaret Walker Alexander Personal Papers.

dialectic in a redemptive narrative model, one that feminist nonfiction like *Jubilee* actively refutes.[30]

Walker's struggle for copyright infringement calls forth a reformation of reproductive justice. *Alexander v. Haley* was framed only in terms of the autonomy of one's (reproductive) body, but reproductive justice is also the right to tell family stories without fear of being accused of "derivative" reproduction.[31] The double entendre creates a reproduction/Reproduction axis where the re-creating of Walker's family's story presents an issue with time. Of course, Haley's text was published after *Jubilee,* yet its cultural acclaim renders it one of the most prominent modern slave narratives of the late twentieth century. *Jubilee* is a text in the tradition of slave narratives, while *Roots* is an iconic example of a made-for-TV book. In the vein of a true scribe, Walker narrativizes these events with anecdotes and facetious tales, sometimes writing in large letters: "I may be David, but you SHO' AINT GOLIATH." By the time Margaret Walker's case was dismissed in 1978, *Jubilee* had been out for ten years and *Roots* had been out for two. National enthusiasm for *Roots* was well established, and Walker had been watching its rise to fame.

As soon as *Roots* was published, Walker began crafting the case. In December 1977, she received a hearing in front of a magistrate of the Southern District of New York to establish a case for unfair competition and unfair use.[32]

how ethical is this? How professional?

How dumb must I be?
Stupid, black and female me?
I am told I cannot beat the system
Tell me why I should have to fight the system
Tell me why
All my family must die

---

30. Orlando Patterson comments upon the afterlife of institutions of slavery in the "premodern world" as producing a relationship in which the freed person must "honor" their "former master, and everywhere certain social obligations were expected" of them. Patterson, *Slavery and Social Death,* 241. Walker was aware of the constraints of these social obligations and the sense of "honor" she and her relatives felt navigating in a white world, and what the story would mean to navigate in an ancestral plane.

31. US Copyright Office, "Definitions."

32. Walker made a total of nine allegations, as she describes in her scrapbook, including "Verbal Threats," "Unfair Competition," "Unfair Appropriation," "Conspiracy (hypothetical and theoretical)," "Copyright Infringement," and "Obstruction of Justice." Box 3, series X, Margaret Walker Alexander Personal Papers.

> If we speak the truth
> And not a lie.[33]

What are truths and lies in the fight for a cultural epoch of African diasporic history moving into the twenty-first century? Walker's short-form poem reveals the unbearing truth of "women's issues," "women's matters," and "women's problems." Most often reserved for discourse around not believing Black women and their relationship with their bodies, Walker's poem illuminates the self-negation as she attempts to be heard in the courthouse and beyond.

The feminist tensions related to the suit are fraught. In contrast to Walker's treatment in court, Harold Courlander, a Bethesda, Maryland, author of *The African,* made out with a settlement of approximately $500,000 (paid by Doubleday). Courlander, a Black male author, was a student of Haley's. While writing *Roots,* Haley made an income lecturing. He attested that students and audience members would pass notes to him while he talked, and he dumped them in a crate and had no idea of knowing the authorship of such contents. Courlander's team alleged that over eighty-one passages had "found their way" into Haley's novel. The court believed him. Most pointedly, Courlander won in the same district court in which Walker lost.[34]

To be sure, in "how ethical is this?," Walker was asking questions not only of the integrity of her opponent, but also of herself, oscillating on many registers of what is real and unreal, validated and unvalidated. But Walker's poem reveals a different relationship to "the system" or institutional upholding of a nontruth, and the intergenerational consequences of being a cultural and state antagonism.[35] The poem also details a different type of death, a spiritual one,[36] which her family is experiencing over and over. "Tell me why my family must die / over and over / if we speak the truth / and not a lie," she writes. Conceptualizing theft of Black feminist memory-keeping as reproductive injustice means an admission that the people who live in the stories are no longer able to be made manifest.

If we think about memory as the surviving ancestors and the lives of descendants that did not survive, then story theft is a violation of reproductive

---

33. Scrapbook, box 3, series X, Margaret Walker Alexander Personal Papers.
34. Lescaze and Saperstein, "Bethesda Author Settles."
35. I will always frame Walker's lawsuit as a state antagonism with cultural consequences. This is to return activity to Walker as an antagonist to the state antagonism for bringing the case against Haley, but also a cultural one for writing a text that reasserts Black women's heritage as foundational to history.
36. Revilla, "Attempted Spirit Murder."

survivability of Black feminist thought. Instead, as Alys Eve Weinbaum writes, "black women's insurgency constitutes a self-evident historical truth rather than verifiable 'fact,' while simultaneously imagining 'refusal.'"[37] This refusal might not lend itself to narratives of refusal that take up more popular space, such as Harriet Tubman's heroic expeditions to free enslaved people. But the women who attempted to escape, planned to but felt that they couldn't leave their children, were there as well. It is in their stories that Black feminism lives, and also where reproductive injustice lives. Authors like Walker would have encountered the "impossibility of telling" such histories, which extends the literary mode of "critical fabulation" where we elaborate—critically, and within reason—to resist the foreclosure of our archives through the imagination, creating an imagination of the survivability of Walker's ancestors, in terms of memory and culture. In fact, imagination would have been the only way her folks could survive. Again, as her mentor writes to her, "Imagination is truer than life; that is the fact which every writer discovers and the fact which every writer discovers and the fact which people usually concede to the conscious mind of the writer."[38] Memory is how our ancestors survive in the present. To threaten those memories is to threaten their ability to be remembered or reproduced in the present.

A Black Feminist Truth: "Despite History"[39]

Unlike with Courland, the media paid no attention to Walker's copyright suit. When the media *did* publish anything related to her case, it came in the form of her own op-eds and letters to the editor. Even more disheartening, news publications used Courland's and others' suits against Haley to question the very foundations of Black memory and history. Reputable sources like the *New York Times*, as seen above, questioned the veracity, or even the possibility, of *any* Black history. The arguments that Walker and her lawyers set forth, however, refuted not only Haley's claim to the histories and knowledges in *Roots* but also the bad-faith historical analyses of the media. One of the primary arguments made on behalf of Walker's case for Haley's derivation of her novel was that Alex Haley did not complete any robust research for this work. While he and his team claimed Haley had "researched" for *Roots* beginning in 1968, nearly ten years before the novel's publication, this research was quickly debunked. Walker found that there was no record of any travel by

---

37. Weinbaum, *Afterlife of Reproductive Slavery*, 64.
38. M. Walker, *How I Wrote Jubilee*, 33–49.
39. McFadden, "Novelist's Suit Charges."

Haley from before 1966, and that he and his editor admitted that they "did not know how to do organized, methodological, or thematic research and kept no records."[40] She plainly cites his method as "hoaxes, tricks, and faux pas." Not to be exalted only by comparison, Walker's research prowess was what she was "trained" for and had been doing her entire life. What became of her trial was a struggle over Walker's own labor and her qualifications to write *Jubilee*. Her methods of poetry, memory-keeping, recitation, and oration—sprinkled with theologian tendencies—were the same challenge to institutional misnomers that the Black Power activists fought against: the teleological assumptions of European history that are quickly debunked by the tradition of African diasporic folklore.

There are many tensions that are enlivened in the reference to African American history as "no recoverable particulars," when it is the descendants of the Middle Passage's survivors who continue to wrestle with such a vague "before" while working from the traces left behind. As Walker maintained strong ties with the literary community around the country, even when she was not as prolific as she hoped, she looked back on the lives of her ancestors for guidance. She conducted genealogical research that required institutional investigation and written correspondence with historical societies. She reviewed her journals from her conversations with her grandmother. She reviewed astrological charts of her ancestors to the best of her ability. She traveled across the country to visit Randall Ware's birth and death place and steel grist in Albany, Georgia.[41] Much like Walker yearned for the days of untethered time for reading and writing—a conundrum to her in-laws[42]—she found ways to make her life continue rather than suppress her writing life. These research trips became easier once her two oldest reached a more manageable age and her parents began to watch them in her hometown of New Orleans. The "before" might have been unattainable for her, but the burning desire to create and write her story was textured by her children's lives instead of robbed by them. Her maternal status allowed her to fully place herself as a type of breaker of karmic tendencies of the family to disremember their history, and for her to solidly mark her place in the lives of strong Black women who independently and collectively fought for their kin to be *free*.

---

40. Scrapbook, box 3, series X, Margaret Walker Alexander Personal Papers; and Journals 1943–48, box 4, series II, Margaret Walker Alexander Personal Papers.

41. Margaret Walker took time away from her family to complete research trips to visit South Carolina, Georgia, and other places. During these times she usually left her children with her mother and father in New Orleans.

42. Graham, *House Where My Soul Lives*, 292–95; and Schwartz, "WPA Narratives as Historical Sources."

Margaret Walker was the granddaughter of Elvira Ware. She was the great-great-granddaughter of Randall Ware. And she intended to tell that story in a world created by a woman named Vyry.

Walker also traveled to these places to understand the dialects of the characters of her novel. In addition to completing traditional research on her ancestors and their lives, she also had more difficult research tasks that took years to investigate around her grandmother's health and her busy schedule. In a word, the relationship building between Margaret and her elders stood between her and relating to her characters. It wasn't until her grandmother's final days of life that she was able to have a conversation with her grandmother that led her to her great-grandmother's birthplace, due to memory issues.[43] This is the painstaking labor of ancestral work: the needling, the sifting against an already-wrought narrative that everything is lost or forgotten, and the body that refuses to remember. In other ways, establishing an emotional distance from her sometimes toxic family dynamics—which included a marriage that was admittedly abusive (verbal on her part and physical on Alex's)—Walker wrestled with the politics of her place in her lineage. She considered how she could help the country to understand that the history of Black women in the United States, and specifically post-Reconstruction, was a life constantly *in* construction.[44] The use of dialect and rhetorical flourish in the characters resurrected the essence of her ancestors, but the process to discover them was hardly "unrecoverable." For instance, in an anthropological move, *Jubilee*'s final words were not of her grandmother, but rather her sister-in-law Daisy, with whom she and her husband lived. It was in Daisy's garden that Walker first heard "Chick, Chick, Chicky," a soft tune that signaled to readers at the end of Vyry's 630-page testimony that light can be found in the small pleasures of a Black woman tending to her flowers on a warm spring morning.[45] In addition, most of the chapter epigraphs begin with sayings or songs that her grandmother would sing around the house.[46] "Despite" nothing—*Jubilee* unearthed the "particulars" of African American history by enlivening it through the living descendants.

Walker was the most high-profile writer to accuse Haley of plagiarism, but the only plaintiff that did not win her case. It is the scrapbook-as-documentation of Walker's struggle against Haley's legacy that puts her in conversation against the state-sanctioned violence against Black maternal memory, and where we can see the activation of scraps. It's a framework for

---

43. Graham, *House Where My Soul Lives*, 293.
44. Graham, *House Where My Soul Lives*, 292–95.
45. Graham, *House Where My Soul Lives*, 292–95.
46. M. Walker, *How I Wrote Jubilee*, 61.

understanding, fundamentally, that the state can also be responsible for supporting the suppression of Black women's memory by way of creative formation. It also speaks to the patriarchy of creation and its general saliency within the space of creativity. Walker arguably lost her case with much more evidence against Haley than her male counterparts, who won undisclosed amounts of money.[47] The primary danger of my writing about this case and Walker's legacy is, of course, only doing so by comparison to Haley's other lawsuits. But it's much deeper than that. In the late 1960s and early 1970s, Margaret Walker occupied a space in her career that was finally not solely defined by childcaring but instead now signposted a return to her craft. She still labored greatly by her service work and teaching at Jackson State University. She was the first director of the Center for Black History, Life, and Culture, which is still present on campus as the Margaret Walker Center in Ayer Hall and houses her archival papers. She was the first Black woman director of any such center in the United States. Her stature as a poet and connected literarian meant that she knew most prominent Black writers and that most, if not all, practicing writers knew her. Alex Haley and Margaret Walker were not strangers by any means. By the late 1960s, Margaret Walker was a legend in the writing community in Chicago, the South, and beyond. She was the writer of *For My People* and many other poetry compilations, and yet she somehow remains overshadowed in the canons of post–civil rights Black literature. Nikki Giovanni described Walker as "the most famous person nobody knows."

The patriarchal theft of Walker's work was, in some sense, multigenerational, as both her student and teacher alternative took (credit for) her labor. In February 1971, Walker leveraged her position as a culture leader and invited Black academics, poets, writers, and culture workers to convene for several days in the National Evaluative Conference on Black Studies. Folks like Ossie Davis, Nikki Giovanni, John Henrick Clarke, Alex Walker, David Driskell, and dozens more led working sessions, gave response papers, and workshopped with students. On one of the last days of the conference, Thursday, February 20, Alex Haley joined the conference for the fifth session as the key addressee for the conference's theme of "Black Heritage: Our Cultural Roots." He presented his talk, "Black Heritage: A Saga of Black History," after a brief introduction by Dr. Vincent Harding, director of the Institute of the Black World in Atlanta, Georgia. The talk was lauded. Only seven years before *Roots* was published, Walker and Haley dined together at Jackson State after Haley's keynote lecture. In that same moment, in a move as tasteless and insulting as it was striking, he sold a complementary pamphlet at the Jackson State University bookstore entitled, "Had I Wrote *Jubilee*." He proceeded to ask Walker twice

---

47. Lescaze and Saperstein, "Bethesda Author Settles."

over the course of the year if she would invite him to lecture at the center or in her writing classes. Haley revered Walker as the literary giant she was known to be, but his admiration consistently demonstrated a lack of ingenuity around the integrity of his own writing.

Men's theft of Walker's labors did not begin with Haley, however. Biographer Maryemma Graham wonders if Walker's fight was one that traveled back to her undergraduate days as a researcher for Richard Wright. Later in life, after the biography of Richard Wright was written and published by Michel Fabre in 1993, Walker received many questions about Fabre's book, especially as it followed her biography of Wright, *Demonic Genius,* published only five years prior. In interviews she vehemently denied any romantic affair or undertones, although there was certainly much confirmation of that in her journals. The biographer didn't consult her before including that revelation, but perhaps more revolting was that he painted Walker as a fawning, newly minted Northwestern undergraduate with a degree in literature who was enamored enough with Wright to do all his secretarial work. In response, Walker maintained to others that it was in fact *she* who taught Wright the basic conventions of grammar. She says in an interview with Claudia Tate, "I helped Wright. He couldn't spell straight. He couldn't write. I had just graduated from Northwestern with a major in English literature. Do you believe that I was just being introduced to literature by Wright?"[48] Walker's writing career was characterized by men stealing her work. It seems that every book she didn't write *wasn't* because of a child born. Every book she hadn't written was because her gifts had been appropriated by a man.

The lacunae (mis)represented as Walker's only exposed the vacancy of substance and creation of those who replicated her words. Much like an originary wound creates scar tissue that overcomes, stiffens, and confuses the muscles and flesh that attempt to heal, the muscle overcompensates, and then can only be broken down through sharp pressure through needles or deep massage. Walker never publicly denounced Wright altogether, citing his immense influence in her understanding of Marxism. Biographer Graham wonders if this impacted her life later on: If it weren't for Walker's impact on Wright's writing, and the misrepresentation about their relationship altogether, would Walker have been so adamant about her case against Haley? Her angst against Haley and the failure of the case would last the rest of her life. When Haley's farm was auctioned off to pay his outstanding debts, it was Walker who received a barrage of phone calls from friends and reporters.[49] Walker's battle with Haley tethered her to him for the rest of her life.

---

48. M. Walker and Tate, "Interview," 195.
49. Graham, *House Where My Soul Lives,* 596; and Journal 108, November 1980–January 1981, box 2, series I, Margaret Walker Alexander Personal Papers.

Toward Historical (Un)knowability

Archives have historically been created by those who held institutional power, and this is no less true for the manuscript collections and public records of the Reconstruction era, in which Walker conducted her research. Wealthy white folks, many of them part of families and communities who had owned Black people, and their biased state-produced memory were not just the issue of African American writers like Walker. They were also the issue of *all* readers and writers of historical writing. In her essay "How I Wrote Jubilee," originally published in 1972, Walker takes up the question that is so often posed to her by the book's audience members: "How much of it is fact and how much of it is fiction?"[50] She answers this throughout the essay in a number of ways, attesting to her years of research,[51] and validates these questions by discussing how they remained within her family. Her father referred to her grandmother's stories as "tall tales," but it was her grandmother who would reply, "indignantly," "I'm not telling her tall tales; I'm telling her the naked truth!"[52] Despite her father's assertions and the many questions around the novel, Walker did wonder at times, "How much of the burden of history can fiction bear?" She asked the question not because she believed she was writing fiction but indeed that it should be read *as* fiction so that it could properly "come alive."[53] Again, truth was not the priority of Walker, but authenticity. This is apparent in her verbs used to describe her grandmother's story in novel form: "What was I trying to prove through this search among the old documents? I was simply determined to substantiate my material, to authenticate the story I had heard from my grandmother's lips. I am using literary documents to undergird the oral tradition."[54] Only once in the essay does Walker attest that "the basic skeleton is factually true and authentic. Imagination has worked with this factual material, however, for a very long time."[55] Walker did not make up the looks, cadence, or events. She even studied Southern dialect so that she could understand the cadence of her characters' speech. What she *does* write is that the middle section of the novel contains the most flourishes, where the bulk of characters are the poor whites also left bruised by

---

50. M. Walker, *How I Wrote Jubilee*, 50.
51. M. Walker, *How I Wrote Jubilee*, 55. She described the book as her "consuming ambition" and explained that wherever she took a job, she would "hound the librarians to help me find books and materials relating to my story."
52. M. Walker, *How I Wrote Jubilee*, 50.
53. During a Ford Fellowship stint at Yale University, her mentor Homes Pearson said to her, "You're telling the story, but it does not come alive." M. Walker, *How I Wrote Jubilee*, 57.
54. M. Walker, *How I Wrote Jubilee*, 56.
55. M. Walker, *How I Wrote Jubilee*, 62.

the end of the Civil War.⁵⁶ To her, they were composites, mere symbols of the white power that desperately clung to the social and institutional hierarchy of a broken Confederate South. Perhaps she took to heart what Richard Wright wrote to her in a letter: "You know Margaret, being a writer doesn't mean that you have a masterful grip on life.... After all, writing comes from the imagination; it proceeds from the plane where brute fact and feeling meet and blend."⁵⁷ Her composites which bore John Dutton, Miss Caline, and Grimes refused to grasp that the only power they had was owning others. None, especially Grimes, Vyry's overseer, was left with any actual power he could have assumed at the Civil War's end.⁵⁸ The liberties that Walker took had very little to do with veracity, however. She wrote a composite, rather than a stereotype, of the poor whites who went on to compete with Blacks during Reconstruction. Vyry's view was that they did not know any better. Walker knew sentiments based on how her grandmother spoke about white folks and their actions toward them. She could speak to that. *Jubilee* posed many inconvenient truths to American history as a whole just by centering a Black woman who insisted on waiting to be free despite being presented with opportunities to pursue freedom. Walker's words illustrated how historical narratives around typically "heroic" women often failed to draw out the complexities of racial capitalism that affected Black women, who existed almost explicitly for breeding on plantations. It also posed uncomfortable truths around Black folks who chose to help and support land- and plantation-owning whites and poor whites alike. The novel runs through all of these actions, asking the reader to question their own presentist assumptions. It also redefined what it meant for a Black woman, a Black mother, to "fight" in the Civil War, how freedom came into and out of one's life as quickly as it did through Vyry's. The novel draws out these complexities and represents the specific toll of reproducing family, place, and heritage until we finally find Vyry in her final home in Alabama.

The media response to Walker's and others' plagiarism lawsuits were critical of the continued accusations and juxtaposed them with Haley's success. This is best illustrated in an April 1977 *New York Times* editorial entitled "Fact,

---

56. M. Walker, *How I Wrote Jubilee*, 62. Walker also admits to writing "imaginatively" when it comes to the "lack of bitterness" of her great-grandmother. Vyry is a notably agreeable character who draws much sympathy for her owners and at times defends them against other enslaved people. Walker writes that she omitted a more angry disposition because the truth was that her ancestor was a "definite product of plantation life and culture" who was "deeply religious" and believed strongly in forgiveness.

57. M. Walker, *How I Wrote Jubilee*, 49.

58. Grimes also admits his lack of power in the Reconstruction era of the novel wherein Walker writes of him and his family groveling for food and heat from Vyry.

Faction, and Roots."[59] Its inaugural question rose up again: "Does it matter if, as seems to be the case, 'Roots' is filled with inaccuracies?" The question is not merely if *Roots* is filled with inaccuracies; inaccuracies, after all, are only possible if one knows the perceived "truth" of certain historical events. The question is *also* not whether Haley's "inaccuracies" can be remedied by the "accuracies" of Walker's family saga. With this adjusted premise, we are equipped to see how the media's framing around "historical accuracy," "truth," and "faction" is a red herring for not talking about the theft of Walker's work. If this were the story fed to the media at the time, no one would know. But what's clear is that in the media's eye, the lawsuits against Haley are simply a result of his practice of inaccuracy, thus misnaming his work as a "family saga" and nonfictional. This may be a question of terminology felt or unfelt by Haley (although evidence shows that Doubleday did settle these cases, and quickly). Instead, the media and the plagiarism suits were unable to grasp the theft of what Toni Morrison has written as "becoming" for Margaret Walker's subjecthood through her publication of *Jubilee*. The result also stole Walker's "becoming" as "Black, Female, and Free," in the sense that it was in the zenith of her career that she was the best poised to tell her family's story with the most success.

Conversely, if "becoming" is not merely "looking at; nor is it taking oneself intact into the other," then Haley *becomes* a new story and new genre of African American literature: an erroneous, patriarchal story that attempts to dissolve the African diasporic opacity around lineage and ancestry. The media's reluctance to criticize *Roots* for its "factional" approach shores up the neoliberal impulse to exploit Black history's opacity and embrace the *factional*. Haley didn't elect to deploy a methodology of faction when he could have used critical fabulation or Black storytelling; rather, he drew a narrative that emphasized male heroism and empty, progressive narratives of hope. Notably, *Jubilee* does not necessarily disrupt similar narratives of progress: Vyry often makes more conservative choices when it comes to relationships with her owners, and she most definitely embodies the "naked truth" Walker's grandmother discussed.[60] The truth was uncomfortable, not just for white audience members, but for Black readers as well. But the suits against Haley don't so much illuminate a liberal relationship with truth as they do the misunderstanding that

---

59. "Faction," a term that Haley had used as a means to describe "'heightened history,'" is quoted in the original article, but never cited.

60. Vyry certainly makes choices that would not be regarded as "revolutionary," particularly when she defends her owner to Innis Brown, her second and spiritual spouse, for the near-death beating she received. M. Walker, *Jubilee*, 487.

Walker's life's work cannot be stolen and then reproduced. It has *become*—not only Walker herself, but her family, again and again.

The means of reproduction also applies here in a very literal sense: Since its original 1968 publication, *Jubilee* has never been out of print.[61] Not for nothing, Walker's work enlivens this opacity by laying bare what she knows as well as what she could never know or what is not hers to share. Here is very much the difference between "fact and truth," as Toni Morrison proposes.[62] Morrison draws a similar conclusion as Trouillot in that facts are "created" through a fact-creation system drawn from power, access, and archival survivability.[63] What was on trial in Walker's suit was not that Haley wasn't representing facts, but rather that he was misrepresenting and plagiarizing from her family's truth. Black women's intellectual labor falls more often into this category, underscoring the gendered dynamic of rejection from the state's cessation of Haley's publishing.

Where does fact creation fall into the scheme of Black feminist history-making, memory-keeping, and *becoming*? Why is this a reproductive injustice to question one's making, keeping, and *becoming*? The issue here is a both/and: Black history has long been accused of "inaccuracies" because of the hierarchies of truth in which stories are held, and because of the opacity of truth. In turn, what this yields is a discussion seeped in anti-Blackness about Black creativity being "verifiable" or "veracious." Acknowledging the inherent anti-Blackness that comes from labeling Black creativity and history as unverifiable, I also acknowledge that fact-creations made by those embodied as Black can still be anti-Black themselves. By this I mean that an argument about not finding *another truth* or an *essential truth* further underscores that Black feminist memory-keeping is not about pinpointing a truth, but rather maintaining an integrity in the stories and lives of ancestral accounts.

Haley continues to mobilize white forms of knowledge-building or "knowing," and the media response with it. *Roots* actually supports the claim that non-Black memory-keeping and storytelling is the baseline for verifiable truth. In this sense, Haley's *Roots* is not separable from the implicit "Americanness" that relies on white American history as the standard for truth. Haley's reproduction of Walker's words assumes a paternalism over other slave narratives published during that time. It also assumes an authority over the narratives from which it copied. The media attention played its role in concretizing the novel as a classic, and the miniseries that followed only a year after its publication was a historic moment for television. A *Time* magazine article from

---

61. Giovanni, "And So We Sing."
62. Morrison, *What Moves at the Margin*, 93.
63. Trouillot, *Silencing the Past*, 26.

February 1977 is preserved in Walker's scrapbook. It was clear that the spectacle of anti-Black violence "so deeply disturbed" one man, emblematic of so many Black communities, "that he had to stop watching after two episodes." The journalist concluded,

> There seemed to be scarcely any black Americans, even ones who thought they were well versed in their race's history, who did not come away from their TVs shaken to the core by *Roots*. Said Aurora Jackson, a social worker in Chicago: "It's one thing to read about this, and another thing to see it. My concept of slavery was always intellectual. For the first time, I really felt I had a picture of how horrible life was."[64]

An interviewed professor of American literature, John Callahan, observed, "We now know our roots are inextricably bound with the roots of blacks and cannot be separated."[65] What audience members did not know was the secondhand harm from watching these shows, pushing a pressure point of violence to elicit some sort of sympathy from white audiences.[66] Marmon writes that many felt "the TV series left whites with a more sympathetic view of blacks by giving them a greater appreciation of black history."[67] Both sympathy and appreciation operate on a logic of attesting that Black history involves feeling "pity or sorry for someone *else's* misfortune." *Roots* paradoxically played to white notions of history by dislocating slavery as a white and colonizer-made institution. It also vacated responsibility for enslavement. It framed the legacy of slavery as Black people's problem. Of course, where my analysis is partial to Walker's novel for a range of reasons, it should not go unsaid that Walker's narratives weren't exactly revolutionary. *Jubilee* was critiqued for employing myths such as a staging of Randall Ware and Innis, Vyry's second husband, as a foil for 1960s discourses between Malcolm X and Martin Luther King Jr. This is the same rhetoric that continues to disable anti-racist efforts today: focusing on shocking spectacle to understand the absent logic of anti-Blackness.

Materialities and Documentation

Walker's approach to writing her book can be summed up in her own words as a "philosophy of history," which is "exactly what one would expect it to be: a

---

64. Marmon, "Why 'Roots' Hit Home."
65. Marmon, "Why 'Roots' Hit Home.
66. Jared Sexton writes about secondhand trauma in *Black Men, Black Feminism*.
67. Marmon, "Why 'Roots' Hit Home."

point of view."[68] She described her "world of 'let's pretend,' with material from a chaotic and disorganized life and experience."[69] This disorganization left behind a novel that consumed a life and mirrored the imagination. I am not suggesting that Walker's story was one of cold, hard facts, while Haley's was one of pure fiction. That dichotomy does not encompass the labor of Margaret Walker and her grandmother. It does not encompass her reproductive labor. What is more useful is that they both fall on a spectrum of memory-keeping that relies on homage to ancestors. Walker considered herself and her family as the forebears of Haley's *Roots*. It was not simply imaginative—a technique she had no issue with—but rather, it was a story derivative of their lives and efforts. Walker delves into questions of "rememory," in which we think about the act of writing and fighting for the case of *Jubilee* as an effort of performativity of the traumatic act done before.[70] Walker elicits her own rememory through a memory-keeping practice as an extension of her own journaling.

Scrap Theory explores corporeal materiality and discovers other forms of materiality, taking up the question of how piecing one's life together is a self-archiving endeavor. In addition to logging Walker's views, motives, and frustrations with her plagiarism lawsuit, her scrapbook also points to an infraction on Black memory. There's more to be plumbed in the number of journals she created and unanswered letters sent. Journaling is the first-person documentation of one's life and journey. Told through the language of her own everyday experiences, Walker documented her thoughts, feelings, doodles, budgeting, and astrological charts. She wasn't *only* interested in the day's residues. She painted a picture of how she was creating the story of *Jubilee* while caregiving and navigating the world as a teacher and writer. In her struggle to find the literary language and vehicle of her life, Walker's scrapbook and journals supplemented the journey to reproducing her life for her own descendants.

The scrapbook, as a medium, has long been regarded as a static repository instead of a living document of archival material.[71] Black people in America have a shared relationship with scrapbooking that moves beyond the original curation of consumerism. As Ott, Tucker, and Buckler point out, scrapbooks

---

68. Marmon, "Why 'Roots' Hit Home." 69. This is very different from the Hegelian sense of philosophical history, where the historian has bracketed distance from the events entirely. For Walker and Black women memory workers, their philosophy of history is simply a point of view that recognizes their own biases based on their and their ancestors' lived experiences. Hegel, *Lectures*.

69. Hegel, *Lectures*, 64.

70. Toni Morrison coins "rememory" in *Beloved*, wherein one of the primary characters, Sethe, is triggered into remembering something that she had suppressed so violently that it felt like the first time she had remembered the event at all. Morrison, *Beloved*.

71. Gilger, "Otherwise Lost or Forgotten."

"manipulate meaning through rupture and the reconstruction that follows," and their "scrap aesthetics" bear more than a passing resemblance to the collage and montage practices of the avant-garde.[72] At the same time, scrapbooks are uniquely grounded in the practices of everyday life and assert the signifying potential of vernacular culture and the processes of textual recycling. Such "creative control" allowed Walker to preserve her experience, her writing (in the form of editorials and opinion pieces on her lawsuit), and her thoughts and doodles on the case. Her intermittent writing also "reconfigures the compiler's relationship to the social economy and to the objects that it produces."[73] Walker attempts to reconstruct a historical record for herself during this time, creating a social economy that centered her labor and its exploitation. It does not create a different account of the events. Rather, it resumes her authority over the event of theft, as her words and scraps mirror the heightened emotional investment of her work. In Walker's hands, the scrapbook shifts from the traditional object of a memento to a compilation of legal notes. She documents the process of her own attempts to bolster the case, and in so doing, she documents the public's reckoning with *Roots* and Haley.

The function of this scrapbook could be engaged on the level of literature as a living entity, wherein the document and material artifact trespass intellectual property and *intellectualism*. Framing intellectual production as (re)production, we can also honor the violation of the documentation of her family and herself—not just the creative output yielded from it but the years of ancestry work and labor that went into excavating a family's story. For the function of analysis of this scrapbook, I'm focusing on this as a theft of intellectual labor and an injustice to the memory of Walker's ancestors. The document also walks us through a Black woman creative's affective experience through the judicial system in a prescient foreshadowing of contemporary rhetoric around #MeToo. Through this lens, the lawsuit is very much an iteration of gendered- and sex-based intellectual violence. As such, this is a reproductive injustice on the abstract register of memory violence, and on an emotional register one that Walker felt as a jab to the work she had been toiling on her entire life.

As a "document within the document," Walker's scrapbook captures her insights on the prominence and legality of the theft of Black maternal and ancestral thought. In Walker's view, Haley had reduced the journey of "going back 200 years and seven generations to an ancestor of the author" to a "gimmick."[74] Put best in her words, "There is real moral principle involved

---

72. Tucker et al., "Introduction to the History of Scrapbooks," 16.
73. Gilger, "Otherwise Lost or Forgotten," 117.
74. Journals 1943–48, box 4, series II, Margaret Walker Alexander Personal Papers.

here, a question of justice, a serious malady running rampant in American society—a condemnation of all creative artists, a lewd mockery of all scholarship—to satisfy the greed of many or a few, for money, prestige and fame."[75] In her critique, Walker gestures toward what could be understood as the end of the "author" and the rise of the neoliberal public intellectual. Who could deserve the status of celebrity author less than a man who, she believed, riffed from her life's work? It is the removal from the role of intellectual to academic, griot to regurgitator.[76] Walker saw this as a moral failure of culture and of the justice system, including academia and publishing houses. These institutions were just as culpable for upholding the fake image of a trained and learned writer in such a critical time in American history. The value of an American "saga" was clearly nothing. The details of the case and the injustices that led to her unrest are evident in her "FACT SHEET," a several-page journal entry written between 1979 and 1980 that begins in emboldened, easy-to-read lettering with no edits. By the end of the timeline, the letters are combined, the pencil has dulled, eraser marks blend into the crossed-out names, and arrows point to the marginalia that crowds the lined writing. Walker struggled with the nonconclusion of *her* saga, the saga that concluded a "hellish decade!"[77] To Walker, the details become the vague post-release of the *Roots* television miniseries (1977) in the years after *Jubilee*'s publishing.

Amid her health issues, the lost battle against cancer her husband fought, and the dismissed lawsuit, Walker created a journal in the late 1980s entitled *Last Rites*.[78] The lens of subject formation activates Walker as a self-documenter and a vindicated, wronged artist. The record preserved in the scrapbook is difficult to locate without prior knowledge of the case itself. The range of emotions displayed, lexicons induced (for example, legal, literary, investigative), and content preserved would indicate a fan of Walker, but at times, rather obsessive. This was her right—we all form a relationship to material reality. The right to this material authority is where Walker constructs, in real time, the injustice done onto her on a personal level and also one in the public sphere. The intersections abound, where Walker simultaneously contributed to the media archive by literally writing some of the pieces that she later pasted into her scrapbook and attempted to influence the media by suggesting they write about her case. This nuance makes the scrapbook three-dimensional in

---

75. Journals 1943–48, box 4, series II, Margaret Walker Alexander Personal Papers.
76. Personal conversations with Frank Wilderson III.
77. Journal 106, December 1979–April 1980, series II, Margaret Walker Alexander Personal Papers.
78. Journal 106, December 1979–April 1980, series II, Margaret Walker Alexander Personal Papers.

a way that many others do not. Where Ott, Tucker, and Buckler point out that the scrapbook highlights an alienated relationship between commodity and subject, these frameworks do little to understand the theory of scrapping as a Black woman. Where author Kristin Gilger corrects their reading on the basis that this theorization does not account for scrapbooking "black life," we must also wonder about the extent that Walker preserved for evidence, and that her scrapbook, and the journal pages pasted within it, are case preparation, and at times, an engagement with legal discovery.[79]

The "scrap aesthetics" bear more than a passing resemblance to the collage and montage practices of the avant-garde. Compilers, through the continual action of separation and reconstitution, undermined the alienation that often characterized social relations under capitalism. Objects may have originated in the prevailing and impersonal marketplace, but individuals converted the unfamiliar into the familiar by cutting up the materials of capitalism and turning them into gifts to themselves."[80]

Doing so may invoke a kind of "archaeology" of Black memory. David Scott takes up the active verb of "archaeology," evoking a sense of digging up, excavating, and a ritual of turning over and over again that which we find in the archives.[81] When we do this, we must also see Walker not just as an object but as a person. Centering her as a Black woman means meditating on what she wanted to be remembered as and for. The same arguments that I am making here could also be made for her role as a writer. They could also easily be made for reading Walker as an activist. But we also have to understand that Walker, and her archival materials, respectively, have their own "reality" that is outside our encounter with her, as Scott suggests. When grappling with this, we disabuse ourselves of binaries that constitute themselves between erasure and amplification. In other words, expanding our knowledge of Walker as an educator does not misdirect our conversation, nor does it redirect it. It actually helps readers comprehend all of her roles as mother, writer, teacher, poet, and descendant.

In this sense, the Walker papers possess a hypervisibility amid the lives of other Black women who have been symbolically annihilated.[82] As Black women archives seem to be rarely collected or comprehensively archived, the

---

79. Gilger, "Otherwise Lost or Forgotten," 116.
80. Buckler, Ott, and Tucker, *Scrapbook in American Life*, 18.
81. Scott, "Introduction."
82. Here, I'm using this term as Caswell, Cifor, and Ramirez do in thinking about the South Asian American Digital Archive. In "To Suddenly Discover Yourself Existing," they use this media studies term to discuss the erasure of marginalized communities in the public sphere. It's interesting, however, to think of the ways that Black women experience similar symbolic annihilation by way of cultural appropriation.

Walker papers impact communities of Black women. Here, we can think of communities as institutionally isolated or not, both general and specific. In the early 1990s, toward the end of her life, Walker published a number of essays that asked specific questions around moralism and plagiarism. It seemed that even after the state failed her, she asked how these questions directly correlated with the development of Black women in America. Scrapbooking and notebooks revealed not only Walker's inner thoughts, but also the (non)linearity of those thoughts.

It is important, too, to expand the traditional notion of the use of scraps in the use of a scrapbook to tether, once again, the freedom of storytelling and believing in a Black feminist truth. Scrapbooks can make memories visually legible. They also create an aesthetic commentary, disrupting linearity, representation, and the authoritative voice of memory. Walker's scrapbook engages the facetious in her use of fairy tales, suspending belief in the regularity of this theft. There's still disbelief, or an undertaking of an illusion, that comes through as an example of the "black belief," a sense of knowing that she took into the afterlife.[83] She knew that freedom was also about not being appreciated. Her free self would never have been accepted and understood. Her potential would have to live out in her archive and the novel she bore. She was the mother to Marion, Firnist, Sigismund, and Little Margaret. She was the great-granddaughter of Sis Hetta, the granddaughter of Elvira Ware, and the only baby girl of Marion and Sigismund Walker. She was her family's light and her family's baby. And *Jubilee* hers.

---

83. M. Walker, "We Have Been Believers." Walker writes about "black belief" as an unstaggering belief of hope in surviving the effects of systemic disenfranchisement, despite the holocaust of Black life survived since and during captivity.

CHAPTER 3

The Corporal Archive of Separation in Contemporary Black Women's Cultural Production

The intimacies surrendered to the witnesses of Black women's cultural production can hardly be understood in their singular presentation. While we may read the stories of Black women's lives within contexts of diaspora, immigration, and separation, Black women creatives engage with the underbelly of relationality that is only fully realized with intentional considerations of space, time, geography, topography, and body politics. This underbelly highlights what Felice Blake describes as the "intentional and strategic indifference to the White gaze" that is illustrated in Black creative writers' depictions of intraracial conflict.[1] The effects of "intentional and strategic indifference" to the writing of one's relationships with kin can circulate the "terrible beauty" found in the messiness of Black women's experiences with their origins.[2] The spaces from which they came, the people from whom they came, and the bodies that reproduce their complicated histories fraught with genocide, enslavement, and sexual violence complicate the reproduced "terrible"-ness of this beauty that is presented in diasporic literature and art. The body in particular is revealed as iterative rather than merely representative of the personal conflicts that arise because of these histories. Reading Black women creatives' work as an exercise of interlocution with space, time, and body draws inconvenient scenes

---

1. Blake, *Black Love*, 7.
2. Hartman, *Wayward Lives*, 4.

of humiliation and violence that would not survive a gaze more interested in preserving triumphant narratives of Black women living with intergenerational trauma.

Conversely, how intergenerational trauma lives within the body alongside Black women's creative practices situates Black women's cultural production as history-telling. Dionne Brand's *No Language Is Neutral* powerfully intervenes to remind us that creativity, the body, and history are one. In it, she centers Black bodies as the holders of their captors' transgressions, living with originary scenes of violence within their corporal realities that often harken back to those of their ancestors: "They say this place / does not exist, then, my tongue is mythic / I was here / before."[3] Brand's concluding words of her poetry collection do not romanticize the place "before," but recognize a history that is not lost on or in the body. The tongue is elevated as a site of supernatural knowing. This chapter reads Black women's writing to understand how these bodies remain "fixed under the ether of history."[4] As such, it subverts the reduction of Black women as the sum of their oral/aural and/or reproductive organs to suggest corporality as a paradigm to read the lasting effects of colonialism on diasporic Black women writers and visual artists who live and create in North America.

Drawing most heavily from Edwidge Danticat's memoir *Brother, I'm Dying* (2007) and novel *Breath, Eyes, Memory* (1994) as well as M. NourbeSe Philip's *She Tries Her Tongue, Her Silence Softly Breaks* (2014), this chapter investigates the nexus of the body and colonialism through literature and visual art throughout the diaspora. Visual artists Firelei Báez (b. 1981, Santiago de los Treinta Caballeros, Dominican Republic) and Wangechi Mutu (b. 1972, Nairobi, Kenya) ask, visually, What of the body's ability to transcend space and time when put under the pressure of ancestral recollection? Taking place in three designated acts entitled "I. The (Mother) Tongue," "II. The Womb," and "III. The Lung," I subvert notions of colonial belonging as conceptually dizzying to the concept of diasporic origins, positioning the body and the parts that compose it as a mirror for the annihilated possibilities for unmitigated filial belonging in colonial lands. This chapter wonders, as a creative text, how the body might be imagined as canvas and map to (re)imagine-as-reproduction the technologies of colonialism in their present moment. The body, rendered a tabula rasa through colonialist means of material vision, still bears this violence. To this point I ask, how might we locate the body—the discursive,

---

3. Brand, *No Language Is Neutral.*
4. Brand, *Map to the Door,* 35.

morphing, transmogrifying body—within the diaspora? What and who does it reproduce? What and who does it resemble?

One way we may connect with the body on diasporic terms, rather than colonialist terms, is water. I situate the body, memory, and trauma in the "oceanic waters of past in present" as a disruptive and generative metaphor for the confusion left by the violent experience of diaspora. Dionne Brand writes, "Water is the first thing in my imagination," and Omise'eke Tinsley argues that "water, ocean water is the first thing in the unstable confluence of race, nationality, sexuality and gender" in the opening line of her essay on imagining the queer interiority of the early enslavement of Africans.[5] *Mami Wata* is the fluid (un)footing of the intimacies situated in this chapter. Where the goal of analysis is connecting the body, land, and origin, *Yemaya*, the water that rises and falls on a whim, whose temper is slow to erupt, whose borders invade shores without permission and create metaphor for the unpredictability of the relationality in the diaspora, is the method. Motherlands do not become less unpredictable under militarized governments and fascist politics; they become increasingly enraged by them. This rage becomes embodied in those who are victimized by these inequities. In such systems of upheaval, the land becomes water and water becomes land, blending into the instability of known space and time. As one Haitian said after the devastating 2008 earthquake, "It's like the earth itself has become liquid . . . like the ocean."[6] My method wrestles with how land and water are as fused as those who claim them as mothers, painting an omnipresent question of origin and bodies in the diaspora. Bodies expand like the water, quake like the earth, and threaten our allegiance to what we know to be true and what we cannot comprehend; we might ask ourselves what it means to purely "be like water."[7] Water, destructive and rejuvenative, is more weighty and destructive when it becomes the sum of its parts. As Isaiah Washington writes, "The water is both death and life."[8]

With Danticat's work serving as the anchor of this chapter, I wrestle with multiple works by women writers and culture workers who have migrated to the United States and Canada who bolster the treatment of corporality, creativity, and memory. In the first section, "The (Mother) Tongue" is shorthand

---

5. Brand, *Map to the Door*, 6; and Tinsley, "Black Atlantic," 191.

6. Danticat, *Art of Death*, 11.

7. Actor and activist Bruce Lee is largely credited with this adage, and it has since been martialed by many activists' movements, especially the anti-government movements in Hong Kong, China, protests against the Fugitive Offenders and Mutual Legal Assistance in Criminal Matters Legislation (Amendment) Bill of 2019. Protestors were known to yell, "Be water!" to initiate quick, synchronized movements against state-sanctioned attacks on crowds. Dapiran, "Be Water!"

8. Washington, "Our Black Ophelias."

for "mother tongue," or that which is taken from one character in Danticat's *Brother, I'm Dying*. This work features a Haitian, male-embodied character who wrestles with medical trauma induced from a radical laryngectomy made in an effort to save his life. After losing his speech, Danticat unravels for us a lifelong story in which the character feels farther and farther removed from his mother tongue, his mother country, and his family in his loss of speech upon moving to America. In the second section, "The Womb," I analyze Jamaica Kincaid's *The Autobiography of My Mother* (1996) alongside Danticat's *Breath, Eyes, Memory* to navigate displacement and separation. I place the body in conversation with origin for a brief analysis of the womb as it appears in characters found in these two books. The quest for origin and the experience of sexual or birth trauma is a journey these characters trace quite easily. This tracing makes possible a reading of the Black matrilineal as often literally imbedded within one's venter. I engage with American poet-scholar Bettina Judd's work with her personal experience undergoing pelvic trauma in her book of poems *patient* (2013), which helps piece together the traumatic excavation of one's reproductive future. The last section, "The Lung," examines the spirit of lineage through the work of Danticat and poet Gerardo Polanco. Often associated with grief, the lung, as it is depicted in the works chosen, manifests as a window into how grief is bestowed upon descendants without choice.

I. The (Mother) Tongue

I start on the note of origin to dislocate the correlation between people being reducible to their bodies. A survey of Black women's literature reveals a historical and present preoccupation with the trouble of origins. Diasporic subjects in the novels of Jamaica Kincaid, Dionne Brand, and Edwidge Danticat reveal the maintenance of filial belonging and national belonging in Caribbean islands of Antigua, Haiti, Trinidad and Tobago, and Grenada.[9] The Caribbean is an important site to explore the diasporic body for two primary reasons. First, the writers and artists listed above demonstrate profuse creative ability to investigate the tropes of kinship and belonging in an African diasporic context. Second, these authors cement the nation-as-mother and the generational torment of the catastrophe of enslavement and the ongoing effects of colonialism laid at their feet as young Black women. These writers more than exposit the "productive tension between attachment and a drive toward intense and

---

9. Kincaid, *Annie John, Small Place, Mr. Potter,* and *Autobiography*; Brand, *Map to the Door*; and Danticat, *Breath, Brother,* and *Dew Breaker*.

idiosyncratic individuation" that proliferates in diasporic life.[10] As Nadia Ellis states, "This productive tension between a quest for affinity and a desire to separate is often marked by frustration."[11] The argument of this chapter traces this marker of frustration through the colonial body as collectively stored and felt. Frustration does not just notate that which we would like to be but that which cannot be in this lifetime. It marks an intergenerational mark, lingering in those who remain unsatisfied with what seems inevitable but will never come. The body is marked by the African diaspora and national and political upheaval left in the wake of the transatlantic slave trade. This is not to further "mark" the body with the atrocities of violence but to show the marker of "frustration" of living and dying under the same colonial flag that claims the unfreedom of those living in the colonized islands of the British and American empires today.[12]

The many locations of dispossession in this chapter also complicate separation as an originary problem for the African diasporic peoples. A quest to belong leads to questions such as, To what? and To Whom? and Toward what end? while pulling the tension of self-definition beyond the identity of the descendant of a stolen enslaved person. Jamaica Kincaid effectively names this conundrum as the "cold bleak wind at my back" in the opening sentence of *The Autobiography of My Mother*: "My mother died at the moment I was born, and so for my whole life there was nothing standing between myself and eternity; at my back was always a bleak, Black wind."[13] "The bleak, Black wind" is the absence of her mother, which propels her protagonist, Xuela, forward. It is not the loss of her mother, but the absence left by the death of her mother, the force she herself comprises of an uncertain past and even more uncertain future. The questionable circumstances of her mother's life and death constitute the impetus of the book and propel Xuela forward. Toni Morrison's Milkman Dead articulates a similar "wind" during his search for his family's history with a similar defeatism in *Song of Solomon*: "I'm already Dead," he says to his friend Guitar as he announces his quest to discover his family's history.[14] However, the examples given above engender an anxiety for redress more than they present a possibility for it. I take for direction M. NourbeSe Philip's calculations made in *She Tries Her Tongue, Her Silence Softly Breaks* to challenge the perception of "wholeness" or the action of being "made whole."[15]

---

10. Ellis, *Territories*, 6.
11. Ellis, *Territories*, 6.
12. Danticat, *Brother*, 250.
13. Kincaid, *Autobiography*, 93.
14. Morrison, *Song of Solomon*, 204.
15. Shockley, "Going Overboard," 815.

These types of phrases double down on the assumption that diasporic individuals are only partly intact because they do not live in their motherlands. Black feminist creative production gestures toward "wholeness" through its depictions of mother and its various disruptions.

For Edwidge Danticat, the rupture caused by separation represents multiple instances of the "discursive reality" caused by the separation of mother and child. Danticat's first novel, *Breath, Eyes, Memory* (1998), follows the journey of a Haitian woman in her late teens to early adult years. The story of Sophie Caco is a journey of tracing her matrilineal line from New York back to Haiti. As a young child, Sophie is left in Haiti to live with her Aunt Atie until her mother sends for her to join her in New York City. Sophie slowly learns that her father was her mother's rapist. As a result of her rape, her mother decides to put Sophie through nightly "checks" for purity that include physical verification if Sophie is still a virgin. These "checks" are traumatizing for Sophie and result in a lifelong struggle with physical and emotional intimacy as well as a self-inflicted experience with body mutilation. Her mother's abuse subjects Sophie to the filial observance of what Rosamond S. King calls the "Cult of True Womanhood" represented in the "Cariglobal manifestations of gender expectations" of "proper" sex and gender practices for young women.[16] The generational traumas of sexual abuse, neglect, and poverty that complicate Sophie's relationship with her mother come to a head when Sophie gives birth to her own daughter and returns to Haiti as an escape from her marital problems. It is only when Sophie returns to Haiti that she can process the culmination of her matrilineal trauma and the many lives she is living in her own.

Her quest to assuage her trauma is intensified more than healed in Haiti. Despite the strong constitution of Caco women, Sophie worries about her daughter's safety and the gratuitous violence she witnesses by the *macoutes*.[17] She is reminded often of her mother's violent rape, which led to Sophie's being, and the sexual violence her mother transferred onto her in return. She recalls meeting her mother in New York for the first time. Upon meeting, her mother asked if she looked like Sophie imagined her: "'Am I the Mother you imagined?' 'No,' I responded, 'you do not look like the Virgin Mother.'"[18] Sophie's mother may not have been the virginal *Erzulie* she imagined her to be, but her mother reminded her that the rape she endured sullied Sophie's purity as well. In Haiti, Sophie recalls her mother's rape as she passes a sugarcane field: "A man grabbed me from the side of the road, pulled me into a cane field, and put you in my body. . . . I did not know this man. I never saw his

---

16. R. King, *Island Bodies*, 125.
17. Danticat, *Breath*, 60.
18. Danticat, *Breath*, 59.

face. He had it covered when he did this to me. But now when I look at your face I think it is true what they say. A child out of wedlock always looks like its father."[19] "A child out of wedlock always looks like *its* father" generalizes Sophie as an outcome of terror, rather *a child* born from it. In addition, her being "put" in her mother's body is much different from her mother becoming pregnant and her body nurturing a child. Sophie stood as a reminder to her mother that she was not born into the world but exists as a repercussion of violence. Danticat herself has accounted for the multiple natural and political disasters visited upon Haiti and its people as a "passive hurt." This hurt, which accounts for the "separation, no matter how it happens," and its "earth shattering," is passed down through Sophie's body and her connection to the land from which she is begot.[20]

Her mother's words also implicate Sophie into an origin story of terror, one to be potentially passed down to her daughter. This origin story could not be wiped clean by a return to her motherland. The rearing of her daughter did, however, present an opportunity for redress. Sophie lives a daily reminder to her family of the violence her mother endured: "I knew my hurt and hers were links in a long chain and if she hurt me, it was because she was hurt, too. It was up to me to avoid my turn in the fire. It was up to me to make sure that my daughter never slept with ghosts."[21]

Sophie's attachment to breaking the cycle of pain caused by her mother fractures her efforts to gain emotional footing on her origins. Sophie's mother's inability to undo the violence she inflicted upon her mother leaves her emotionally weary and origin-less. Shortly after we learn of Sophie's mother's suicide in the book, Sophie recalls when her mother sang "her favorite Negro spiritual" to her. She sings,

> Sometimes I feel like a motherless child.
> Sometimes I feel like a motherless child.
> Sometimes I feel like a motherless child.
> A long ways from home.[22]

Sophie feels maternal estrangement is shared by her mother. Their desire for belonging manifests as intergenerational trauma passed through the body. The lyric "A long ways from home" is applicable to Danticat's feeling of being away from her motherland and distanced from the legacy of her granddaughter. In her lamentation of feeling motherless, her mother is still a child, frozen

---

19. Danticat, *Breath*, 61.
20. Clitandre, "Mapping the Echo Chamber," 171; and Danticat, "Lòt Bò Dlo," 257.
21. Danticat, *Breath*, 203.
22. Danticat, *Breath*, 215.

in the emotional state she occupied when she was assaulted as a teen. She could not protect herself from sexual violence, nor could she protect Sophie from it; she even became the perpetuator of sexual violence. However, Sophie concludes on the final page of the novel that her mother's pain was the solution to her mother's crisis for "home." For Sophie, the suicide was anything but conclusive. Her mother's suicide forces Sophie to reckon with her desire for protection by naming the dysfunctional origin that lay behind and ahead of her: "I come from a place where breath, eyes, and memory are one, a place from which you carry your past like the hair on your head."[23] Her breath (read: spirit), eyes (read: sight for the future), and memory (read: past) manifest in even the places of her body that are perceived as dead, like her hair. Danticat's afterword, written in a love letter to Sophie, says that "her body is being asked to represent a larger space than your flesh."[24]

This chapter proposes the creative practice as a space through which healing from the pain of Black dispossession may or may not be sought. *What was/is it like for Black women coming to America through forced or coerced means?* There is no singular answer to this question. Nor may the answer be found inside imaginative contexts. Mother tongue is the archive and archive is the mother tongue: the language through which a series of resonances, repetitions, and discursive uses of (textual) language are able to speak or are unable to do so. This section turns to language, or originary language as the medium through which creative use of language is explored as an exploration of mother.

M. NourbeSe Philip's *She Tries Her Tongue, Her Silence Softly Breaks* questions the mother tongue and its double bind of anxiety for origin and of attempt for redemption. In "On the Discourse on the Logic of Language," Philip writes,

I have no mother
tongue
No mother to tongue
No tongue to mother
To mother
Tongue
Me[25]

---

23. Danticat, *Breath*, 234.
24. Danticat, *Breath*, 236.
25. Philip, *She Tries*, 30. The rest of this portion goes on to dissolve the "father tongue" or the role of the patrilineal in the formation of language as a formation of one's identity. Philip is positioning the mother tongue and father/tongue as two sides of the same coin of colonialism and control. The mother tongue, here, is complicated by its appearance of protection.

The text is also accompanied by a subnarrative that runs along the left-hand margins and two edicts. The first page contains the above stanzas and "Edict I." The second page contains the poetry and a progression of the subnarrative, "Edict II," where the poetry provides a meditation on the mother tongue and the removal of one's speech from their origin. An edict, or pronouncement or announcement of a law (particularly in monarchal societies), states, *"Every owner of slaves shall . . . ensure that his slaves belong to as many ethnolinguistic groups as possible. If they cannot speak to each other, they cannot then foment rebellion and revolution."*[26] The second edict reads, *"Every slave caught speaking his native language shall be severely punished. Where necessary, removal of the tongue is recommended. The offending organ . . . should be hung on high in a central place."*[27] In addition to the passage being reminiscent of lynchings in which "offending organs" were sexual, lynchings of Black men sought to annihilate the phallus, especially after inadequately accused of sexual aggression or rape. The scene Philip sets forth is the broader mnemic scene of the violence of the sexual trauma of losing one's mother tongue. The tongue (also a sexual and reproductive organ when deployed to give care to an infant) would be severed to separate one from their language, food, taste, and ability to give and receive pleasure, and to *rebel*. The reproductive corollary with the question, "What is my mother tongue?" The broken stanza prioritizes the question of "What is my mother?," for us to understand the mother as a "what" as well a "who." Unwrestling motherhood from the sole notion of embodiment, while using the body as an *instrument* through which this unwrestling occurs, tells us everything about the multivarious forms of motherhood that cannot be dislodged from dichotomies of violence/care, protection/violation, and mother/mother(less). This subnarrative indicates the use of the "tongue" as the first initiation of mother–child attachment. The mother's tongue is seemingly the one of purification: "She had tongued it clean of the creamy white substance covering its body."[28]

This "creamy white substance" is vernix caseosa, a waxy substance that coats fetuses in the womb and keeps their body protected from the moisture of amniotic fluid. Although humans do not lick vernix off their young when they are born like other mammals, humans wipe off the vernix, and usually prematurely (upon birth). Removing the vernix prematurely, rather than letting the protective layer be reabsorbed by the skin, can lead to a lifetime of epidermal problems for the child. Vernix interacts with the newborn's outer

---

26. Philip, *She Tries*, 30.
27. Philip, *She Tries*, 32.
28. Philip, *She Tries*, 32.

layer of skin for lifelong optimal epidermal composition.[29] The text along the side of the page, along with the dominant text, produces a conversation between the conflicting effects of a mother's attempt at protection. The mother's tongue establishes attachment with unforeseen negative effects.[30] It also reaffirms the tongue's classification as a reproductive organ, where, much like a breast, it can be used to nurture a child, as it does in the act of licking vernix caseoa or giving or receiving pleasure. It can be used to utter spells or revolution, otherwise bonding parents with their children.

Danticat recalls her Uncle Joseph reminding her, "*Pitit moun se lave yon bò, kite yon bò,*" or, "When you bathe other people's children, . . . you should wash one side and leave the other side dirty."[31] As Danticat and her brother leave for the final time to join their father and mother in New York City, she recites this Creole phrase and wonders if it's how her uncle felt letting them go. Uncle Joseph is confronted with their departure a long eight years after Danticat and her brother leave Haiti. Who is also left unprotected in the washing? We have yet to understand if Uncle Joseph leaves one side of her dirty to stave off his own attachment to the children. But it is more likely that he does it to leave hope for the parents to return, and to remind her that her parents are still her primary caretakers.[32]

As much as Uncle Joseph kept her clean, he kept her dirty—a reminder that she would one day leave him for her biological father. Despite his effort to perform a detachment from his niece, Danticat conveys that he was never able to shake Danticat as his daughter. Throughout her childhood, he affectionately refers to her as "*sa fille.*" The children of the family often helped Uncle Joseph on his daily errands, but none more than Edwidge. When asked by a bank teller confused by her relation to him as companion, "'Ta fille?' Your

---

29. The World Health Organization and many other organizations recommend rubbing vernix into the skin rather than wiping it off. Vernix has also been collected to make burn creams for adults that are more effective than those without it as a base. G. Singh and Archana, "Unraveling the Mystery."

30. The tongue is how young girl-child Clare in Michelle Cliff's *Abeng* knows her history: "Clare thought about the great house. The time which had passed through it. The salt taste of the walls. She sometimes imagined that the walls of certain places were the records of those stories of the people who and lived within the walls. She did not remember where she had gotten this idea, but she held onto it. The walls might not be able to reveal exactly what they had seen, but perhaps they could indicate to a visitor or something, if only a clue, about the time which had passed through them." Cliff, *Abeng*.

31. Danticat, *Brother, I'm Dying*, 120.

32. Brendane Tynes writes about the impossibility of protection for Black girls, women, and femmes in the diaspora: "Gendered violence, perpetrated by individuals and institutions, against those in the realm of Protection is unimaginable; their violations necessitate Justice through legal punishment." Tynes, "Reimagination."

daughter?," her uncle nods, "the same blissful nod he used to indicate agreement when something was suddenly clear to him," and pats Danticat on the head.³³ His attachment to *sa fille* does not waiver even as he nears death. Yet when he is dying in his hospital bed, Danticat urges her uncle to "hold on" for her so she has time to assume the role of caregiver she finds most familiar. He is unable to hold on and dies before she can see him while in Miami government custody, where he was kept with other Haitian migrants. Uncle Joseph kept Danticat close to his heart but refused to be cared for by her again. Although he could not speak, they were bound by the love and tragedy that comes from the licking mother of Uncle Joseph.

The symbolic "tongue" ties Danticat and her uncle throughout the novel. The scene described in the previous paragraph is one that Danticat remembers vividly. A young girl without early responsibility she was not. His damaged voice box left her uncle able to speak to his family and congregation only in whispers. But by the age of fifty-five, it was recommended he have a radical laryngectomy, which would mean losing his voice box completely. He flew to New York and had spoken his last words to his family in Haiti before he left. When he would return, he would be speechless.³⁴

Uncle Joseph's loss of tongue meant relationships between him and his family must be newly founded. Young Edwidge would become his primary interpreter and one of the only people who could understand his gestures to speak for him. Later, she would become the only person who could interpret him threefold to translate the words his body spoke to Creole for her parents and then to English for their doctors.³⁵ Without the children around to translate, Uncle Joseph was subject to a kind of ridicule that exiled him from his ministry and his community in Bel Air. Danticat feared for the emotional toll of his community exile the most: "Back then, all I could think to do was imagine a wall around him, a roaming fortress that would follow him everywhere he went and shield him from derision."³⁶ Where Uncle Joseph did not lose his tongue literally, his loss of "Kreyol," the language of the communiqué of the religious center of Bel-Air, was lost. His mother tongue was taken and created a fortress around his relatability and contact. Here, mother tongue is embodied by a man but was the way that Uncle Joseph engaged with what

---

33. Danticat, *Brother*, 66.
34. Margaret Walker describes a similar loss of voice she noticed in her aging father, a native Jamaican who lived out most of his life in New Orleans, Louisiana. Biographer Maryemma Graham writes, "Soon Jamaica disappeared from his conversation. Because he grew more silent as he became older, she always thought his longing for Jamaica had taken his voice." Graham, *House Where My Soul Lives*.
35. Danticat, *Art of Death*, 51.
36. Danticat, *Brother*, 64.

Trinh Minh-ha would call "mother's talk," or a gendered form of wisdom that brings the "impossible within reach" for young Edwidge.[37] Speaking mother tongue was how Uncle Joseph enacted his place in Bel-Air and as the Haitian caregiver of Danticat and her brother.

"It is not our way to let grief silence us,"[38] Danticat's father reminds her. His words speak loudly through Haitian-Dominican born, Brooklyn-based artist Firelei Báez's *Voice after Memory (June 20th)* (2015). Made on Yupo paper, a heartier, synthetic alternative to conventional paper, Báez's spiraling figure of inks allows the ink of dark green, seafoam, turquoise, and red to create an arterial figure that appears to be a head, insofar as bright blue eyes gaze behind the audience. The arterial imagery mirrors the dismemberment of the diaspora and the metaphors between separation and the body drawn in this chapter. Her work focuses on the body "in context with history and nature," and the surfaces she works with reflect this context. She says, "Paper itself is something that reacts to the environment, it's very flexible, it absorbs a humidity or a dryness and it will expand and contract like our bodies often do."[39] *Voice after Memory (June 20th)* expands like "the body archive" in which the "body is a visual sign of the body's exterior limit," but "our bodies extend into space well beyond the skin."[40] Like the figure, there is no outside or inside to the body, nor is there to diaspora. There is no boundary to sense, either. The visual fluidity of this conceptual voice is most heard as Báez's ability to challenge what Kobena Mercer calls the "implicit hierarchy of bodily senses that assumes inherent dichotomy between the aural and the visual."[41] Speaking through the visual, we see the oozing of the diaspora into the bodily, visual, and textual in concert to muddy the body within colonialism. The painting exhibits a feminine form that echoes Báez's sentiments that women have "special abilities" developed because of their social environment. Such precarious conditions have allowed them to exist between cultural boundaries and to even build resistances to external restrictions placed upon them.[42]

Báez's color choices also resist the implied dichotomy of silence and unsilencing often applied to Black women's representation in artistic forms.[43] The paints blend within one another, leaving marks of blacks and red-oranges that

---

37. Ha, "Mother's Talk," 28.
38. Danticat, *Brother*, 267.
39. Andy Warhol Museum, "Firelei Báez."
40. J. Singh, *No Archive*, 30.
41. Mercer, *Travel and See*, 227.
42. Rocío, "Bodies of Color," 58.
43. For more on this, see Carter, "Things Said and Unsaid," 224. Thompson's *Shine* discusses the traditions of representation in African diasporic art and how to forge new paths of inquiry beyond questions of representation.

refuse to marry. Vibrant colors are not blended completely to make new, more prevalent colors, nor are they denied their organic movement. The feminine figure created from these colors is not forced to practice active resistance to invisibility to overrepresent itself.[44] The lack of a clear mouth does not render the figure as unable to speak through voice. Instead, Báez's figure communicates a different subject somewhere to the audience's left. It does not directly interact with the gaze of the audience with eye contact. It suggests that the focus of its memory is somewhere beyond the audience's comprehension; invisibility cannot be spoken against in clear terms. Communication is both transformed and performed through the figure's body position and the originality of color.

Danticat's work soars in the subtleties of voice and its disruptive power in the silencing/unsilencing framework set forth by Báez's image. In her critical work and interviews, Nadège Clitandre writes that Danticat's emerges as a literary voice that links the untold and forgotten histories of her illiterate ancestors.[45] The refusal to be silenced, even under metaphorical silencing measures such as political oppression and sexual violence, is an honoring of the ancestor by the descendent. Uncle Joseph, who finds new ways to speak to his community even in the moments he wishes to speak with his voice the most, uses his body to perform grief for his mother-in-law. In his performance is a similar performance of grief and resistance. It weighed heavily on Uncle Joseph that Grandmè Melina, the family griot, was unable to be laid to rest in her mother tongue. Reverent throughout the service at his church, Uncle Joseph ran to the pulpit upon the ceremony's conclusion. Standing "motionless," Uncle Joseph amplifies his voice and grabs a microphone: "Had he forgotten that he couldn't speak? Should they expect some kind of miracle?" Danticat writes. As he pauses and then mouths "goodbye" to his mother-in-law, the congregation gasps in disbelief.[46]

Danticat elaborates, "This, he seemed to want to say, was not like all the other funerals he'd attended. . . . This was a woman, an old woman, who had traveled a long way from home and had lived a *long* life. He too was hoping to live a long life. He had traded his voice for a cure. But now he couldn't even properly say good-bye."[47]

To be sure, Uncle Joseph's voice was taken, but he was not silenced. Throughout the memoir, it is important for Danticat's father to remind her more than once, "It is not like us to let grief silence us." Although grief can be

---

44. Fulton, *Speaking Power*, x.
45. Clitandre, *Mapping the Echo Chamber*, 181.
46. Danticat, *Brother*, 74–75.
47. Danticat, *Brother*, 75.

arresting, Danticat's family draws an apex between grief, silence, and nationalism to show that the use of the voice—or expression, broadly understood and performed—is the substance of liberation.

Later in the novel, during the initial traumatic event that led to Uncle Joseph's radical laryngectomy, he managed to call his brother and Edwidge's father, Mira: "'Frè, map mouri.' Brother, I'm dying."[48] Years later, Mira's struggle with pulmonary fibrosis worsens as his worry for his brother's condition in an immigrant detention center worsens.[49] Dionne Brand writes, "The new migrants remain immigrants until they too can disappear their origins."[50] Both Mira and his brother could never disappear their origins, despite the loss of their breath and tongue. The irreconcilability of becoming a citizen (remaining an "illegal immigrant") results in the loss of origins. Mira's decline in health is characterized by his loss of liberties, as is his brothers'—made possible by physical presence in Haiti. In the initial scene of the novel, Danticat worries for her father's ability to drive a gypsy cab and continue to work amidst his coughing and wheezing. Later, his coughing and wheezing is what prevents him from speaking on the phone with his family in Bel Air. Speaking to one another keeps the brothers vibrant and connected to their homeland.

Her father's relationship with his motherland is precarious. His early days growing up in Bel Air are rocked by poverty and the instability of the Haitian government. "Then, as now, leaving seemed like the only answer, especially if one was sick like my uncle or poor like my father, or desperate, like both."[51] Leaving Haiti seemed like the only choice for Danticat's father. Lineage travels through the memoir as iterations of separation and the overwhelm of specters of separation.[52] The unresolved grief of Mira and Uncle Joseph intensifies these specters and takes on a life of its own—or takes over a life of its own, literally sucking the breath from Danticat's father's lungs.

Grief from separation is also portrayed as physically crippling for Sophie's Grandmè Ifè, causing a condition she refers to as "chagrin," a disease caught if you get too used to a loved one before they must leave: "To my grandmother, chagrin was a genuine physical disease. Like a hurt leg or a broken arm."[53] Sophie later asks her aunt if one can really die from the mysterious disease:

---

48. Danticat, *Brother*, 41.
49. Danticat, *Brother*, 249. "He's getting worse," Danticat's brother tells her, "and this thing with Uncle's not helping."
50. Brand, *Map to the Door*, 63.
51. Danticat, *Breath*, 54.
52. Brand, *Map to the Door*, 26. Brand writes, "In the diaspora you are overwhelmed by the specters of captivity."
53. Danticat, *Breath*, 24.

"She said it was not a sudden illness, but something that could kill you slowly, taking a small piece of you every day until one day it finally takes all of you away."[54] Danticat's father is likely suffering from chagrin, his grief manifesting as pulmonary fibrosis. Lungs, the organ often associated with grief in Chinese medicine, bear the brunt of the brutality of yearning for Haiti and his brother Joseph.[55]

II. The Womb

The reduction of Black bodies to the sum of mere parts is a dangerous practice. The isolation of body parts in this chapter names the physical and emotional occupation of separation in the human body as trauma. Kenyan artist Wangechi Mutu grapples with a similar challenge when working with the dismembered parts of Black women's bodies to make a collage of twelve fragmented pieces in *The Histology of Different Classes of Uterine Tumors* (2006). In the Mutu's piece, dismemberment of Black women's bodies is parsed out to make a "histology" of a colonial body in twelve distinct portraits. Mutu makes large what seems too small to the naked, colonized eye, as if we are looking through a microscope. Illuminated by Mutu's microscope are oversized lips, eyes, and noses, mixed with images from medical gynecological texts. Where one expects eyes, we see a speculum with a vagina. Instead of a chin, we see nipples. In a type of post-/subhuman collage made from newspaper, medical textbooks, and magazine images, Mutu's page asks us to consider uterine dysfunction and disease. The microscopic analysis of the tissue of Black women is one put together in an unrecognizable way with manifested effects. Who they are and who they are not is defined by disease rather than who or what individually appears on the page.

Mutu's depiction of tumors could liken them to captors, inhabiting the captive's body as an extension of themselves, with a curious association to present-day health crises that affect Black people with uteruses in the Americas. Every day 77 percent of self-identified Black women in America are more likely to miss work because of uterine fibroids or other severe uterine symptoms that reportedly affect their ability to be intimate with their partners, children, and families.[56] Comprehensive medical research has yet to isolate the determining factors for Black women's disproportionate experiences with the social isolation (for example, having to stay home from work, or being unable

---

54. Danticat, *Breath*, 25.
55. Pacific College, "Emotions."
56. Stewart, "Burden of Uterine Fibroids."

to travel, walk, or spend time with loved ones) caused by severe uterine pain. But most studies point to a deficiency of Vitamin D and prolonged exposure to stress. Both variables evince the trauma from separation from motherland laid manifest in the body.[57] Prolonged deficiency from the sun, especially for dark skin, which is evolutionarily designed to prevent too much absorption of humans' primary source of Vitamin D—the sun—has manifested in descendants' bodies. The argument for stress and transgenerational post-traumatic syndrome hardly needs to be argued.[58] The womb's desperation for a "manufactured" origin manifests in the "tyrannical" body. The troubled venter is both the symptom and the answer to the fibroids' growth.[59] Although Mutu's collage is abstracted, the work puts together medical biology and its abiding racist technologies, violently put back together with medical instruments like a speculum that make Black women's visages unrecognizable and opaque. The contemporary colonized body is made clear through things like uterine deficiencies and other health ailments. For Mutu, a microscopic look into the tissue we are made of tells this story. As Brand writes in *A Map to the Door of No Return*, "The body is the place of captivity."[60]

The Black body and the semblance of its parts connects contemporary artist Firelei Báez's and Mutu's work in a contemporary context. That which I previously framed as "arterial imagery" of the body's tissue, artery, and organs exposed in Báez's work overlaps the methods of Mutu. In Mutu's material choice of cutting pieces from books and magazines and Báez's method of ink and paint, the substances invade one another as a reminder that diasporic Blackness distinguishes itself through the "translative drive of appropriation that always transforms the various cultures and ethnicities it comes into contact with."[61] Bodies—human bodies, bodies of water, even bodies of knowledge—also remain changed by diasporic Blackness and its bellicose affects. Even still, diasporic Blackness becomes untenable against the multiple abrasions of colonialism, breaking down the walls of identity and creativity that come to make up the hybridity that is the Black Atlantic.[62] So too dissolved in this hybridity is the origin from whence we come. The origin as mother dies over and over, turning each hybrid, transformation, altering as a continual process of exile. Reproduction is a process of reduction and excess. The scenes of transfer inform an imagery of diaspora beheld in its constituents' bodies.

---

57. Brand, *Map to the Door*, 30.
58. Brakta et al., "Role of Vitamin D"; and Gallagher et al., "Effects of Vitamin D Supplementation."
59. Brand, *Map to the Door*, 64.
60. Brand, *Map to the Door*, 35.
61. Mercer, "Art History."
62. Gilroy, *Black Atlantic*.

Black enslaved bodies built the foundation of the institutions that went on to literally sell them and the banks, schools, and government centers that would oppress their decedents. La Vaughn Belle excavates this foundation through the abstraction of the material walls of the body: blood, effort, extraction made legible through the rubble. The water that gives life to coral, the water that cohabitates with its tides and storms, both figurative and literally, affects those that broke pieces of coral. Corals are marine invertebrates, distinct from plants because they do not make their own food. Enslaved Africans were sent into the ocean to cut coral to be used for the foundations of the institutions in St. Croix.[63] Those sent out would cut the living animals and haul them to shore. Working among such a beautiful animal would also be dangerous, as coral cuts are known to be slow to heal without proper care. Some of the beautiful but sharp exoskeletons contain nematocysts, an organ consisting of a minute capsule that ejects thread and causes a sting in the seemingly harmless lacerations.[64] The animals secreted themselves into the bodies of the enslaved, fighting for their lives while the enslaved Africans were forced to work for their own. Belle's capture of the foundational stones, posed in a rectangular, transparent case, presents the lacerated coral fossils as testimony of their experiences. Christina Sharpe argues for the "staying power" of human blood in saltwater oceans for over "260 million years." The equivalent of "staying power" in human blood and DNA is potentially endless.[65] The forced environmental antagonism against the coral and against the enslaved person is told through the piece. The pieces of coral are stacked and removed from their plastered containment that hid the shards to the buildings that were not in ruin. Evident in *Trading Post (Articulated Hierarchies and Visible Displacements)* (2015), standing at 36″ × 18″ × 18″, is the inverted "hierarchy" of visible narratives.[66] It also makes clear the narrative kept hidden, but also the environmental captivity of enslavement in the Caribbean: isolation in the saltwater paddies Mary Prince writes of in her groundbreaking 1831 narrative, and the use of the nonsentient animal wounded in the project of colonization. Despite the coral's nonsentient status, I echo Alexis Pauline Gumbs's offer to re-recognize memory and breathing through collectivity: "Maybe it's time to remember that there is more than one way to breathe in icy depths or summer heat. To thank your ancestors for how you have evolved in the presence of polar bears, harpoons and other threats."[67] The water did not just evolve

---

63. Belle, "La Vaughn Belle."
64. Plantz, "Coral Cuts."
65. Sharpe, *In the Wake*, 41.
66. Belle, "La Vaughn Belle."
67. Gumbs, "Undrowned." See also the book of the same title: Gumbs, *Undrowned*.

with the enslaved African, they were both differently brutalized together. Even after the enslaved are gone, the coral fossils stay stacked in Belle's image of this inversion, showing that history is extricable from the body, the body from the wound, and the wound from the water. The history of these animals, and its entanglement with the bodies of the enslaved, evolves the sea, the coral itself, unravels the "ancestor" as purely human-embodied. The 3D case allows spectators to envision themselves in the afterlife of the captivity, encased for voyeuristic inquiry and remembrance. Descendants of the coral are looking at their ancestors and in turn themselves, watching the inversion of ancestor (past) to descendent (present), and further disarticulating the hierarchy Belle punctuates in contemporary storytelling.[68] The fossilized, organic material goes through physical change, moving from animal to foundation to remnant according to its extracted use in that given moment. Caribbean visual art incorporates the material and the corporal (in all the various "bodies" previously stated) to produce greater insight into the symbiosis between colonization and their actual bodies. Along with "polar bears, harpoons, and other threats," the enslaved ancestor evolves its breath with coral, salt, and water to weather the injury of enslavement. The motherland, and the waters that surround it, continues to violate the enslaved and those forced to be there. Not because it is the mother who is inherently violent, but because colonization has taken her over to abandon those who were forced on her shores and whom she once called kin.

III. The Lung

The body resurfaces as a map in written and visual texts. Danticat, Philip, Kincaid, Mutu, Belle, and Báez ask what, if any, independence is gained through the legacy of the child, separated from their mother. Captivity looms over their work as that which is ultimately unable to be redressed in histories of Black women's lives.

The retrospection of Danticat's mother's, uncle's, and father's deaths is concomitant not with a certain age of ascertainment of mother wit herself, but with her own experience with pregnancy: "My father is dying and I'm pregnant."[69] The memoir is impossible to contextualize without Danticat's pregnancy in mind. It is impossible to ignore Danticat's deliberate connection between the beginning of life and the end of life because her parturition

---

68. Trouillot, *Silencing the Past*.
69. Danticat, *Brother*, 15.

bookends the book. The first sentence of the memoir is, "I found out I was pregnant the same day that my father's rapid weight loss and chronic shortness of breath were positively diagnosed as end-stage pulmonary fibrosis."[70] It comes most into focus in the first and last essays of the book, which figuratively bookend the story of her father's and uncle's deaths with conception, proposing the beginning and an end as reliant on one another. This move draws a circle of legacy for us, imagining that as one door closes, another opens. Danticat, or at least her body, is the hinge of this door if not the door itself. Here again, the patrilineal line is disrupted, making the woman's body a subversive body. Origins veer wayward as the coding of origin depends on Danticat's pregnancy.[71]

Thinking of the Danticats as exemplars of embodied grief, African diasporic bodies tell us something specifically about the contentions and prolonged relationships with mother-as-tongue and homeland—all metonymic devices for the mother to which we belong. I end this chapter with the first part of Gerardo Polanco's two-part poem, "Ringing Inside the Open Spaces of My Lungs, and: Neruda, Please Explain a Few Things" (2016). I quote this piece to use the creative to summate the semblance of the colonial body amalgamated through Danticat, her father, and her uncle. To conclude this chapter with the suggestion that these three people are born from one another reinforces the reflexive and fluid relationship between ancestor and descendent, mother and child, and the linearity of inheritance. This relationship is not necessarily one of migrants, immigrants, and family, but iterations of separation between mothers and children and children who bear the scars of that separation. Polanco writes:

> The sound of my mother forcing a tired heart to beat   one more time.
> The sound of my mother's weeping   forcing sanity despite thinning veins.[72]

The bodies here are transitional sites of memory in which belonging becomes exacted in the Black maternal body. The sound of a wail is what births the male subjectivity, further erasing the presence of the Black maternal body. Polanco's description of the sound of his mother and grandmother's "weeping" and "crying" reifies the maternal figures' "pain as the matrix of his becoming," which he "must leave behind in order to claim a future for himself."[73] Where Danticat's father and uncle do not necessarily "become" from her wail of pain (Danticat's subversion of the patriarchal biblical story that women are born

---

70. Danticat, *Brother*, 3.
71. Mwangi, "Silence Is a Woman."
72. Polanco, "Ringing Inside the Open Spaces," ll. 623–25.
73. Yates-Richard, "What Is Your Mother's Name?"

from Adam's rib), it is through Danticat's memories that the pain of losing motherland and mother tongue that mother–child separation appears for us as acute and indiscriminate as one could fear. Borders, between the motherland and new land, the border that marks the migrant or the immigrant, are also perpetuated by the myth of corporality. That bodies are not separate from one another, nor can they be separated by land. The body intensifies the unstable logic behind nationalist state legacy as patriarchal.

The Black maternal body is the one in which "the dead and the living are already linked" in blood.[74] The mother here is not redeemed as the author herself but appears to us as a disappearance. The mother, unable to be reclaimed, exists only in the intent of achieving the impossible goal of retroactive care and the undoing of loss.[75] A notable figure in Saidiya Hartman's depiction of Venus first appears to us naked and hung by her ankles on a transatlantic slave ship. It is this same girl who remains as nothing more than *Black Venus* in Janelle Hobson's work (2005), and in similar to other works by Marisa Fuentes (2016), and by Sasha Turner as a mere "unnamed girl" (2017). This young girl is best articulated by Spillers's Black woman as the "present-absence," or that which exists only to draw stark opposition to construct notions of being to her white counterparts.[76] Here, the mother is similarly lost and unrecuperated in color, narrative, and personal story, reconstructed through the violent, intimate ways in which Black mothers and their kin are rendered legible. In the next chapter, I probe further into the politics of remembering and artistic practitionership as it takes material and digital forms by Black mothers. By pairing the literary and the material together, I demonstrate how Black women produce artistic and cultural artifacts from which memory is read and produced. In the case of Tamir Rice, a twelve-year-old boy who was disappeared from his neighborhood a mere block from his home, and his mother's subsequent efforts to memorialize him, we can engage in the aesthetics of archiving Black death that Bambara composed as a touchstone for grieving mothers who deploy the same artistic expressions of grief into the twenty-first century. The abstracted forms of the mother that I emphasized in this chapter, and the embodied form of the mother, further undo that which undoes its own embodiment through the parsing of organs, experience, and exile. The tongue that the mother speaks, then, is the tongue that violates as it utters the material of dispossession, making the body the canvas of its own details of separation.

---

74. Danticat, *Brother*, 249.
75. Hartman, "Venus in Two Acts," 3.
76. Spillers, "Mama's Baby, Papa's Maybe," 64.

CHAPTER 4

Refused Memorials and the Black Feminist Archival Praxis of Samaria Rice

Many will easily recall the murder of twelve-year-old Tamir Rice in 2014. His untimely death was a flash point in the ongoing protest against state-sanctioned deaths in the new century. Following the death of Trayvon Martin in 2012, Tamir's death joined a cadre of other high-profile police killings that rallied national outcries and birthed new political movements. Unlike in previous generations, these new racial and political reckonings were largely formed by the digital age in which they occurred, such as #BlackLivesMatter and the Movement for Black Lives.[1] The 9-1-1 call from the person who first speculated that a "Black man was throwing a gun around" visualized the scene of Rice's death for listeners. Surveillance footage from the Cleveland park in which he was killed, a cement-posted and wooden gazebo in the background, was released soon after his death. It rapidly reached hundreds of millions of viewers, thus allowing anyone with internet access to witness a child taking his last sentient breath.[2] In many ways, the lasting legacy of the digital footprint of Tamir Rice's death is the most material thing we have of his memory. Stills from this video are what replays the actual events and normalizes the mass viewership of Black death, remnants of the lynchings in our not-so-distant past that attracted crowds of over ten thousand people.[3]

---

1. Social media has shaped the political movements and their corresponding uprisings, especially as it pertains to the movements. Barber, "Can You Be?"
2. *Los Angeles Times* staff, "Hear the 911 Call."
3. Minnesota Historical Society, "Duluth Lynchings."

In the same era in which the death scenes of Korryn Gaines, Eric Garner, and Tamir Rice circulated the web, a concurrent public memory crisis erupted around the institutional and structural legacies of the Civil War and Confederate "heroes." The ire to remove Confederate monuments was part and parcel of the same social fabric of this time, displacing the impossibility of erecting physical memorials for slain Black folks while the digital allowed us to relive their deaths over and over—sustaining grief as a permanent condition of Black life.[4] This condition is often defined as the social position of being Black. Critical Black theorists engage in mourning in myriad ways; most applicable here is their attending to the "slow death" of Black mothers and how mourning prolongs the spectacle created by Black death.[5] These spectacles manifest physically in memorials, monuments, and the bodies and minds that contextualize them within their own experiences with mothering and parentage.[6] Material memorials for Black people—meaning three-dimensional sites, statues, or plaques commemorating the slain—were and remain defunct for a society still living the original event, at the click of a button and the never-ending evidence of gratuitous anti-Blackness.

What is less frequently recalled about the murder of Tamir Rice and those also killed by state-sanctioned violence in the digital age is the difficulty of erecting material memorials of their lives and the abhorrent circumstances through which it becomes difficult to materially manifest Black memorial. Historiographies of monuments and memorials attend to this difficulty in analogous terms of events such as the Vietnam War and the Holocaust. The death of Black children like Tamir Rice and public resistance to figure state culpability within the grammar of memorialization continues to demand critique that escapes these analyses.

My critique relies on Samaria Rice's grief as a framework to understand the object of the gazebo as a generative object for a multitude of efforts. For one, it could foster healing for Tamir's mother. But beyond that, the material is critical in reframing narratives about state-sanctioned violence against Black children as violations of reproductive rights.[7] At the time of writing in 2020, no physical memorials—beyond plaques—have been successfully erected for

---

4. Rankine, "Condition of Black Life."
5. C. Smith, "Slow Death"; and Williams, "Black Maternal Grief."
6. D. Fuentes's article draws a connection between the visuality of Black maternal separation and her own experiences. Vivid remembrance that crosses intergenerational lines is a common hook in writings about Black motherhood and mourning, including Rankine's and William's articles mentioned above. Fuentes's begins with an intergenerational anxiety in which she divulges a dream about her newborn daughter being taken from her. Fuentes, "Visible Black Motherhood."
7. McClain, "Murder of Black Youth."

the aforementioned slain, with the exception of Tamir Rice.[8] This chapter is invested in the materiality of dispossession—what comes from material, what is born from it, and how the dispossession of children takes up two- and sometimes three-dimensional form to articulate kinship separation. It also asks how the material exhibits collective, inter-, and transgenerational grief and its dynamic in remembering contemporary victims within the historical contexts of victims of the past. Specifically, it locates Samaria Rice's erection of *Objects of Care: Material for Tamir Rice* (2018) as an archival practice of her son's death.

In recent years, Black women's scholarship in the humanities has engaged in the "scraps" of the archive as a method to understand the interior lives of Black women. In the years following her son's death, Samaria Rice's relationship to the gazebo fluctuated in response to the public vandalism of the gazebo and the city's decision to demolish it.[9] This chapter interrogates her exploration with the refused object of the gazebo as "scraps" left behind by similar oppressive structures of memory that situate Black women's archival praxis as unrecognized labor. *Objects of Care* poses an exemplary opportunity for archival studies scholarship to incorporate the theorization of Black feminist archival praxis, specifically through engagements with refused objects or "scraps" of Black life and death as documentation. As an assemblage of refused objects, *Objects of Care* is an exemplar of how *Black visuality* usurps the collection of Black archival matter. Samaria Rice's enacting also helps distill the "function to refuse Blackness itself" by moving Blackness and identity to the fore of her archival praxis. What is lost in the stringent adherence to archival studies' articulations of archives and "the archive"? How must we imagine Black women's archival labors differently to fully articulate all their historiographical and intellectual interventions into archival study? How does a critical undertaking of scraps punctuate the epistemic violence that precedes a study of Blackness? By engaging in Rice's work as part of a historical Black feminist archival praxis in which Black women elicit greater understandings of archival studies and what is deemed a practitioner, my analysis intervenes on institutional articulations of memorial and Black women's contemporary memory work by situating Black maternal grief as a site for archival production and transcendence.

---

8. There have been memorials that have been constructed by the communities of which the slain belonged, however, but none that include the construction or preservation of a physical memorial such as a building or statue. I am not making this distinction for the convenience of argument but more to juxtapose the resistance to memorials that resemble the size and weight of those to commemorate the Confederacy. For more, see Maynor, "Response to the Unthinkable."

9. S. Rice and Gates, *Samaria Rice*.

Archiving Black Maternal Grief

After the immediate aftermath of her son's murder, Samaria Rice sought to remove and prosecute the person who killed her son and his accompanying coworker. In so doing, she entered a high-profile year-long legal battle rife with public unrest between herself, the city of Cleveland, and the Cleveland Police Department. An unsuccessful prosecution of the officers led to a civil suit against the city of Cleveland, and Rice was awarded a $6 million settlement, along with the tentative agreement that the gazebo would be demolished.[10] She first offered the gazebo to multiple cultural institutions and museums in Cleveland, all of which rejected it. As owner of the materials, her primary objective was to locate a storage space to store the materials safely. Rice had become fearful that the gazebo was too vulnerable to vandalism in its original place of Cudell Park. Her artist-activist contacts from Cleveland, who were instrumental in organizing protests on Tamir's behalf, connected her with Hank Willis Thomas. He then suggested Theaster Gates as a possible person to help store the materials. Combining Samaria Rice's rejection of Cleveland's attempt to "erase any memory" of Tamir's murder, Gates took up her call to thwart the city's effort to "erase that material object that was allowing other people to mourn. They were trying to reset protest by getting rid of the object."[11] In 2019, the stored, deconstructed materials were titled *Objects of Care: Material Memorial for Tamir Rice,* housed at Gates's archival and exhibition space, the Stony Island Arts Bank, based in Chicago (figure 2).

Set in a back room on the first floor, the exhibition room was un-enterable, walled off by text on the front-facing wall with a list of demands penned by Rice.[12] In 2018 the materials were reerected in their original form outside, on the north side of the Stony Island Arts Bank, and complete with a concrete picnic table inside the structure that was available to Arts Bank visitors through a single concrete sidewalk path. The piece was dedicated that same year with a celebration that included remarks from Samaria Rice, the Rice family lawyer, and a few local artists.[13] One artist, Yaw Awgeman, sang

---

10. M. Smith, "Tamir Rice's Family."
11. S. Rice and Gates, *Samaria Rice.*
12. The demands: "1-2-3-4 / open up your door I've been waiting outside for a very long time // 1-2-3-4 / open up your door I've been waiting so long just to sing my song // 1 / I want the badges / I want their guns / Pink slips for blood / Pink slips for blood // 2 / The government shall recognize / the price of his life / The weight of my tears / The burden of Service // 3 / Tim Loehmann / And / Frank Garmback / Should be charged / Should see jail / For the murder / Of my boy // 4 / If you can't protect us / If you cannot serve / Give the moneys to the babies / Fund the education of these children / And not your fear."
13. Rebuild Foundation, "Objects of Care."

FIGURE 2. Samaria Rice (American, b. 197?), *Objects of Care: Material Memorial for Tamir Rice*, 2018. Photo taken by author.

the demands written by Rice that appeared on the facing wall of the original installation.

The installation now occupies the north lawn and is surrounded by a fenced-in grassy space; Rice said she intended it to be a "community space" "to bring people together as a meeting spot."[14] A plaque titled "Memorial for Tamir Rice" faces pedestrians and drivers traveling south on the 1600 block of South Stony Island Avenue (figure 3).

It reads in full:

> On November 22, 2014, 12-year-old Tamir Rice was murdered by a Cleveland Police Officer while playing with a toy pellet gun at the Cudell Recreation Center in Cleveland, Ohio. In 2016, at the request of Samaria Rice, Tamir's mother, artist Theaster Gates and Rebuild Foundation deconstructed and

---

14. Rebuild Foundation, "Objects of Care."

FIGURE 3. Samaria Rice and Rebuild Foundation, *Objects of Care: Material Memorial for Tamir Rice* plaque, 2018. Photo taken by author.

transported the gazebo, a park structure immediately adjacent to where Tamir was killed, to the Stony Island Arts Bank. Ms. Rice sought to preserve the structure as a community space for reflection, public interaction and healing. The Material Memorial for Tamir Rice provides a space for visitors to publicly and privately reflect upon the racial, political and economic crises of this country. The gazebo, a visible testament to Tamir's memory, serves as a site of reflection and dialogue and a call for change.[15]

The plaque explicitly mentions Samaria Rice's effort to "preserve the structure as a community space for reflection, public interaction and healing" through the iteration of a "material" memorial. This materiality "provides a space for visitors to publicly and privately reflect upon the racial, political and economic crises of this country." Despite being titled "Memorial for Tamir

---

15. Personal photograph, taken July 19, 2019, in Chicago, Illinois.

Rice," the placard illustrates that the memorial is a "material," with viewers left to imagine what other forms of memorial exist for Tamir in the context of materiality, and the dispossession of an object from its original homeplace.

Objects of Care joins a surviving material culture of the remarkable intimacy of Black kinship without denying the dimensions of violence that shape it. Because Tamir Rice was not already included in the vision for Cleveland's futurity, it stands as a reminder of separation from his mother. Samaria Rice's reerection of the gazebo joins the fragmented legacy of Black mothers' public-facing responses to the deaths of their children. The most prominent example remains Mamie Till-Mobley's choice to display the image of her son Emmett's tortured body in the 1955 issue of *JET*. Today, Emmett Till's memorial placard, at the suspected site of his death, has been reerected four times after being vandalized and shot at since its original commemoration.[16] In our current era of highly publicized Black death, an era that converges with the advent of the Black Lives Matter movement and the wide circulation of images, rhetoric, and public memorial and sometimes reliving the deaths of slain Black children, Black mothers have reached a particular visualization remnant of Mamie Till-Mobley. Like Till's photo, the video of Tamir's death was a preceding visual accompaniment to a material memorial that lives to visually tell the story of his death. The gazebo allows for visitors to physically and spiritually partake in the memory-making of his death without leaving the history of violence against young Black boys behind.

Artistic Disruptions in Historical Space(s)

Positioning videos or images as documentation of an original event is approximate, but distinct from the memorialization of that event.[17] The attempt to memorialize Black child victims of state-sanctioned violence remains undertheorized by the historical institutions that do not house them and its actors who seek to uphold the impunity of police violence. Samaria Rice's stewardship, management, and reerection of the gazebo allows for a continued reading of how Black mothers enter archival practice via visuality, objecthood, and memorial-making. Singular to Samaria Rice's attempts to materially memorialize her son is its convening through the artistic space and medium. This convening, albeit accidental, does not remove her from nor necessarily include her in the history of artists whose work engenders disruptions of

---

16. Siemaszko, "City of Cleveland Settles."
17. Noble, "Teaching Trayvon."

tradition and nostalgia by situating Black death as explicitly state sanctioned. A clearly enunciated part of this genealogy includes Fred Wilson's *Mining the Museum*, which offered an explicit artistic interrogation of the literal archives of the Maryland Historical Society and located the tension between the state's archive and its exploitative and anti-Black histories.[18] Instead of operating in overworked frameworks of silence or omission, Wilson worked to "disembed artifacts from fixed narrative templates" and question the racial assumptions the museological space makes available to its artifacts as well as those who view them.[19] Wilson's work made available both the museum space and the archives from which his materials drew the violence that made the cultural, social, and economic organization of early America possible. It mediated the scene and the apparatus of the museum using the very objects it claims. Just as Wilson's work utilized the archives of the Maryland Historical Society for contemplative use, Rice's use of the Stony Island Arts Bank is part of a tradition in which arts practice makes clear the illegibility of violence in historical narratives shored up in museums. This tension between the museum space and its artifacts made evident through arts practice exceeds this chapter and has been pronounced in many other works.[20] Where Bridget R. Cooks productively articulates the tension about the space in the context of Black life's various historical events,[21] I focus on the process of creating and appraising art-as-documentation after the rejection of the gazebo. This analysis demands the figuration of archival practitionership where Black mothers produce archival objects, records, and collections for creative use of the gendered and racialized matrices of violence that occlude them from memorializing their kin.

In recent years, archival approaches via visual studies and archival studies have talked to and past each other, widening the breadth of their lines of inquiry through a focus on Black women's lives.[22] The reframing of key archival terms such as "document,"[23] "record,"[24] and "artifact"[25] is made possible through inter- and multidisciplinary approaches to Black women's experiences with the public visuality of grief. These renegotiations innovate a Black archival studies subfield that includes a growing body of literature beginning around the publication of Trouillot's *Silencing the Past* (1995). Trouillot's

---

18. Wilson, *Mining the Museum*.
19. Mercer, *Travel and See*, 38.
20. Corrin, "Mining the Museum"; and Corrin, "Audience Responds."
21. Cooks, *Exhibiting Blackness*.
22. K. Brown, *Repeating Body*; and Campt, "Black Visuality."
23. Sutherland, "Reading Gesture."
24. VanDiver, "Off the Wall."
25. C. Smith, "Sorrow as Artifact."

analysis attended to the void of content on Black people's lives and forms of knowledge and the material, cultural, and visual material they produced *as* archival preservation. While the interdisciplinary scholarship of Black studies and historical studies has made the largest contributions to the historiography on the archival lives of Black mothers, there yet remains a gap. Studies have failed to understand how Black mothers document the moment of separation from their children and the emotional, physical, and spiritual vacancy left from being without them. Scholars across the humanities continue to discuss the "silences" and "absences" of Black women's history without discussing the noninstitutional methods used to document their lives. In this respect, artistic approaches to archival work have yielded opportunities to investigate Black women's cultural production as archival labor.[26] Special issues, monographs, and articles concerning critical feminist approaches to the archive have focused on white feminist genealogies. This scholarship simultaneously inflicts a violence of displacing other iterations of feminism (for example, Black feminism, transnational feminisms) and provides openings for scholars of literature and art to critique their oversights with decolonial and anti-racist methods.[27] The 2020 special issue of *feminist review* attends to this gap, featuring a number of pieces concerned with what could be considered "decolonial archival praxis."[28] In this issue is "Listening with Gothenburg's Iron Well: Engaging the Imperial Archive through Black Feminist Methodologies and Arts-Based Research," an exemplary article in which Lena Sawyer and Nana Osei-Khan attend to the required methodologies of performativity and art, announcing arts-based approaches *as* Black feminist praxis, especially when it comes to "understanding and creating decolonial meanings" of statues and monuments.[29] Past failures to theorize Black feminist archival praxis on its

---

26. For instance, arts scholar Diana Taylor's work to multiply the cultural and archival repertoires of daily life articulates the overlapping struggles between artists and their ancestors, and the arts-based approaches of Ann Cvetkovich have exposed the unique ways "trauma" requires "new forms of documentation and the ways they are seen." Taylor, *Archive and the Repertoire*; and Cvetkovich, *Archive of Feelings*, 7.

27. Swaby and Frank, "Archival Experiments." There are also multiple journal special issues, namely in *Social Text* (2015), which has an excellent focus on eighteenth- and nineteenth-century histories. Kate Eichhorn's *The Archival Turn in Feminism* (2013), however, falls flat and does not address Black feminism, let alone women of color feminisms. This is especially severe in Eichhorn's monograph. Swaby and Frank's edited issue is the first to make specific mention of Black feminism. For more on creative approaches to archiving Black life and death, see Brand, *Map to the Door*; and J. Singh, *No Archive*.

28. "Decolonial archival praxis" is coined by Tonia Sutherland in "Reading Gesture."

29. Sawyer and Osei-Kofi, "'Listening,'" 58.

own terms, rather than through analogous terms of oppression,[30] animate future archival studies that theorize everyday Black women's archival praxis. In other words, Black feminist arts-based approaches to the archive "supplement a sparse historical archive" to testify to "the persistence of the trauma of slavery into the present" and to understand the archive of Black death.[31]

I source archival studies and visual studies to pronounce Samaria Rice's artwork as archival praxis and to further attend to the gaping void in literature around Black women's lives in archival studies. Engaging the gazebo on the level of documentation—and the state's failure to preserve said documentation—distinguishes how material and visual artifacts contribute to the cultural construction and dissemble traditional notions of archival matter. Archival studies literature on Black and oppressed lives often takes optimist approaches, citing archives as a possible place of "recovery" and redress, while visual studies scholars critique Black visuality and the visibility of Black suffering within it, and how it toggles between creating around racial trauma and yielding to its inevitability.[32] I use Black feminism to trouble both of these bodies of literature, which often displace mothers like Samaria Rice in the materiality of mother–child separation, showing that the many extensions of state-sanctioned violence are archival as well as reproductive issues. In this dynamic source of literature we are able to attend to the role of mothering in the preservation of one's image and material likeness after they are killed, thus expanding the term of "memory worker" to include the labor of lay archivists and everyday artists.[33]

This multi- and interdisciplinary treatment centers Black feminist curatorial and archival practices. Black feminism neither saves these women from their pain by finding redress in their practices, nor does it bar them from seeking ways to cope with their experiences. It underscores the importance of the "connections between the politics of Black women's lives, what we write about and our situation as artists."[34] As art critics have demonstrated, a more

---

30. Hartman, *Lose Your Mother*. Many decolonial approaches to the archive in archival studies have articulated atrocities such as those visited upon the victims of the Khmer Rouge regime in Cambodia (Caswell, *Archiving the Unspeakable*) and the victims of the Yugoslav Wars (Gilliland and Caswell, "Records and Their Imaginaries"). As Saidiya Hartman writes on the singularity of the crisis of archiving African diasporic history: "Dispossession was our history." Hartman, *Lose Your Mother*, 74.

31. Weinbaum, *Afterlife of Reproductive Slavery*, 64.

32. Fleetwood, *Troubling Vision*; D. King, *African Americans*; and Mitchell, *Living with Lynching*.

33. Drake, "Liberatory Archives."

34. B. Smith, *Toward a Black Feminist Criticism*.

direct conversation with archival theory and the arts opens up the possibilities of archival latitude of the gazebo. For Okwui Enwezor, artistic practice "undomesticates" archives and the materials that may not be institutionally housed or stewarded: "So thoroughly has the archive been domesticated that it has come to serve as a shorthand for memory; whether its images are lifted from newspapers and magazines or downloaded from digital cameras, it presses upon its users and viewers new kinds of ethical, social, political, and cultural relationships to information, history, and memory."[35] He argues that his main object of study, photography, is more than a practice of "representations of the catastrophe," but is rather the "unmediated evidence of it."[36] Samaria Rice's stewardship, installment, and erection of her son's memorial is an archival endeavor facilitated through artistic practice. Her preservation of the gazebo contributes to the project of undomesticating Black archival matter and practices that are unwieldy for archival spaces. She does this by enacting a Black feminist archival praxis that includes (1) naming the gazebo as "history" and artifact (signaling her son's killing as a refused object that signifies an inconvenient history)[37] and (2) engaging with a feminist standpoint of appraisal that embraces her positionality as a Black mother. Naming Black feminist archival praxis as an emerging form of memory work that embraces the affective and creative dimensions of memory-making, we can see how Black women's archival practices are made more visible through arts practice while still considering the biases that relegate us and our intellectual labors to "alternative" spaces of archivy such as art. In a general sense, this chapter meditates on Samaria Rice's memorial for her son in its two forms as an example of how the intellectual contributions of Black women expand notions of archival theory and practitionership via materiality and memorial making.

Although the archival turn is an important theoretical and scholarly moment in the evolution of archival theory, Black women articulated diverse and discursive modes of documentation long before Derrida's, Trouillot's, and Foucault's contributions in the late twentieth century. As mentioned in the introduction of this book, both critical and encouraging discourses of inter- and transdisciplinary approaches to "the archive" often undertake the Holocaust as its exemplar of the problems state-sanctioned violence presents to historicity.[38] Rarely is the genocide of the transatlantic slave trade used as an

---

35. Enwezor and International Center of Photography, *Archive Fever*, 34.
36. Enwezor and International Center of Photography, *Archive Fever*, 34.
37. S. Rice and Gates, *Samaria Rice*.
38. Manoff, "Theories of the Archive." Michelle Caswell's *Archiving the Unspeakable* is a really good exception to this, however.

example of genocidal violence. Taking after Du Bois's early twentieth-century proffer of the Negro as a "problem" for life and historiography, visual and art studies scholars such as Enwezor and Tina Campt have taken African diasporic experiences of violence as similar "problems" for practical applications of archival theory, showing the ways photography and imagery intervene on Eurocentric archives of diaspora.[39] Their work also mitigates the reinscription of Eurocentric tendencies of analyses that underscore African diasporic archival materials of utility, and especially leisure, as nonexistent and/or annihilated and thus unavailable for study. Humanities scholars, writers, and poets have fought to study the assumption of Black archives' unavailability, while remedying these gaps with speculative histories as ancestral testimony.[40] Their work helps undo the "epistemic violence" that comes with articulating a "method of encountering a past that is not past."[41] Under analytics such as Christina Sharpe's "wake work," Black women's literature and visual making is thus part of a long tenure of Black feminist archival practitionership that is illegible to rigid traditions of archivy when it comes to "plotting, mapping, and collecting the archives of the everyday of Black immanent and imminent death."[42]

Samaria Rice and the other Black women artists mentioned in this chapter propose a more direct invitation for Black feminist artistic practice. Their work, rather than being caught up in an archival turn that asserts their work might be legible, stakes its own claim in the field and makes archival expansion possible. Such dynamic meditations are made clear through the refused materials with which Black women engage and the ways they prove useful in coping with the terror of surviving a child's death. Black women continue to develop a necessary method of "wake work" that requires "sitting with, gathering, and tracking" this condition of Black motherhood in our highly visible and digital age of Black nonage death.[43] Their meditations converge with contemporary thought that seeks to expand understandings of the archival turn. It is because of Black women like Samaria Rice and their embrace of artistic practice that we are able to sit, gather, and track the life and death of children like Tamir Rice.

---

39. Du Bois, "Souls of Black Folk." See also Chandler, "Originary Displacement."
40. For instance, *Zong!*, written by M. NourbeSe Philip and Evie Shockley, is cowritten by an ancestor, Setaey Adamu Boateng. See also Shockley, "Going Overboard."
41. Sharpe, *In the Wake*, 13.
42. Sharpe, *In the Wake*, 13.
43. Cullors and bandele, *When They Call*.

Theorizing the Scraps: A Practice of Refusal[44]

Tina Campt's *Image Matters* begins with an anecdote about discovering still photographs of her ancestral heritage. Upon visiting her aunt's house and inquiring about family photos, Campt was offered some materials her aunt had saved from "the well-worn route to the trash can." Campt recalls: "To my surprise, she called back from an ill-defined location in the maze of her house: 'Well, I got rid of a lot of them and was thinking I'd just throw the rest of them out. I didn't think anybody would want them and they take up so much space.' I immediately yelled back, 'I'll take them!,' startling myself with the vehemence of my own reply. . . . I had barely gotten a word out of my mouth when my aunt suddenly reappeared, dragging a large, black garbage bag full of photos."[45] Campt's aunt's "large, black garbage bag" of photos, barely saved from disposal, provided some of the last visual documentation of her family members' lives. As candid photos, they helped construct a more textured interior to the preferences and desires of daily life. Such materials allowed Campt to imagine how much of Black people's visual legacies are relegated to the literal and figurative garbage bags that lie in one's attic. Campt's aunt also allowed for her to engage in the kind of memory work that was voided in the institutional archives Campt scoured to find evidence of Black families living in Europe. Much of what goes into remembering Black people's lives requires the use of found, refused, and unwanted objects. This methodology of scraps, then, infuses a public discussion around the sanctity of Black images, objects, and other materials through which we are remembered.

Memorialization, or the process of preserving memory of a person or event, demands a theorization of scraps because of the ways Black life and death have received singular resistance in archival documentation, preservation, and appraisal. At the very least, it demands a process of extramaterial engagement to address the lack of symbolic, social, and juridical justice of remembering the whole of who Black folks were. Processing grief of loved

---

44. Again, a chapter of Eichhorn's *The Archival Turn in Feminism*, "The Scrap Heap Reconsidered: Selected Archives of Feminist Archiving" begins its chapter with Susan Faludi's words: "Feminism's heritage is repeatedly hurled onto the scrap heap." I evoke scraps as the material manifestation of the fragmentation of Black history and what is relegated as scraps by a politics of refusal that is governed largely by an observation of the systems that refuse Blackness in visual and material forms. Eichhorn's analysis text does not include a conversation about Black feminism or any kind of women of color feminism in any one of its chapters. Her conversation between the archival turn and feminism is more concerned with the archivist and preservationist's work to preserve materials from white feminist unrest, such as zines, making her use of "feminism" synonymous with "white feminism."

45. Campt, *Image Matters*, 2.

ones through materiality does not always gesture toward the refused, however. Black mothers also engage with "life-sizes." These life-sized cut-outs of slain loved ones sprinkle the lawns and homes of grieving families. Memorial is also enacted on the body. Novelist and memoirist Jesmyn Ward brings the memorial T-shirt to life in her memoir *Men We Reaped* (2013). She reminds us that the memorial T-shirt puts grief into a wearable object that extends the grieving period during the months or years the T-shirt is worn.[46] These T-shirts take "wearing" an emotion out of metaphor and into a material practice of mourning and grief. Black women's deploying of the material, visual, written, and performed, is singular in their creative use to document their lived experiences in a particular moment. Their mourning practices also allow them to place their mourning in step with other mourning Black people. As anti-Black racism is embedded in our culture, Black women have challenged the degrees to which Black mourning has been normalized.[47] Ephemera-as-memorial is one aspect of materiality that alters the memorial as one fixed in landscape and/or space. This means the memorial encounters its viewers rather than the viewers encountering it. This type of memorial could be categorized as an anti-monument, or "an action, a performance," that resists "the fetish of the site, the fetish of representation of power."[48] T-shirts and cut-outs are often fixed, imposing structures that usher memory into public spaces. A mundane piece of clothing like a T-shirt is unassuming and nonimposing for those who want to wear it and those who may passively encounter it. T-shirt-wearing occupies a unique intersection of personal and public mourning, while transforming mundane material into documentation—of mourning and the mourned.

Dynamic use of the material offers Black families an opportunity to renegotiate personal histories with other forms of state-sanctioned violence, such as mass incarceration. In material practice, these objects may be engaged as refused materials, or those that are unwanted. The Philly People's Paper Co-op offers a specific internship program for mothers who have experienced incarceration and have a demonstrated interest in book arts, paper-making, and social justice. Paper-making interns have the opportunity to engage in a performative healing practice of obtaining copies of their criminal records, shredding them, and using them to produce pulp for homemade paper. They use

---

46. Ward, *Men We Reaped*. T-shirts often feature a young photo of the deceased with the years of their birth, or "sunrise" as it can be stylized, and the death date or "sunset." Many T-shirts offer a picture of the deceased around the time of death or a complimentary photo chosen by the family.
47. Rankine, "Condition of Black Life."
48. Lozano-Hemmer et al., "Alien Relationships," 155.

that paper to print anti-incarceration messages and posters that are then sold to pay for bail for mothers.[49] The transformation of an unwanted "record" brings new meaning to recycling experiences and redefining one's present identity with past experiences with the state.

All of these practices make a much larger intervention into what it means to engage with objects and materials that are unwanted, neglected, or used for purposes other than their intended use. Enacting the "practice of refusal," which defines "the contours of an emergent Black visuality that itself constitutes a practice of refusal as . . . creating radical modalities of witness that refuse authoritative forms of visuality which function to refuse Blackness itself," imbricates material objects as artifacts of feelings.[50] How might we imbricate material objects into *Black visuality* as they symbolically and physically structure sites of death? The "leftovers" of permanent loss also manifest in the physical to evoke what we might call the lasting materiality of dispossession.[51] Archival practice, reliant as it is on a universal and assumed understanding of what constitutes textual evidence, perpetuates Black grief as unseen and unthought, rather than acceptable and accessible. Materiality, by contrast, inspissates the historical study of Black dispossession by pushing the bounds of how it appears: as visual and tactile evidence of grief. If we imagine the coffle or perhaps chains of the stultifying chain gang, materiality is how enslaved Africans were *of* but not *in* relation to one another. What's more, refused objects empower a surreptitious language of permanency that destabilizes an audience's perceptions that the precarious conditions of Blackness existed at one point in time but no longer, making all the more real the *afterlife* of slavery.[52]

Situating the Gazebo within Black Women's Archival Praxis Histories

Contemporary artists often reorient refusal and refused materials for archival and aesthetic function. Most notably, Betye Saar—a self-described "recycler"

---

49. The People's Paper Co-Op, "People's Paper."
50. Campt, "Black Visuality." See also C. Smith, "Sorrow as Artifact."
51. Skakur, *Assata*, 146–47. The poem "Leftovers—What Is Left" laments the material and emotional loss of Assata Shakur after her infant daughter has been stolen from her while incarcerated. She writes, "I mean like, where is the sun? / Where are her arms and / Where are her kisses? / There are lip-prints on my pillow— / i am searching. / What is left?"
52. Hartman has said that the afterlife of slavery is the "normative condition of Black death in civil society." Hartman and Siemsen, "Working with Archives."

and "junkie"[53]—creates her assemblages from found materials. Saar's work engages scavenged objects from others' trash cans to make political and Black feminist statements of identity and genealogical exploration. Her famous *Black Girl's Window* (1970) is a silhouette of Saar's head surrounded by an arrangement of images, symbols, and materials such as a tintype of a white woman and a skeleton figure. The refused materials decorate the partition between a Black feminist exploration of identity and an outside world that persists in its destruction. Below the silhouette of her head is a self-scribed poem beginning with the line "My roots are tangled. . . ."[54] The centered silhouette disavows the hegemonic compulsion to decenter ourselves as creators. Looking out from the domesticated space of a "Black girl's window," a Black feminist archival praxis peers onto the rest of the world while admiring its own practitioner. The glass of the window separates us from the vantage point Black women occupy to explore their own identities as universal truth through others' refused materials.[55]

Both Rice and Saar, through their work, join a powerful constellation of Black women artists who use refused objects to symbolically engage Blackness and other cultural materials. Chaikaia Booker (b. 1953) and Vanessa German's (b. 1976) practices use literal trash as well as materials that have been "trashed," such as homes in historically Black communities. Their work remarks upon the capitalistic tendencies of urban renewal. German created Art House, a house located in Homewood's neglected Black neighborhood. The exterior is formed from glass, paint, roof tiles, and ceramic tiles she found in abandoned homes on the very same block.[56] German uses the house and front porch as a studio space to make sculptures from other refused objects to convey messages of transformation. She manipulates the materials to construct larger forms alone and sometimes with children who live nearby. Her message also admits their inability to shift the systems of value that caused their own refusal. A Black feminist orientation toward scraps asks important questions about the processes of preservation and how "embodiment and

---

53. Cotter, "It's About Time!" Almost all of Saar's materials are found materials from antique shops, swap meets, flea markets, and trash cans. She says, "I've been that way since I was a kid, going through trash to see what people left behind. Good stuff."

54. Cotter, "It's About Time!"

55. VanDiver, "Off the Wall." VanDiver offers an excellent reading of Saar's *Hattie's Box* (1971), which explores a personal history of Saar as well. VanDiver, "Off the Wall," 41. VanDiver writes that the works made from Saar's inherited objects underscore an archive that "does not promise closure, and questions remain."

56. Cascone, "Artist Vanessa German." German is also resisting the framework of gentrification by reusing the scraps of the neighborhood to "revitalize it" without displacing its current residents.

subjectivity frames curatorial approach."⁵⁷ And, as Rebecca VanDiver writes, such an approach positions archives as a "repository of historical things as well as an aperture through which to construct narratives about art history," meaning Black women's curatorial and creative production changes the pitch of art's historicity as well.⁵⁸

Samaria Rice is singular in her memorial making by transforming refused materials for her original goal of healing, while also being the solitary steward of her son's material legacy. She has been involved in her son's image and likeness in arts exhibitions and remains vigilant in monitoring initiatives that try to use it without her permission. This is demonstrated in an installation exhibit curated and produced by the then artist-in-residence of SPACES (Cleveland, Ohio) Michael Rakowitz (b. 1973). With Rice's blessing, Rakowitz aesthetically anchored the installation with the toy gun Tamir was holding when he was shot. The artist and curator used the color orange to annotate the lack of public safety available to Black citizens in the pro-gun, open-carry state. Tamir's toy did *not* have an orange tip, and the curator used the color to denote an ineffective gun with an enabled safety. Rakowitz collected refused orange materials found throughout Cleveland.⁵⁹ Cleveland residents collected and donated orange objects found in gutters, garages, and people's homes throughout the city to meditate on the meaning of "public safety" and symbols, and how the color orange denotes assurance for some and lethality for others.⁶⁰ This exhibit included a stand-alone installation by Samaria Rice after a successful relationship formation between Rice and Rakowitz.

Artists and institutions are typically not successful in incorporating Tamir's legacy without his mother's authorization. Local institutions regularly deny artists' requests to use the gazebo and Tamir's likeness if they have failed to obtain her approval.⁶¹ In 2018, Samaria Rice participated in speaking engagements worldwide, including with the Cleveland Museum of Art. Although Rice collaborated with Beyoncé for *Lemonade* (2016), perhaps the artistic work that will remain in public and cultural memory, Rice does not typically engage in popular culture uses of her son's image.⁶² Essential to Rice's memorial-making practice is not so much her resistance to all public

---

57. Joachim, "'Embodiment and Subjectivity,'" 36.
58. VanDiver, "Off the Wall," 41.
59. Weber, "Samaria Rice."
60. *A Color Removed.*
61. Rice is a close friend and collaborator of Amanda King, a Cleveland-based photographer and the director of Shooting Without Bullets, a youth photography project. Dafoe, "'We Need to Tell a Different Story.'"
62. "Freedom."

depictions without her guiding hand, but her apprehension about the demonstrated lack of care for Black death. Rather than recalling her son's life and whole personhood, her son's image is often used as a cheap flash point for audiences. Rice's assertions into the art world suggest a desire to play out the creative life of her son after his death. The creative and experimental efforts that incorporate her son's memory are successful because she can position her son's memory within broader archival issues that dispense visual and material forms of Black life for shock or spectacle.

Black women's assemblages of gathered objects detemporalize memory from an otherwise static existence, creating scrapbooks of remembrance that connect past and present fears of separation. Some may provide possibility for the future, while others foreclose upon it. Samaria Rice's work assembles refused materials to display the unwanted gazebo as a space to reflect on its original use and its power to transform her son's memory as a refused one, while contributing to the genealogy of Black women assemblage artists.

Proposing Black Feminist Standpoint Appraisal

Samaria Rice found political and affective value in the gazebo that Cleveland did not want. Many community members supported the city's calls for its demolition.[63] Citizens characterized the structure by the terrible memories associated with the gazebo, while Rice steadfastly named it a "pure" space: "My son was murdered here and his purity is sacred."[64] For Cleveland, the gazebo sat as a negative "site of memory," where a site acts "to stop time, to block the work of forgetting, to establish a state of things, to immortalize death, to materialize the immaterial."[65] The title of the memorial gestures toward an implied but fundamental difference between recalled histories between the state and Samaria Rice. This chasm is materialized in *Objects of Care* and its profound appellation, which underscores its fragmented state.

Samaria Rice's specific positionality as a mother-activist-artist may not be accompanied by a sustained artistic "practice" but is called to the artistic realm for its availability for collaboration with other activists.[66] Arts practice allows her to engage in public-facing archival work while accessing collective mourning that Black mothers are not always afforded. Calling for the state to account for Black death is all too often considered controversial. Samaria Rice and

---

63. Neely, "Tamir Rice Gazebo Demolition."
64. S. Rice and Gates, *Samaria Rice*.
65. Ater, "Challenge of Memorializing Slavery," 143.
66. *A Color Removed*.

other grieving Black mothers enact a social practice through "uncomfortable" documentation methods, gathering and creating with sacred materials like their children's bodies or their death places.[67] M. Carmen Lane, a 2016 collaborator with Samaria Rice, has said, "There's a history and a term for the way that artists and the sacred interact and I think we call it social practice in 2018."[68] Refused materials inhabit an uncomfortable dialect between the production of value and noncompliance with its capitalistic formations. Art and memory practices that include scraps of Black life and culture work together to bring affective meaning to the aesthetics of scraps.

Using wood slats, dirtied stuffed animals, and the gazebo's shingles, Rice stages an appraisal process of the scraps themselves. Appraisal, as defined by the Society of American Archivists, is "the process of determining whether records and other materials have permanent (archival) value. Appraisal may be done at the collection, creator, series, file, or item level."[69] The value of scraps in Black feminist archival praxis becomes most clear under what Michelle Caswell calls "feminist standpoint appraisal," which leverages the marginalized identity of the appraiser as an asset. In addition, feminist standpoint appraisal lends archival and intellectual legitimacy to those who get "dismissed, devalued, and, in some cases, labeled false by dominant power structures" within past traditions of appraisal.[70] The radical form of valuation not only verifies those doing the appraising as experts, but also awards legitimacy to the results of said appraisal. It also allows for a greater weight on the process of acquisition and appraisal, which has so often determined which identities are kept out of mainstream archival discourses of accessioning/appraisal, arrangement, and description. As Caswell argues, identity has long been disregarded in discourses of appraisal.[71] Traditionally, the exclusion of identity came with a tacit underscoring that the "dominant" white, educated, upper-middle-class male positionality was the universal standpoint for appraisal. This perspective was considered unbiased in exercising the most fair

---

67. The mothers of Trayvon Martin, Eric Garner, Sandra Bland, and many others formed a collective called Mothers of the Movement, and they have appeared at highly public events such as the 2016 Democratic Convention. Samaria Rice did not attend because she personally endorsed Bernie Sanders.

68. Lane, *Ken'nahsa:ke/Khson:ne,* also uses installation of objects to stage personal confusion and familial trauma over her grandmother's murder and the necropolitical colorism her family experienced when a Cleveland Black-owned funeral home would not process the body because she appeared to be white. Lane's grandmother was Black/Indigenous. SPACES, "SWAP #68."

69. Society of American Archivists, "Appraisal."
70. Caswell, "Dusting for Fingerprints," 9.
71. Caswell, "Dusting for Fingerprints," 9.

and accurate appraisal of political and affective value because it purported to eschew appraisal based on financial value.

An embrace of Black feminist standpoint appraisal means rethinking how scraps make up most of the archival material of Black death. They may (but do not always) first undergo a juridical, social, and symbolic process of rejection before they are made publicly or privately available. A Black feminist standpoint appraisal provides a specific mode of appraising that resists dominant institutional barriers that disallow Black women as recognized archival practitioners.[72] Feminist standpoint appraisal acknowledges that both the process and the end archival product are deeply dependent on one's positionality and embodiment. Where Caswell remarks aptly that "feminist standpoint epistemologies help us rethink both the process by which archival value is determined and the archivists' role in that process," a Black feminist take on standpoint appraisal cannot be an errant martialing of identity politics. Often positionality becomes collapsed with one's identity, which reduces feminist standpoint appraisal to a mere matter of identity-forward archival practice.[73] We must also identify Black motherhood as a social location bound by separation and recognize how appraisal quantifies and prices the public spectacle of Black death, while also participating in the same cache of ownership caused such separation. We might also think about the ways appraisal can be Black feminist in terms of its refusal of ownership.[74] Scraps are generated by refusing ownership and acknowledging discursive modes of creation. This is why many institutional archivists use the term "memory work" to describe their institutional work, for neither they, nor the institution they work for, can ever "own" a scrap of Black life or Black death. It is and will always be a material manifestation of a past characterized by the unknown more than the known.[75] Memory workers revive, recall, and shape materials to make connections to the present for collective archiving. Under Black feminist standpoint appraisal, materials can be both priceless and forbidden, invaluable but immaterial, because they will never be valuable under the auspices of traditional archival institutions themselves.[76]

---

72. The 2022 Administrator's Report (A*Census II) of the Society of American Archivists found that just 16 percent of archives administrators were BIPOC (Black, Indigenous, and People of Color), while 84 percent were white. Skinner and Hulbert, "A*CENSUS II."
73. Caswell, "Dusting for Fingerprints," 12.
74. Morrison, *Beloved*, 124.
75. Drake, "Liberatory Archives."
76. Powell et al., "This [Black] Woman's Work." There are many community archives doing this work right now, and too many to name. Some excellent examples are Project Row Houses in Houston, Texas; the Black Archives of Mid-America in Kansas City, Missouri; and the Black in Appalachia Digital Archive.

Mining for "nuggets" is the insatiable task of historians, archivists, and culture workers, regardless of subject matter or line of inquiry.[77] Black feminist standpoint appraisal animates dimensions of discrimination that render Black life and death unworthy and Black archivists and identity as subjective. The process of mining is inevitably shaped by personal relationships to materials. Historical mining also brings the present in painful relief from histories fragmented by the precarity of Black materiality. Scraps are the dominant findings of one's pursuits of Black women's lives and the ways that each artifact appears to the intended. As indicated by Tina Campt's anecdote about her aunt's literal garbage bag full of photos, Black women's preservation of seemingly unwanted materials is governed by the domain of Black feminist archiving. Perhaps methods of acquisition, preservation, and appraisal have not been legible to traditional archival theory or practice because of the lack of cultural capital exchanged for said materials, and the implied lack of value tied to objects that Black women find valuable.[78] Also, infusements of Black death and life both uproot models of beauty and sanctity, thus making such objects disposable and perpendicular to state narratives of white heroism. Samaria Rice still hopes to fulfill her originary desire for the gazebo to stay in Cleveland, even as it now stands in Chicago.[79] The state's inability to grapple with the "sacredness" of the object and its affiliation with Tamir Rice's death diverged from its ability to produce and maintain comfortable histories that uphold white supremacy.[80] "Uncomfortability" is a named method of Samaria Rice.[81] Her acquisition of the gazebo materials put value in that which caused institutional discomfort. The gazebo was made "pure" upon her son's shooting and laid as a pile of "pure" scraps with the same political and affective value attendant to all material memorials. Her use of feminist standpoint appraisal of a perceived unwanted site is a metaphor for the ways Black children's lives are thrown away in service of state narratives that actively devalue Black lives, even after their death by erasing the material memory from everyday life.

---

77. Hamilton et al., "Introduction."
78. Black studies scholar Kathryn Lawson reminds me that there are multiple terms of donation of materials that are not always exclusive of the desire to donate funds to a space. Acquisitions is a wide practice, to be sure.
79. S. Rice and Gates, *Samaria Rice*.
80. Ramirez, "Being Assumed Not to Be."
81. S. Rice and Gates, *Samaria Rice*.

Exclusion and Black Archival Practice

The correlative histories of excluding Black women archivists and Black women artists in their respective institutional spaces is an example of the overall erasure of Black women's archival practitionership, both private and public. Ashley Farmer writes that "Black exclusion from archival spaces" is much more than an architectural problem; it's a problem of preserving history and the contents of these archives.[82] As I have argued, Samaria Rice's expansion of documentation and appraisal practices attends to this type of exclusion through artistic engagement. The implications of art practice *as* archival practice is deeper than an aesthetic engagement with scraps. The attempted literal and symbolic destruction of Tamir Rice's would-be memorial site changed the landscape of activism on Rice's behalf: "People in Cleveland aren't making enough noise," she said, "and I don't really know why. So I guess I got to make it with the center, and they have to make it with their art."[83] Black feminist frameworks of archival praxis disrupt conventional models of archival processing such as documentation and appraisal. Samaria Rice's Black feminist archival praxis illustrates the invisible distinction between arts making and archival making.

Contemporary convergences between highly public killings of Black people call for new material constructions of memory. Tonia Sutherland's landmark essay "Reading Gesture" puts the archival praxis of Samaria Rice into a much longer genealogy that decenters the archival turn altogether. We may witness the "archival praxis" of Black Caribbean dancer and choreographer Katherine Dunham through performative and gestural document to changing Caribbean experiences under colonial rule in the early twentieth century. Sutherland argues that developing a "visual literacy" to understand visual forms of communication bursts open the potential for new reading practices of Black life and death.[84] Black feminism makes "readable" the "gestures" of women done and undone in their creative and cultural work. Archival praxis made evident by Black women in their situation dissolves boundaries of art making and archival practitionership as archival praxis. Just as Sutherland undertakes digital archivist Jefferson Bailey's assertion of a reconsideration of twenty-first-century *respect de fonds* toward the digital, Black feminist archival praxis explicates colonial practices of reading and archivy—especially of the "embodied, gestural, or otherwise."[85]

---

82. Farmer, "Archiving While Black."
83. Steinhauer, "Artist Honors Tamir Rice."
84. Sutherland, "Reading Gesture."
85. Sutherland, "Reading Gesture."

Black feminist archival praxis, then, is not so much reading "against the grain," as it were, but drawing a correlative reading practice to the materials that associate and evidence Black life and death.[86] Samaria Rice's memorial making utilizes the arts space to make legible a history of resistance to documentation, while reenacting a documentation process herself. This contradiction generates a political agitation with implied archival practitionership, barely recognized beyond the final product through which it appears at the Stony Island Arts Bank.

The undermining of Black women's contributing archival practices attempts to position Black women on the peripheries of artistic spaces too. Black women's exclusion from artistic spaces is reflected in the amount and quality of Black women's work that is acquired and exhibited. According to Artnet News's 2018 research, Black women's work makes up only 3.3 percent of all acquisitions.[87] A gendered anti-Blackness that erases Black women and nonbinary artists from archives also raises questions about the structural barriers to Black women's work, which is subject to patriarchal methods of appraising artwork. In archival and librarian practice, anti-Blackness is rampant behind the reference desk as well, as recent controversies show that anti-Blackness also overdetermines Black women's professional lives in libraries and archives.[88] Samaria's work affirms such statistics, both inasmuch as Black women artists are made visible by Black male curatorial prowess, and by how Black women have more difficulty attaining success simply because of their embodiment. This can be simply understood as gatekeeping that occurs in practice but also is embedded in the infrastructure of sites of culture and memory, both material and referential. While I am sure that the opportunity for Rice to contribute the gazebo to the Stony Island Arts Bank was and is a trans-local community space for "reflection, public interaction and healing,"[89] we must also be sure to understand how similar archival praxes are foreclosed upon by the illegibility of Black scraps as artifact and the efforts to preserve them. Where Theaster Gates attests that the gazebo is neither "art" nor "artifact—It's history," we must also be attuned to the ways that Black women are often only able to contribute historical objects for view through artistic spaces and via connection to well-resourced male leaders.[90] Gates's ability to own and

---

86. Stoler, *Along the Archival Grain*. I mean this in the sense that Stoler's work draws alternative readings of European texts, and Black women's cultural memory practices deny the premise of the "primary" document, thus destabilizing what is a "primary" source altogether.
87. Halperin and Burns, "Museums Claim."
88. McKenzie, "Racism and the American Library Association."
89. S. Rice and Gates, *Samaria Rice*.
90. S. Rice and Gates, *Samaria Rice*.

direct the archival and artistic space spells more trouble than respite for Black women's abilities to own and operate archival spaces and for their archival labor to be accounted. The announcement that the gazebo will be temporarily available to the Arts Bank is more metaphor for the ways that Black women's archival and artistic labors are only made legible when passing through the purview of Black male artists. Gates's words undergird the importance of the piece as a memorial in the context of the Confederate statues being taken down. To be sure, his remarks were not meant to disenfranchise Rice's labor but rather to be a testament to the gazebo structure's work to be read as both a transitory and a historical artifact in a world where art is increasingly used to puncture national consciousness. Unable to preserve its sanctity in a public space, Rice sought a private, artistic one that still had attending elements of gatekeeping. Her story illustrates how Black women's activism-as-documentation is illegible to traditional institutional archives.[91] Even in those arenas through which "noise" is more easily made, the noise must first be heard by gatekeepers.

A revival of Black feminist creative modalities of archival contribution will not so much bring forward a Black feminist archival turn as much as expose how Black feminism revives the archival turn itself. When Michelle Caswell critiques recent humanities undertakings of archival forms of practice and theory, she takes for granted the use of the term "the archive" as a site of fragmentation and misunderstanding for Black scholarship itself. Black feminism exposes the blind spots of scholars of the humanities and social sciences and the dangers of articulating the archive as a metaphor for memory.[92] The semantic issue of even using the term "the archive" unsettles archival studies scholarship that celebrates the long history of librarianship and archival practitionership and its reliance on women's labors. Critical discussion of Black women's lack of access to library and information science programs or professions must be addressed. The "baggage" that goes along with decades of intellectual discovery by archivists must also be the weighted baggage of anti-Blackness that demonized Black women memory workers as witches. These women and nonbinary people developed skill sets that were available to local institutions that we were neither allowed to work in or attend as students.[93] Samaria Rice's archival praxis intervenes on the concept of archives and doubles the exclusion that white women archives and librarians have contributed. The erasure of noninstitutional intellectual labor of Black women archivists

---

91. Gumbs, "Eternal Summer." Black gender scholar Omise'eke Tinsley rejects this use of metaphor, however. Tinsley, "Black Atlantic."

92. Caswell, "'The Archive.'"

93. Lingel, "This Is Not an Archive."

is immeasurable because we do not think of storytellers, clothes makers, memorial makers, art makers, chefs, fiction writers, singers, or performers as archivists enough. Their work staves off the renewed symbolic deaths of loved ones' scraps being demolished. Can we live?[94] We are living as long as we are remembered.

---

94. "Can I live?": "An expression of frustration with one's current situation. Or expression of growing impatience with requests being made of oneself." Urban Dictionary, "Can I Live."

CONCLUSION

The Black Maternal Superbody

How can a theory of scraps help us understand Black women's praxis for coping with death? I have set out to plumb this question in the preceding chapters to ultimately conclude that the question of praxis and death is unresolvable in the ongoing specter of state violence. Where Black women's memory-making practices are shaped by this violence, they refuse to be underdeveloped by the registers of violence that attend them. Black mothers refuse to document practices that reproduce their children's deaths and to capitulate to the violences of institutional navigation around these deaths and their documentation practices. In sum, a new strategy has manifested the material, spiritual, and cultural memories of slain, unborn, and too-soon-gone children.

The History of the Superbody

Deirdre Cooper Owens's term of the "medical superbody" isolates the Black woman's reproductive body as an originary site of obstetric violence.[1] Cooper Owens's work argues that Black women's bodies were outside the perceived parameters of humanness, thus constituting the lack of ethical medical treatment Black women experienced during the early formations of gynecological

---

1. Cooper Owens, *Medical Bondage*. See also Schwartz, *Birthing a Slave*.

practice. Cooper Owens also argues that the "medical superbody" may have been deemed unhuman despite being a prone subject for medical experimentation. The violence Black women experienced benefited larger society because their bodies served as the literal testing material for advances in reproductive health.

The Black maternal superbody returns the "medical superbody" to a scene of reproductive justice within the contemporary Movement for Black Lives. I see this term as part of a reproductive justice analysis of the Black feminist archive. It at once de-centers *and* centers Black women's lives and bodies in the Movement of Black Lives. It also reveals the ways that maternal bodies converge with other definitions, such as "Black activist mothering," or "Black women as mothers who are engaged in community work and are intentionally living in the margins and do so as acts of resistance and transformation," to show how political action impacts the maternal body and Black mothers' daily lives in such bodies.[2]

The concept of the Black maternal superbody and an analytic of reproductive justice work together to allow for a space to experiment messily with identity formation in the social, medical, and public activist spheres, through the aperture of the reproductive body. One of the primary thrusts of this book is that Black mothers' activism and memory-keeping form a counternarrative to the assumption that activism is an inherently patrilineal affair.[3] The assumptive logic that the most potent activism is practiced and instituted by male-identified people erases not only the myths that have long affected Black women's bodies, but also the ways that our activism is embodied. Rather than taking Black women's struggles for bodily autonomy and safety as central to our activism, they are too often portrayed in public discourses as mere coincidence. The Black maternal superbody as a framework derives from the superwoman myth that Michele Wallace formulates. Wallace also finds origin, as does this book, in Patricia Hill Collins's "controlling images," or images manufactured to "control" imagery rooted in the juxtaposition of white Victorian womanhood.[4] The superbody-as-myth overdetermines the formulation of activism-as-cultural-memory as a masculine story, and thus Black mothers are inherently oppositional to the supremacies of whiteness and womanhood.[5] This explosion leads to a conceptualization of the archive of activism

---

2. Sakho, "Black Activist Mothering."

3. In *Living for the Revolution,* Springer provides an excellent account, told through the oral histories of Black women activists active during the Black Power era. See also Spencer, *Revolution Has Come.*

4. Hill Collins, *Black Feminist Thought,* 79.

5. NPR staff, "Emmett Till's Father."

as multimodal.[6] This "grammar of Black feminist futurity" hones imaginative expression as consequential to forming lasting historical narratives around Black women's bodily liberation from destructive myths. If we are to critique the social, legal, and cultural injuries that shape Black women's bodies, relationships, and identities, we must also undertake these injuries as wounds to Black women's imaginative and activist labors. Tina Campt's grammar of Black feminist futurity outdoes its own bounds of the optical to other senses, as well as the kinetic. The process of Black futurity *in motion* also perceives activisms through the body politic, such as giving birth or the simple refusal of a Black body to rise from a diner counter. Black feminist futurity accounts for the ways that Black cultural expressions of Black maternity enact their own vision of "living the future *now*," where Black women express maternity viably, and without fear of dispossession. It in no way conflates the future, let alone the now, as a utopia. This grammar I enact views Black maternal activism as compulsory inclusion when imagining the foundations of cultural activism.

The Black maternal superbody is a framework that exposes the expectations that are imposed on Black maternal bodies. Where I divulge a very capacious meaning of mothering that includes biological male actors, I anchor the Black maternal superbody as a myth that affects Black femmes and women's bodies, which are indeed *as* extraordinary as the amount and type of pain and struggle we endure, rather than succumbing to them. In a contradictory turn, I conclude with the ways the Black maternal superbody exists in excess and extraordinariness, and is codified as a super-entity—because it is. In the institutional, systemic, and public orders that ordain Black mothers as "dangerous," I imagine the homicides of Chantell Grant and Andrea Stoudemire as an attempt to quell Black mothers' ability to initiate radical change for their children.[7] This change meant taking a stand against gun violence in the South Side of Chicago. As they paced between the corners of 75th Street and Stewart Avenue in Chicago, Illinois, in the summer of 2019, I imagine their murderers thought they were sending a very clear message to their organization, Mothers and Men Against Senseless Killings: This is our home to protect, not yours.[8] A block occupied for every day of every summer since 2015, this corner was the home of gun violence feared by the neighborhood's parents and children. Mothers had diffused an otherwise-active shooter zone for nearly four years, until Grant and Stoudemire's deaths.

We can imagine those who killed them were doing so to stake a claim on space they perceived as theirs, rather than the neighborhood's. We can also

---

6. K. Brown, *Repeating Body*; and Taylor, *Archive and the Repertoire*.
7. Gumbs, "We Can Learn," 193; and Ramos, "2 Mothers Killed."
8. "About: Mothers and Men."

imagine that they saw themselves disenfranchised not only by the state but also by the neighborhood from which they attacked—so much so that they could only find a place in it by replicating the ultraviolent tactics of the state. Despite Grant and Stoudemire's physical killings, the homicide of Erica Garner and the attempted homicides of all Black maternal bodies, these women cannot be killed. Their bodies become ingrained in an activist tradition. The deaths of Grant and Stoudmire especially show how permanent separation affects larger formations of kinship bonds, like communities, both local and global. It was through their activism, and the sacrifice of their bodies, that we can tie the enduring stress from Black dispossession to the death of Black mothers. I conclude with their stories to suggest the imagination can also be embodied and an as-yet blank canvas through which dispossession is not simply downloaded into our DNA.[9] I do it to suggest that even when Black mothers aim to imagine their lives differently, they do it artistically and from the inside out, or in Dionne Brand's words, in a unique way for us to "find our liberation, our freedom, our energy, by exploding it—from the inside."[10]

Because creative contributions (for example, corporal and activist) are often overlooked as cultural artifacts dissimilar to archival artifacts, I consider this close reading of Black feminist futurity important to pushing the bounds of how Black maternal activism can be canonized. Campt writes that this grammar "is a performance of a future that hasn't yet happened but must. It is an attachment to a belief in what should be true, which impels us to realize that aspiration. It's the power to imagine beyond current fact and to envision that which is not, but must be. It's a politics of prefiguration that involves living the future *now*—as imperative rather than subjunctive—as a striving for the future you want to see, right now, in the present."[11] Black feminist futurity as a grammar of looking, and looking as a reading practice of the visual, is not to be isolated to the optical sense. Mothers commence. Mothers organize. Mothers utter. Mothers hail. Mothers reign.

As creative expressions drive the iterations of social, legal, and bodily abuse, the archive of Black motherhood exceeds traditional notions of archives. We must imagine that archival documents and records may be used for something beyond their original contexts, to reflect and produce fundamental discursive reality in their own right.[12] Black maternal activism exists outside the "who gets remembered, who gets forgotten" binary that seems to sit at the fore of discussions about archival injustices. *Who is remembered?* and

---

9. Yehuda and Lehrner, "Intergenerational Transmission of Trauma Effects."
10. Saunders, "Defending the Dead," 67.
11. Campt, *Listening to Images*, 17.
12. Scott, "Introduction," xvi.

Who is forgotten? are very important questions to interrogate. When Michel-Rolph Trouillot posed iterations of these questions in his four steps of fact creation, scholars were left to contend with how much of our history is the history of the power-full. Yet these questions do not penetrate the dimensions of archives that suggest *what* can remember and how nonsentient objects and concepts, like the body and imagination, can hold memory—especially through the present. Perhaps the potential of archival materials lies beyond our interactions with them, and beyond where the imagination bespeaks a greater eventuality, rather than just an elusive potential. The excessiveness of Black motherhood, then, is less of a burden to the archive and more of a prism through which we can understand dispossession and structural anti-Blackness as a whole.

For mother-activists of the diaspora, the Black maternal superbody helps us "interrogate this paradox of myth and motherhood, situating their bodies at the crossroads between self-possession and collective intention—a longing for the visuality of wholeness," Kimberly Juanita Brown writes.[13] Imagination is where Black women creatives imagine a self that belongs and is moved with intention toward collectivity, even within repeating violences. Thinking Black mother-activists' lives, bodies, and prowess as reiterations of enslavement's intense imagery, Black women creatives honor the reiteration not just as a projection into a so-called racial imaginary, but as a site of knowledge.[14] These imaginative works then inform back on the body, where Black women's understandings of themselves do work—or harm—to re-create affective experiences of dispossession for their audiences. Totalizing these activists as mother, activist, daughter, and citizen, we see that Black mother-activists are not only witnesses to, nor mere vessels of, their slain kin's untimely demise. Rather, they are transformative vessels whose bodily truth as mothers converted "corporality into transformative speech."[15] To continue their transformation of speech, we read the corporal, the activist, and the imaginative as spaces of reckoning. Black mothers' activism is liberation that exceeds a politics of myths.

If the condition of life is Black mourning, how do we imagine Black relationships as defined by anything other than harm?[16] To answer this question, we may follow the treatment of the "queer theory of the potential meaning of motherhood" set out by Alexis Pauline Gumbs.[17] This means that the

---

13. K. Brown, *Repeating Body*, 95.
14. The definition of the body that reiterates violences enacted upon it is also the definition of Brown's "repeating body." K. Brown, *Repeating Body*.
15. Mwangi, "Silence Is a Woman."
16. Rankine, "Condition of Black Life"; and Cullors and bandele, *When They Call*, 97.
17. Gumbs, "We Can Learn," 194.

definitions of mothering must also extend to the relationship one has with themselves. For Alexis Gumbs, the radical potential of living in the conditions of grief is in mothering ourselves as well as others. Gumbs martials Audre Lorde's maxim "We can mother ourselves" to contend care as a site of self-valuation and resistance. "Black mothering," Gumbs writes, is "the production of radical difference, when done for 'ourselves' as a reclamation of labor and a reflexive intervention against the reproduction of sameness."[18] Sameness here functions as those who have been socialized into biological mother/daughter relationships.

The Black maternal superbody—exposed under the condition of mothering ourselves and others, in relationship with the reflexive self, with or without support from others—changes how Black women activists are able to effect change. The popular, commodity-driven concept of "self-care" has replaced this form of mothering. Black women cannot be expected to care for the world and themselves, even under the guise of "mothering." Still, mothering ourselves presents an "alternative logic" not only "at the point of reproduction," as Gumbs describes, but into and out of their reproductive years. In essence, Black activist mothers, in an embrace of the myth of the Black maternal superbody that has been weaponized against them, extend their reproductive lives into infinitude as they fight to preserve the right to constitute the conditions of viability for themselves. Out of the Black maternal superbody emerges a challenge to familial, economic, and reproductive structures that are illegible in popular narratives that overdetermine Black women's lives and bodies. In attending to issues impacting their reproductive rights, Black women have often found that their specific history of being subjected to sexual abuse from doctors, forced sterilization, and biased access to birth control was erased by white feminists' fight for the legalization of abortion during the 1970s.[19] Black women's activist efforts are often erased by white feminist coalitions because Black women's relationship to oppression is a structural injury *and* an experiential one. We must then consider Black women's reproductive rights as different from white women's reproductive rights, because the reigning (white) framework of rights is not expansive enough to account for the uneven distribution of structural oppression. A discourse of intersectionality can only speak *symptomatically* to the history of violence that attends Black women's experiences with activism and maternity.

How we are to contend with the contradiction of Black women's exceptionalism with their endurance of trauma is also made clear through Black

---

18. Gumbs, "We Can Learn," 107.
19. T. Frazier, "Birthing Black Mothers," 156–57.

mothers' bodies en masse, through time, and in dynamic use. Naming this chapter's mothers as exemplars of a "superbody" emphasizes the contradictions of Black women's experiences with Black dispossession.[20] I do not use this term to reduce Black maternal activists or their bodies to an impersonal category. Rather, I seek to expand the term to include Black women's bodies, which challenged the contradiction of their ability to endure insurmountable pain of the heart, and yet were strong enough to physically challenge the conditions of their oppression. The question of origin is imagined through the matrilineal line, where children, stolen and sold, creatively wade through a Black feminist history and its attending vastness. Slain mother-activists' legacies usurp the cultural depictions that frame African origins as patrilineal (like Alex Haley's *Roots*), and thus generally code African origins through men and as a male entity.[21] This is not only a cultural fallacy maintained in contemporary visual and material cultures but defunct in the Black feminist imagination Black maternal activists embody.

Making Black mothers visible in the public is a way to make and remake them as superhuman for ameliorative and pejorative gains. The ways in which Black mothers are called again, then re-called in the name of their slain children, allows them to appear to us outside the body and only in the name of their maimed kin. They are only imagined, beyond body, personality, or the tactile stuffs that make them appear to us as flesh.[22] They are used as the evidence that the slain were once here, but only once they are gone. They are removed from their bodies at the moment they supersede them in public discourse. Their bodies, now gone, only matter once they are erased, much like the lives of their slain kin.[23] As discussed throughout this book, racist mythologies shape public opinions about Black mothers and their ability to make prudent decisions about their reproductive lives.[24] These same mythologies contend that Black mothers do not know what is best for their bodies or lives during their reproductive years. Under patriarchal family movements, their involvement in activism marked their inability to make positive choices for their bodies and unborn children. In these framings, engaging in overt social justice campaigns disrupted patriarchal family models; women were to stay home taking care of children. In other words, a depoliticized form of mothering does not result in forms of mothers in which the state is rewarded.[25]

20. Cooper Owens, *Medical Bondage*, 8. See also Hull et al., *All the Women*.
21. Mwangi, "Silence Is a Woman."
22. Mwangi, "Silence Is a Woman."
23. Much of this paragraph's formulation is owed to Mwangi.
24. Roberts, *Killing the Black Body*, 300.
25. Gumbs, "We Can Learn."

Black mothers do not fit into state formations of proper state subjecthood.[26] These formations are replicated in social justice movements that erase Black women's activist labor, leading to further marginalization. White women's second-wave activism of the late 1960s to '70s for the right *not* to parent reinscribed the violences of racial slavery for Black women, whose rights to parent were always under attack on US soil.[27] African-descended women have been fighting for reproductive rights ever since they resisted the theft of their children from the continent of Africa.[28]

Many Black Panther Party members experienced indirect and direct retaliation to their maternal status from the state as a result of their activism. In 1977, Ericka Huggins was the defendant of a manufactured lawsuit about welfare fraud, which stated that the state must "recover" welfare money used to support her three-year-old son, who lived with his father while Ericka attended to her activist commitments.[29] Her contemporary Assata Shakur was and still is famously exiled from the United States because of her involvement with the Black Power movement. Her autobiography, *Assata: An Autobiography* (1988), intimates the polyvocal voices of Black Panther women who were dispossessed of their children and right to parent during this intense historical time. Afeni Shakur, one of the Panther 21, was beaten, jailed, and tried while pregnant with her son. Even an article written in a 1973 issue of *The Black Panther* reported how the state of Pennsylvania "postponed" welfare checks to dozens of Philadelphia families without explanation. Several hundred welfare recipients held a demonstration in protest of their late checks. Black women and children were disproportionately affected by these late payments, both because of the lack of receipt and the subsequent state responses to retaliation. In a neighborhood-organized protest against the state's unlawful withholding, the Philadelphia police force not only arrested women *and* children, but also ran a car through protestors, crushing the legs of one elderly man who was unable to move out of the way of the car in time.

"From the intricate web of mythology which surrounds the Black woman, a fundamental image emerges," Black feminist culture critic Michele Wallace

---

26. Many would argue "humanness" to be the appropriate term here. See Hartman, *Scenes of Subjection*; and Wilderson, *Incognegro*.

27. Combahee River Collective, "Black Feminist Statement," 211.

28. Both Morgan, *Laboring Women*; and Turner, *Contested Bodies*, document the resistances to the theft of their children.

29. "Black Panther Sued." Ericka Huggins was sued by Alameda County for recovery of welfare money used to support her young son, who lived with his father while Ericka attended to the commitments of anti-dispossession work. The receipt of welfare was an instrument used by the state to control Black communities' involvement in the Black Power struggle. Archival evidence found in the 1973 vol. 10, no. 11 issue of *The Black Panther*.

writes in her famous *Black Macho and the Myth of the Superwoman* (1979). Wallace's book composes a canonical fabric of memoir and theory to dispel the myth that is "difficult to let go," that "naturally Black women want very much to believe," for "in a way, it is all we have."[30] In a moment of literary call-and-response, this "difficulty to let go" has also been reinforced by time.[31] In 2019, writer Dani McClain wrote the mythology of the superwoman as ever-present in the political life of Black motherhood. This mythology justifies the scrutiny around Black women's bodies, their reproductive decisions in particular, and their attempts to fight against this regulation.

Many Black feminist scholars engage with paradox to describe Black women's shifting social locations throughout history.[32] This social location seeds deep into subject-making and cultural depiction, making the Black interior a space for Black mothers to articulate their opposition to disenfranchisement.[33] The superwoman myth describes the concept that women have "inordinate strength, with an ability for tolerating an unusual amount of misery and heavy, distasteful work."[34] What Wallace calls "work," Hartman might describe as Black women's "labor," both cumulative and productive, as simply existing in the world, bearing the brunt of violence and defining the afterlife of slavery.[35] Spillers asserts a Freudian analysis to think through the captive body as coming into *being* for the captor while still being absent from a subject position.[36] Black motherhood arrives as the vertex of this seesaw, one form of paradox in which liberation is possible, and one in which the violence of the slave is made real on the flesh. Black women's experiences are wrought with social and cultural grammars that fail to balance the precarity of their social locations as both marginal and integral to the system of enslavement. Mythmaking is a tool to make sense of this paradox. Superimposing the self into the absence Black women (don't) occupy leaves us looking for new ways to appear legible in contemporary feminist movements.

In a transformation of Audre Lorde's *Sister Outsider,* Patricia Hill Collins elucidates a tenet of feminism that marginalized Black women during the 1970s and '80s, known as the "outsider-within" status.[37] Through imaginative

---

30. Wallace, *Black Macho,* 107.
31. Wallace, *Black Macho.*
32. Marginalization is an organizing principle in the schema of Lorde's *Sister Outsider* (1984), hooks's *Feminist Theory: From Margin to Center* (1984), and Patricia Hill Collins's "outsider-within" formulation (*Black Feminist Thought*).
33. E. Alexander, *Black Interior*; and Quashie, *Sovereignty of Quiet.*
34. Wallace, *Black Macho,* 107.
35. Hartman, "Belly of the World"; and Spillers, "Mama's Baby, Papa's Maybe," 65.
36. Hill Collins, "Learning from the Outsider Within."
37. Hill Collins, "Learning from the Outsider Within."

praxes, Black women creatives inform the present by illustrating the lives of Black women who were weathered by these structural political antagonisms upon enslavement. Regarding the formation of Black womanhood under chattel slavery, Angela Davis writes that the nineteenth-century ideology of femininity, which emphasized women's roles as mothers, rendered Black women "anomalies" whose work did not take place in the realm of domesticity (wet nursing, cooking, and house chores). This may be a quintessential example of Black women's lot during slavery: private *and* public, domestic *and* public, "breeder" *and* mammy, wet nurse *and* rape victim.[38] Our lives are multi-parted. Audre Lorde remembers for us that Black women do not live "single-issue lives," and liberation cannot be reduced to one facet of their oppression.[39] Lorde's maxim is often cited as an intersectional approach to situating Black women within Black liberation struggles especially. Maintaining the complexity of Black women's womanhood during slavery, however, informs one of the many pitfalls that overwhelmed Black feminist activism in the later twentieth century, by framing it as an appendage to second-wave white feminism.

Black women creatives and intellectuals, situated both within and outside of institutions, have explored marginality and Black women as marginalized subjects in liberation movements. Toni Cade Bambara's "On the Issue of Roles," in her edited series *The Black Woman: An Anthology* (1970), assessed heteronormativity and patriarchy as the stain on the Black liberation movement. In addition, Bambara wrote that the movement's incessant need to regulate Black women's activist prowess to the private sphere and *only* in service of their male counterparts neutered the potential of the movement and reinscribed notions of marginality. A disquieted bell hooks named this as a primary goal of *Feminist Theory: From Margin to Center* (1984), where Black women's intellectual labor was not lost on the movements of Black and women's liberation. Black women's voices and leadership merely needed to be reasserted on the authority of their own lives and experiences, demanding to formulate their own goals, solutions, and stakes to avoid white feminism functioning as white supremacy. As the trope of marginality incited a movement of Black feminist creativity, it also ignited the neoliberal adoption of diversity models in liberation movements. This institutional adoption of intersectionality first appeared to make feminist knowledge production more capacious for those who do not live single-issue lives. But as Jennifer C. Nash elucidates, it also rendered Black feminism synonymous with intersectionality, making it a lens that was

---

38. Davis, *Women, Race and Class*, 5.
39. Lorde, *Sister Outsider*, 138.

blindly applied to most analyses and without heavy scrutiny.[40] Because marginalization emerged as a "principal analytic," we have yet to understand the ways marginality was metabolized by Black women as an intellectual-activist praxis. Further, we have yet to capture how marginality reinforces the trope that Black women's voices do not matter and therefore must start, instigate, inform, plan, structure, and enact whole political movements.[41]

The myth of the Black maternal superbody challenges traditional definitions of reproduction as a biological act requiring a mother and child. Black maternity, then, is the period during or after care is practiced. This definition explains why the work of Black reproductive rights activists will never be done, even after traditional reproductive justice goals are achieved. It asks us to redefine reproductive justice along much more sweeping terms, including analyzing creative expressions that feature Black motherhood and its continuation with state antagonisms that occur in spaces of intellect and knowledge production.

This book circulates in the uneasy synonymy of self-determination and Black women; Black women's political prowess to both live (and die) a politics of liberation can damage our health. It departs from simply asking in what ways Black women are called to solve crises that affect their ability to raise children into adulthood. It moves beyond this question by showing that the destructive myths about Black women are bought and paid for wholesale in public spheres. And despite its reductive slippage, it also exposes how the myth of the Black maternal superbody successfully brings reproductive rights to the fore of the Movement for Black Lives. Also, it is through an investigation of the interior of these activist-mothers' lives that we can animate how the myth of the Black maternal superbody makes meaning of the imposition of myths generally, and how creative and kinetic forms of activism create new grammars of self-valuation that position Black lives and bodies inside their own paradigm of knowledge production.[42]

The interior of our lives exposes bodily trauma (which is sometimes, but not always, sustained from the parturient period). This trauma is a component that sustains the Black maternal superbody myth. That Black women must solely attend to the crises created to oppress their ability to live and parent without fear creates detrimental effects that often take the lives of Black women activists. The emotional, political, and intellectual labor of attending to crises that affect their children is a reproductive crisis atop other crises that have long affected the lives of Black women and their families. The myth of

---

40. Nash, "'Home Truths,'" 446.
41. Nash, "Home Truths,'" 447.
42. Hill Collins, "Learning from the Outsider Within."

the Black maternal superbody is imposed on Black women who cannot rely on state or community resources to protect the futurity of their families, substantiating superwoman myths that Black women "can do it all."

Recent discussions of Black feminism contemplate Black motherhood, reproductive politics, and the ways reproductive politics, as an ethic, expands beyond matters of Black bodies and the act of reproduction itself. Black motherhood studies includes theoretical and philosophical concerns about the state of Black women's survival. Reframing political journalist Dani McClain's emphasis on reproductive rights within a study of Black motherhood is fundamental to a reproductive justice analysis. In 2015 Jared Sexton combined McClain's Black feminist framework as an approach to the "conceptual lens of reproductive justice" to understand that "Black women and girls *also* suffer the forms of state-sanctioned violence typically associated with Black men and boys" and that it is the conceptual lens of reproductive justice which "encompasses the broad capacity of Black people to reproduce *as a people* . . . that might constitute conditions of viability."[43] To push the bounds of McClain's theory and Sexton's analysis a bit further, we may understand reproduction not only to be the right to birth Black children at all (or to constitute conditions of "viability," as Sexton would have it), but the ability for Black women to autonomously "constitute *conditions* of viability" themselves in a way that does not live in direct contestation with the simultaneous care of other things or other people. Reproductive justice is a person's ability to elicit their own ethics of care with/out systemic or institutional interventions by the state. Not only are Black women expected to solve problems caused by institutional violence within their own communities, many Black mothers directly injured by police brutality and gun violence have integrated mainstream politics. Reproduction is also the act of (re)producing traditions of protest for and about activism, self-defining the roles and desired outcomes for whole movements and causes.

This book ultimately asks us if Black motherhood can be understood through a different set of relations beyond those of fragmentation and dispossession. It concedes that "Black" preceding "motherhood" in a contemporary context of social and cultural relations names motherhood in a complete and totalizing way. But this text also asks us to wrestle routinely with the social, cultural, and political ramifications of motherhood as a personal project as well. The set of relations in this context may have already been determined, but the creations of Black mothers continue to express in ways that require interdisciplinary analysis of the creation's occurrences and embodiments.

---

43. Sexton, "Unbearable Blackness," 169.

EPILOGUE

The Infinitude of Black Motherhood

Every year Black mothers are recognized for their struggle to reproduce, literally and figuratively. Since 2018, only weeks before Mother's Day, Black Maternal Health Week has pre-shadowed this day as a nationally recognized time to focus on "amplifying the voices of Black Mamas, and centering the values and traditions of the reproductive and birth justice movements."[1] At time of writing, on Mother's Day 2023, social media accounts are flooded with the unbearable truth that Black maternal and infant mortality rates are up by 40 percent since the CDC last reported its "3–4× more likely" statistic in 2019.[2] Every year on Mother's Day, I try to draw special attention to Black mothers whose bodies and lives tell an even more complex story about motherhood: a story that lays bare the truth that the horrific death rates of pandemics,[3] reproductive injustice, and gun violence affect Black mothers and their children the most in America. There are many mothers whose lives and deaths intersect with this day in this exact paradox; they are mutually celebrated and mourned. This Mother's Day, and weeks before what would be Erica Garner's thirty-third birthday, I celebrate the infinitude of Black motherhood in and through Erica's story.

---

1. "Reps. Adams, Underwood and Sen. Booker."
2. Centers for Disease Control and Prevention, "Working Together"; and Inskeep and Pfeiffer, "Maternal Deaths."
3. Morehouse School of Medicine, "Two Year Study."

Many will recall Eric Garner, who was killed in 2014 in a chokehold for selling loose cigarettes outside of a Staten Island bodega. Eric's death was a major event in creating publicity around the Black Lives Matter movement, especially after activists successfully shut down the Verrazzano Bridge, which connects Staten Island and Brooklyn. It is because of Erica that her father's last words, "I can't breathe," became a national battle cry against the policing of Black people and Black men especially. After the murder of her father, Erica Garner's fight against police brutality combined with her embodied health struggles. While fighting against the police injustices in the streets, Erica privately contended with the American health care system, which structurally determines Black people can't feel pain.[4] This is the same system responsible for the majority of Black maternal deaths.[5] When she became pregnant with her second son, she developed pre-eclampsia, a condition caused by severe, persistent high blood pressure. It is one of the leading causes of US-born Black maternal death in the United States.[6] Her mother warned her of the perils of working too hard while pregnant: "You have to slow down, you have to relax and slow down," she told her daughter.[7] In August 2017, despite a relentless schedule of community organizing, Erica welcomed her second child via cesarean section. She named him Eric, after her father. During the operation, she suffered heart failure but survived to raise her son for the first few months of his life.[8] Shortly after, Erica had her first heart attack, but returned to organizing work. The doctors determined the pregnancy put a strain on her heart, and the heart attack caused it to be enlarged.[9]

After an asthma attack in December 2017 at the age of twenty-seven, Erica went into cardiac arrest and died shortly thereafter. She died where she was born, in Woodhull Hospital, in Brooklyn, New York. Certainly, Erica died of a broken heart, her body succumbing to the routine of life *and* death that inflicts Black mothers' bodies as the carriers of their ancestral damages. Her two sons now live without their grandfather and mother. In the short years that followed the death of Eric Garner, a victim of police brutality, young Eric's mother suffered similar repercussions of generational death due to the combined effects of police brutality and a health care system that upholds Black maternal death. Erica lives on through young Eric, as her father lived through her. In "Poem Number Two on Bell's Theorem, or The New Physicality of

---

4. Hoffman et al., "Racial Bias in Pain Assessment."
5. Burris et al., "Black-White Disparities."
6. Hatch, "Race Alone."
7. Levenson, "Activist Erica Garner."
8. Carrega and Tracy, "Eric Garner's Daughter."
9. Rouse, "Family and Faith."

Long Distance Love," Black feminist and mother-poet June Jordan (1936–2022) suggests that "there are no parts." When families appear to be fractured or separated through death, their families gather around those left behind to keep alive the memory of the mothers lost:

> There is no chance that we will fall apart
> There is no chance
> There are no parts.[10]

Quantum physicists continue to argue about the controversial notion of "quantum immortality," or the impossibility of death—an unproven but often proffered reality reliant on the "role of the observer." When a particle is observed, it becomes definite. When matter goes unobserved by the human eye, such as a body in ground, or a body cremated and then put in an urn, it resumes an infinite space. (Whether or not the definite particle goes into an alternative reality is up for constant debate.) Jordan pieces together this poetic and scientific merger, expanding the horizons of how connection can be felt and conceived to create the rhetoric of separation: Imagine the embodiment of scraps is an activation of political and cultural activism. Scrap theory, in the vein of quantum immortality, asks how the activism of Erica Garner and mothers like her reveals the fullness of what it means to labor, reproductively. In a very basic understanding of scraps and the material body, Black bodies live in the liminal space of a figuration of what denotes a "healthy" body. In a history of those framed as outside the conceptions of human, we can also understand the circuity of nonhumanness from the conception of Erica Garner's second pregnancy and her parturient experience as a whole. The goal is not essentially to "tear her apart" or impose a fragmentation on a sacred, whole life.

On January 30, 2023, it was tweeted that Atatiana Jefferson's sister died. Two years earlier, her mother died at age fifty-five, and only one year before that, her father died at fifty-eight. And four years earlier, Atatiana was murdered while she was playing video games with her nephew, Zion. Now Zion walks through the world without his favorite aunt, his maternal grandmother and grandfather, and his mother. Their deaths are the ripples from state-sanctioned violence. What is the infinitude of Atatiana Jefferson, and now of Zion? The finality is the compression of state-sanctioned violence, how we move through the world and who we are to be without our loved ones. If there are no parts of the Jeffersons, what is left of Zion? His life is now part of the "chance" June

---

10. Jordan, "Poem Number Two."

Jordan disavows existing: There are no parts, she asserts. What of the infinitude of Erica Garner, Atatiana Jefferson, and now Amber Carr? *There are no parts* between a mother and child. *There is no chance we will fall apart.*[11]

There are many ways the literary, visual, and social allow us to return to the structural characteristics of Black motherhood. To that end, Black motherhood is subject to a set of relations of foreclosure and also what TK Smith reminds us is therefore "infinite": subject to no limitation but, perhaps more importantly, without totalizing external determination.[12] It is in the infinitude that the Black mother may finally repose but never fully rest, for full rest requires an absolution of the future. An infinitude—outside a temporal boundary of a "future," for the future is a reductionist space contingent on a world that says Black kids don't exist. Our task is not to conjure Black mothers, suture them, set and cast their brokenness to make them anew, nor grind them up and piece them back together to make convenient memories of them and the children they left behind. They are immortal; they are infinite. Extending beyond, lying beyond, or being greater than any preassigned finite value, however large. Black mothers are infinite after they are gone, and only made finite by a world observing, a world watching and judging. It is in the infinitude that the Black mother may finally repose. Where she may finally find peace without fear of the theft of her children's lives. In their honor, we lay our hands on our children's backs before they leave home for school, for work, for play, in hopes that one day we will not have to weep for ourselves, nor for the generations of our foremothers who, too, lost their children, and who must always remain gathering their bones to make memories of skeletons. It is for them that we *will* play with our children forever in an infinite "time of not-to-end."[13]

---

11. Jordan, "Poem Number Two."
12. TK Smith, "Embracing."
13. Brooks, "Aspect of Love," in *Blacks*.

BIBLIOGRAPHY

Archives, Artistic Works, and Museum Exhibitions

The Andy Warhol Museum. "Firelei Báez: Bloodlines at The Andy Warhol Museum." April 14, 2017. YouTube video. https://www.youtube.com/watch?v=qfcV7OH6Wy8.

Belle, La Vaughn. "La Vaughn Belle." Accessed December 8, 2022. http://www.lavaughnbelle.com/#/cities/.

Belle, La Vaughn. *Trading Post (Articulated Hierarchies and Visible Displacements)*. 2015. Sculpture, 36 x 18 x 18 in. http://www.lavaughnbelle.com/home-1#/cities/.

A Color Removed. SPACES (Cleveland, OH), July 14–September 30, 2018. https://www.spacescle.org/exhibitions/2018/07/14/a-color-removed.

Corrin, Lisa G. "The Audience Responds." In *Mining the Museum: An Installation by Fred Wilson*, edited by Lisa G. Corrin, 59–67. New York: The New Press, 1994.

Corrin, Lisa G. "Mining the Museum: Artists Look at Museums, Museums Look at Themselves." In *Mining the Museum: An Installation by Fred Wilson*, edited by Lisa G. Corrin, 1–22. New York: The New Press, 1994.

Davis, Noah, curator. *Non-Fiction*. The Underground Museum (Los Angeles, CA), May 2016–April 2017.

"Freedom." Featuring Kendrick Lamar. Track 10 on Beyoncé, *Lemonade*. Columbia, 2016.

Guerrier, Adler. *Conditions and Forms for blk Longevity*. California Museum of African American Art (Los Angeles), February 1–August 26, 2018.

Jackson, Maynard. Mayoral administrative records. Atlanta University Center Archives, Robert W. Woodruff Library, Atlanta, GA.

Lane, M. Carmen. *Ken'nahsa:ke/Khson:ne: On My Tongue, On My Back (Family Tree)*. 2018. Mixed media construction with Black Body Bag. https://mcarmenlane.com/prjcts.

Marshall, Kerry James. *Heirlooms and Accessories*. 2002. Three ink-jet prints on paper in wooden artist's frames with rhinestones, 57 × 54 1/4 × 3 in. The Studio Museum in Harlem. https://studiomuseum.org/collection-item/heirlooms-accessories.

SPACES (Cleveland, OH). "SWAP #68: Michael Rakowitz." December 4, 2018. YouTube video. https://www.youtube.com/watch?v=2fVZkMksok8.

Toni Cade Bambara Collection, 1939–1996. Spelman College Archives, Atlanta, GA.

Walker, Margaret. Personal papers. Margaret Walker Center, Jackson State University, Jackson, MS. https://cdm17311.contentdm.oclc.org.

Wilson, Fred. *Mining the Museum*. Maryland Historical Society (Baltimore, MD), April 2, 1992–February 28, 2013.

Published Works

"About: Mothers and Men Against Senseless Killings." Accessed January 13, 2020. http://ontheblock.org/about/.

Alexander, Elizabeth. *The Black Interior: Essays*. St. Paul, MN: Graywolf Press, 2004.

Alexander, M. Jacqui. *Pedagogies of Crossing: Meditations on Feminism, Sexual Politics, Memory, and the Sacred*. Durham, NC: Duke University Press, 2005.

Appadurai, Arjun. *The Social Life of Things: Commodities in Cultural Perspective*. Cambridge: Cambridge University Press, 1986.

Arnheim, Rudolf. *Visual Thinking*. 35th anniversary printing. Berkeley: University of California Press, 2004.

Ater, Renée. "The Challenge of Memorializing Slavery in North Carolina: The Unsung Founders Memorial and the North Carolina Freedom Monument Project." In *Politics of Memory: Making Slavery Visible in the Public Space*, edited by Ana Lucia Araujo, 141–56. New York: Routledge, 2012.

Avilez, GerShun. "The Aesthetics of Terror: Constructing 'Felt Threat' in *Those Bones Are Not My Child* and *Leaving Atlanta*." *Obsidian: Literature in the African Diaspora* 13, no. 2 (2012): 13–28.

Ayres, B. Drummond, Jr. "Atlanta Mayor Refuses to Oust Black." *New York Times,* April 18, 1975, 17. https://www.nytimes.com/1975/04/18/archives/atlanta-Mayor-refuses-to-oust-black.html.

Baldwin, James. *The Evidence of Things Not Seen*. New York: Holt, Rinehart, and Winston, 1995.

Bambara, Toni Cade. *Those Bones Are Not My Child*. New York: Pantheon Books, 1999.

Barber, Tiffany E. "Can You Be BLACK and Make This?" *Rhizomes*, no. 35 (2019).

Bentley, Rosalind. "Atlanta Mayor Signs Bill Changing Confederate Street Names." *Atlanta Journal-Constitution,* October 3, 2018. https://www.ajc.com/news/local/just-atlanta-confederate-streets-get-new-names/uStM5kDReX0Y5CmemAygrM/.

"Black Panther Sued for Welfare Fraud." *Oakland Chronicle,* November 11, 1977.

"Black Women and the Suffrage Movement: 1848–1923." Wesleyan University. Accessed January 18, 2021. https://www.wesleyan.edu/mlk/posters/suffrage.html.

Blake, Felice. *Black Love, Black Hate: Intimate Antagonisms in African American Literature*. Columbus: The Ohio State University Press, 2018.

Bonaparte, Alicia D. "'The Satisfactory Midwife Bag': Midwifery Regulation in South Carolina, Past and Present Considerations." *Social Science History* 38, no. 1–2 (2014): 155–82. https://doi.org/10.1017/ssh.2015.14.

Bradley, Rizvana. "Vestiges of Motherhood: The Maternal Function in Recent Black Cinema." *Film Quarterly* 71, no. 2 (2017): 46–52.

Brakta, Soumia, et al. "Role of Vitamin D in Uterine Fibroid Biology." *Fertility and Sterility* 104, no. 3 (2015): 698–706. https://doi.org/10.1016/j.fertnstert.2015.05.031.

Brand, Dionne. *A Map to the Door of No Return: Notes to Belonging.* Toronto, ON: Vintage Canada, 2001.

Brand, Dionne. *No Language Is Neutral.* Toronto, ON: Coach House Press, 1990.

Brand, Dionne. *A Map to the Door of No Return: Notes to Belonging.* Toronto: Doubleday Canada, 2001.

Braxton, Joanne M., and Andrée Nicola McLaughlin, eds. *Wild Women in the Whirlwind: Afra-American Culture and the Contemporary Literary Renaissance.* New Brunswick, NJ: Rutgers University Press, 1990.

Brehman, Caroline. "Photos of the Day: Caged Bear." *Roll Call,* November 16, 2020. https://rollcall.com/2020/11/16/photo-of-the-day-caged-bear/.

Brooks, Gwendolyn. *Blacks.* Chicago: Third World Press, 1987.

Brooks, Gwendolyn. *In the Mecca: Poems.* New York: Harper & Row, 1968.

Brown, DeNeen L. "Emmett Till's Mother Opened His Casket and Sparked the Civil Rights Movement." *Washington Post,* July 12, 2018. https://www.washingtonpost.com/news/retropolis/wp/2018/07/12/emmett-tills-mother-opened-his-casket-and-sparked-the-civil-rights-movement/.

Brown, Kimberly Juanita. *The Repeating Body: Slavery's Visual Resonance in the Contemporary.* Durham, NC: Duke University Press, 2015.

Burris, Heather H., Molly Passarella, Sara C. Handley, Sindhu K. Srinivas, and Scott A. Lorch. "Black-White Disparities in Maternal In-Hospital Mortality According to Teaching and Black-Serving Hospital Status." *American Journal of Obstetrics and Gynecology* 225, no. 1 (2021): 83. https://doi.org/10.1016/j.ajog.2021.01.004.

Butler, Octavia. *Kindred.* 25th anniversary ed. Boston: Beacon Press, 2003.

Campt, Tina. "Black Visuality and the Practice of Refusal." *Women and Performance,* February 25, 2019. https://www.womenandperformance.org/ampersand/29-1/campt.

Campt, Tina. *Image Matters: Archive, Photography, and the African Diaspora in Europe.* Durham, NC: Duke University Press, 2012.

Campt, Tina. *Listening to Images.* Durham, NC: Duke University Press, 2017.

Carlisle, Lois. "Atlanta's Berlin Wall." Atlanta History Center. May 14, 2021. https://www.atlantahistorycenter.com/blog/atlantas-berlin-wall/.

Carrega, Christina, and Thomas Tracy. "Eric Garner's Daughter Erica Declared Brain Dead After Heart Attack." *Los Angeles Times,* December 28, 2017. https://www.latimes.com/nation/la-na-erica-garner-brain-dead-20171228-story.html.

Carter, Rodney G. S. "Of Things Said and Unsaid: Power, Archival Silences, and Power in Silence." *Archivaria* 61 (2006): 215–33.

Cascone, Sarah. "Artist Vanessa German Needed Money to Repair Her Steps in Pittsburgh. Then She Won $200,000 from the Crystal Bridges Museum." *artnet news,* December 18, 2018. https://news.artnet.com/art-world/vanessa-german-crystal-bridges-prize-1423390.

Caswell, Michelle. "'The Archive' Is Not an Archives: Acknowledging the Intellectual Contributions of Archival Studies." *Reconstruction: Studies in Contemporary Culture* 16, no. 1 (2016).

Caswell, Michelle. *Archiving the Unspeakable: Silence, Memory, and the Photographic Record in Cambodia*. Madison: University of Wisconsin Press, 2014.

Caswell, Michelle. "Dusting for Fingerprints: Feminist Standpoint Appraisal." *Journal of Critical Library and Information Studies* 3, no. 2 (2021): 1–36. https://doi.org/10.24242/jclis.v3i2.113.

Caswell, Michelle, Marika Cifor, and Mario H. Ramirez. "'To Suddenly Discover Yourself Existing': Uncovering the Impact of Community Archives 1." *American Archivist* 79, no. 1 (2016): 56–81.

Centers for Disease Control and Prevention. "Working Together to Reduce Black Maternal Mortality." April 3, 2023. https://www.cdc.gov/healthequity/features/maternal-mortality/index.html.

Chandler, Nahum Dimitri. "Originary Displacement." In *X—the Problem of the Negro as a Problem for Thought*, 129–70. New York: Fordham University Press, 2014.

Christian, Barbara. "Fixing Methodologies: Beloved." *Cultural Critique* 24, no. 24 (1993): 5–15. https://doi.org/10.2307/1354127.

Clarke, Cheryl. *"After Mecca": Women Poets and the Black Arts Movement*. New Brunswick, NJ: Rutgers University Press, 2005.

Cliff, Michelle. *Abeng*. Trumansburg, NY: Crossing Press, 1984.

Clifton, Lucille. "Why Some People Be Mad at Me Sometimes." In *Next: New Poems*, 20. Brockport, New York, 1987.

Clitandre, Nadège T. "Mapping the Echo Chamber: Edwidge Danticat and the Thematic Trilogy of Birth, Separation, and Death." *Palimpsest* 3, no. 2 (2014): 170–90.

Cohen, Cathy J. "Punks, Bulldaggers, and Welfare Queens: The Radical Potential of Queer Politics?" *GLQ: A Journal of Lesbian and Gay Studies* 3, no. 4 (1997): 437–65.

Coleman, Monica. "Octavia Tried to Tell Us: Parable for Today's Pandemic." *Beautiful Mind Blog*, May 3, 2020. https://monicaacoleman.com/octavia-tried-to-tell-us-parable-for-todays-pandemic.

Collins-White, Mali. "Rethinking the Human: Anti-Respectability and Blackhood." *American Quarterly* 71, no. 1 (2019): 141–49.

Collins-White, Mali, et al. "Disruptions in Respectability: A Roundtable Discussion." *Souls: A Critical Journal of Black Politics, Culture, and Society* 18, no. 2–4 (2016): 463–75.

Combahee River Collective. "A Black Feminist Statement." In *This Bridge Called My Back: Writings by Radical Women of Color*, edited by Cherríe Moraga and Gloria Anzaldúa, 211. Watertown, MA: Persephone Press, 1981.

Combahee River Collective. "The Combahee River Collective Statement." 1977. https://www.blackpast.org/african-american-history/combahee-river-collective-statement-1977/.

Connolly, N. D. B. *A World More Concrete: Real Estate and the Remaking of Jim Crow South Florida*. Chicago: University of Chicago Press, 2014.

Connor, Michan Andrew. "Metropolitan Secession and the Space of Color-Blind Racism in Atlanta." *Journal of Urban Affairs* 37, no. 4 (2015): 436–61. https://doi.org/10.1111/juaf.12101.

Cooks, Bridget R. *Exhibiting Blackness: African Americans and the American Art Museum*. Amherst: University of Massachusetts Press, 2011.

Cooper Owens, Deirdre. *Medical Bondage: Race, Gender, and the Origins of American Gynecology*. Athens: University of Georgia Press, 2017.

Copeland, Huey. "Tending-toward-Blackness." *October* 156 (Spring 2016): 141–44.

Cotter, Holland. "'It's About Time!' Betye Saar's Long Climb to the Summit." *New York Times*, September 4, 2019. https://www.nytimes.com/2019/09/04/arts/design/betye-saar.html.

Cullors, Patrisse, and asha bandele. *When They Call You a Terrorist: A Black Lives Matter Memoir.* New York: St. Martin's Press, 2018.

Cvetkovich, Ann. *An Archive of Feelings: Trauma, Sexuality, and Lesbian Public Cultures.* Durham, NC: Duke University Press, 2019.

Dadzie, Stella. "Searching for the Invisible Woman: Slavery and Resistance in Jamaica." *Race and Class* 32, no. 2 (1990): 21–38.

Dafoe, Taylor. "'We Need to Tell a Different Story': Why Tamir Rice's Mother Samaria Is Collaborating with Contemporary Artists to Honor Her Son's Legacy." *artnet news,* July 30, 2019. https://news.artnet.com/art-world/art-tamir-rices-mother-samaria-turning-tragedy-teaching-opportunity-1612330.

Danticat, Edwidge. *The Art of Death: Writing the Final Story.* Minneapolis, MN: Graywolf Press, 2017.

Danticat, Edwidge. *Breath, Eyes, Memory.* New York: Soho Press, 1994.

Danticat, Edwidge. *Brother, I'm Dying.* New York: Alfred A. Knopf, 2007.

Danticat, Edwidge. *The Dew Breaker.* 1st Vintage Contemporaries ed. New York: Vintage Books, 2005.

Danticat, Edwidge. "Lòt Bò Dlo: The Other Side of the Water." In *Haiti after the Earthquake,* by Paul Farmer, edited by Abbey Gardner and Cassia Van Der Hoof Holstein, 261–70. New York: PublicAffairs, 2012.

Dapiran, Antony. "'Be Water!': Seven Tactics That Are Winning Hong Kong's Democracy Revolution." *New Statesman,* August 1, 2019. https://www.newstatesman.com/politics/2019/08/be-water-seven-tactics-that-are-winning-hong-kongs-democracy-revolution-2.

Davis, Angela Y. *Women, Race and Class.* New York: Vintage Books, 1983.

Dennison, Alicya. "African-American History Spotlight: Ida B. Wells." *The DePaulia* (blog), February 27, 2015. https://depauliaonline.com/9953/nation/african-american-history-spotlight-ida-b-wells/.

Derrida, Jacques. "Archive Fever: A Freudian Impression." *Diacritics* 25, no. 2 (1995): 9–62.

Drake, Jarrett M. "Liberatory Archives: Towards Belonging and Believing (Part 1)." *Medium,* October 22, 2016. https://medium.com/on-archivy/liberatory-archives-towards-belonging-and-believing-part-1-d26aaeboedd1.

Du Bois, W. E. B. "Souls of Black Folk." In *DuBois' Writings,* 357–547. New York: Library of America, 1986.

"Eaves Convicted on Three of Four Counts." *AP News,* May 2, 1988. https://apnews.com/article/2c19b2dd713d20bc268c1f9101da7096.

Eichhorn, Kate. *The Archival Turn in Feminism: Outrage in Order.* Philadelphia, PA: Temple University Press, 2013.

Ellis, Nadia. *Territories of the Soul: Queered Belonging in the Black Diaspora.* Durham, NC: Duke University Press, 2015.

Enwezor, Okwui, and International Center of Photography. *Archive Fever: Uses of the Document in Contemporary Art.* New York: International Center of Photography, 2008.

Falzetti, Ashley Glassburn. "Archival Absence: The Burden of History." *Settler Colonial Studies* 5, no. 2 (2014): 128–44.

Farmer, Ashley. "Archiving While Black." *Black Perspectives,* AAIHS, June 18, 2018. https://www.aaihs.org/archiving-while-black/.

Fett, Sharla M. *Working Cures: Healing, Health, and Power on Southern Slave Plantations*. Chapel Hill: University of North Carolina Press, 2002.

Firestone, David. "The Census Shows Growth in Atlanta's Population." *New York Times*, March 23, 2001. https://www.nytimes.com/2001/03/23/us/the-census-shows-growth-in-atlanta-s-population.html.

Fleetwood, Nicole R. *Troubling Vision: Performance, Visuality, and Blackness*. Chicago: University of Chicago Press, 2011.

"Forgotten History of Ellicott City and Howard County MD: Tom Randall and the Howard House." *Forgotten History of Ellicott City and Howard County MD* (blog), February 19, 2018. http://historichomeshowardcounty.blogspot.com/2018/02/tom-randall-and-howard-house.html.

Frazier, E. Franklin. *The Free Negro Family*. New York: Arno Press, 1968.

Frazier, E. Franklin. *The Negro in the United States*. New York: Macmillan, 1957.

Frazier, E. Franklin, and Anthony M. Platt. *The Negro Family in the United States*. Notre Dame, IN: University of Notre Dame Press, 2001.

Frazier, Tyralynn. "Birthing Black Mothers: A Short History on How Race Shapes Childbirth as a Rite of Passage." In *Black Motherhood(s): Contours, Contexts and Considerations*, edited by Karen T. Craddock, 147–64. Bradford, ON: Demeter Press, 2015.

Fuentes, Danielle. "Visible Black Motherhood Is a Revolution." *Biography* 41, no. 4 (2018): 856–75. https://doi.org/10.1353/bio.2018.0082.

Fuentes, Marisa J. *Dispossessed Lives: Enslaved Women, Violence, and the Archive*. Philadelphia: University of Pennsylvania Press, 2016.

Fulton, DoVeanna S. *Speaking Power: Black Feminist Orality in Women's Narratives of Slavery*. Albany: State University of New York Press, 2006.

Gallagher, J. Christopher, et al. "Effects of Vitamin D Supplementation in Older African American Women." *Journal of Clinical Endocrinology and Metabolism* 98, no. 3 (2013): 1137–46. https://doi.org/10.1210/jc.2012-3106.

Gibson, Campbell, and Kay Jung. "Historical Census Statistics on Population Totals by Race, 1790 to 1990, and by Hispanic Origin, 1970 to 1990, for Large Cities and Other Urban Places in the United States." Popular Division Working Paper No. 76, US Census Bureau, February 2005. https://web.archive.org/web/20120812191959/http://www.census.gov/population/www/documentation/twps0076/twps0076.html.

Gilger, Kristin. "Otherwise Lost or Forgotten: Collecting Black History in L. S. Alexander Gumby's 'Negroana' Scrapbooks." *African American Review* 48, no. 1 (2015): 111–26.

Gilliland, Anne J., and Michelle Caswell. "Records and Their Imaginaries: Imagining the Impossible, Making Possible the Imagined." *Archival Science: International Journal on Recorded Information* 16, no. 1 (2016): 53–75.

Gilroy, Paul. *The Black Atlantic: Modernity and Double Consciousness*. Cambridge, MA: Harvard University Press, 1993.

Giovanni, Nikki. "And So We Sing of Jubilee." In *Jubilee*, by Margaret Walker Alexander, viiii–xiii. 50th anniversary edition. Boston: Mariner Books, 2016.

Gordon, Avery. *Ghostly Matters: Haunting and the Sociological Imagination*. Minneapolis: University of Minnesota Press, 2008.

Graham, Maryemma. *The House Where My Soul Lives: The Life of Margaret Walker*. Oxford: Oxford University Press, 2023.

Griffin, Farah Jasmine. *"Who Set You Flowin'?": The African-American Migration Narrative*. New York: Oxford University Press, 1995.

Gumbs, Alexis Pauline. "Eternal Summer of the Black Feminist Mind: A Queer Ecological Approach to the Archive." In *Make Your Own History: Documenting Feminist and Queer Activism in the 21st Century,* edited by Lyz Bly and Kelly Wooten, 59–68. Los Angeles: Litwin Books, 2012.

Gumbs, Alexis Pauline. *Undrowned: Black Feminist Lessons from Marine Mammals.* Chico, CA: AK Press, 2020.

Gumbs, Alexis Pauline. "Undrowned: Black Feminist Lessons from Marine Mammals: Why We Need to Learn to Listen, Breathe and Remember, Across Species, Across Extinctions and Across Harm." *Soundings* 78 (2021): 20–37.

Gumbs, Alexis Pauline. "We Can Learn to Mother Ourselves: The Queer Survival of Black Feminism, 1968–1996." PhD diss., Duke University, 2010.

Ha, Trinh-Minh T. "Mother's Talk." In *The Politics of (M)othering: Womanhood, Identity, and Resistance in African Literature,* edited by Obioma Nnaemeka, 26–32. London: Routledge, 1997.

Halbfinger, David M. "Maynard H. Jackson Jr., First Black Mayor of Atlanta and a Political Force, Dies at 65." *New York Times,* June 24, 2003. https://www.nytimes.com/2003/06/24/us/maynard-h-jackson-jr-first-black-Mayor-atlanta-political-force-dies-65.html.

Haley, Sarah. *No Mercy Here: Gender, Punishment, and the Making of Jim Crow Modernity.* Justice, Power, and Politics. Chapel Hill: University of North Carolina Press, 2016.

Halperin, Julia, and Charlotte Burns. "Museums Claim They're Paying More Attention to Female Artists. That's an Illusion." *artnet news,* September 19, 2019. https://news.artnet.com/womens-place-in-the-art-world/womens-place-art-world-museums-1654714.

Hamilton, Carolyn, et al. "Introduction." In *Refiguring the Archive,* edited by Carolyn Hamilton, 7–18. Cape Town, South Africa: Kluwer Academic Publishers, 2002.

Hartman, Saidiya. "The Belly of the World: A Note on Black Women's Labors." *Souls* 18, no. 1 (2016): 166–73. https://doi.org/10.1080/10999949.2016.1162596.

Hartman, Saidiya. *Lose Your Mother: A Journey along the Atlantic Slave Route.* New York: Farrar, Straus and Giroux, 2007.

Hartman, Saidiya. *Scenes of Subjection: Terror, Slavery, and Self-Making in Nineteenth-Century America.* New York: Oxford University Press, 1997.

Hartman, Saidiya. "Venus in Two Acts." *Small Axe* 26, no. 3 (2008): 1–14.

Hartman, Saidiya. *Wayward Lives, Beautiful Experiments: Intimate Histories of Social Upheaval.* New York: W. W. Norton & Company, 2019.

Hartman, Saidiya, and Thora Siemsen. "On Working with Archives: An Interview with Writer Saidiya Hartman." *Creative Independent,* February 3, 2021. https://thecreativeindependent.com/people/saidiya-hartman-on-working-with-archives/.

Hartsfield-Jackson Atlanta International Airport. "History of ATL." https://www.atl.com/about-atl/history-of-atl/#1458248596122-ebbde128-a73d.

Hatch, Caslon. "Race Alone Does Not Account for Higher Preeclampsia Rates for Black Women, Study Finds." *HUB (Johns Hopkins University),* January 7, 2022. https://hub.jhu.edu/2022/01/07/american-black-women-face-higher-preeclampsia-risk/.

Hegel, Georg Wilhelm Friedrich. *Lectures on the Philosophy of History.* London: Bell, 1914.

Herzog, Melanie, and Elizabeth Catlett. *Elizabeth Catlett: In the Image of the People.* Chicago: Art Institute of Chicago, 2005.

Hill Collins, Patricia. *Black Feminist Thought: Knowledge, Consciousness, and the Politics of Empowerment.* New York: Routledge, 2000.

Hill Collins, Patricia. "Learning from the Outsider Within: The Sociological Significance of Black Feminist Thought." *Social Problems* 33, no. 6 (1986): S14–S32. https://doi.org/10.2307/800672.

Hobson, Janell. *Venus in the Dark: Blackness and Beauty in Popular Culture*. New York: Routledge, 2005.

Hoffman, Kelly M., et al. "Racial Bias in Pain Assessment and Treatment Recommendations, and False Beliefs about Biological Differences between Blacks and Whites." *PNAS* 113, no. 16 (2015): 4296–301. https://doi.org/10.1073/pnas.1516047113.

hooks, bell. *Feminist Theory: From Margin to Center*. Boston: South End Press, 1984.

Horton-Stallings, LaMonda. *Funk the Erotic: Transaesthetics and Black Sexual Cultures*. The New Black Studies Series. Urbana: University of Illinois Press, 2015.

Hull, Gloria T., Patricia Bell-Scott, and Barbara Smith, eds. *All the Women Are White, All the Blacks Are Men, but Some of Us Are Brave: Black Women's Studies*. Old Westbury, NY: Feminist Press, 1982.

Inskeep, Steve, and Sacha Pfeiffer. "Maternal Deaths in the U.S. Spiked in 2021, CDC Reports." *NPR*, March 16, 2023. https://www.npr.org/transcripts/1163786037.

Jackson, John L., Jr. *Harlem World: Doing Race and Class in Contemporary Black America*. Chicago: University of Chicago Press, 2010.

Joachim, Joana. "'Embodiment and Subjectivity': Intersectional Black Feminist Curatorial Practices in Canada." *RACAR* 43, no. 2 (2018): 34–47.

Jones, Milton, et al. "Oral History Interview of Milton Jones." October 5, 2015. Veterans History Project collection, MSS 1010, Kenan Research Center, Atlanta History Center. https://album.atlantahistorycenter.com/digital/collection/VHPohr/id/481.

Jordan, June. "Poem Number Two on Bell's Theorem, or the New Physicality of Long Distance Love." Poets.org. https://poets.org/poem/poem-number-two-bells-theorem-or-new-physicality-long-distance-love.

Judd, Bettina. *Patient: Poems*. New York: Black Lawrence Press, 2014.

Kincaid, Jamaica. *Annie John*. New York: Farrar, Straus and Giroux, 1985.

Kincaid, Jamaica. *The Autobiography of My Mother*. New York: Farrar, Straus and Giroux, 1996.

Kincaid, Jamaica. *Mr. Potter*. New York: Farrar, Straus and Giroux, 2002.

Kincaid, Jamaica. *A Small Place*. New York: Farrar, Straus and Giroux, 1988.

King, Debra Walker. *African Americans and the Culture of Pain*. Charlottesville: University of Virginia Press, 2008.

King, Rosamond S. *Island Bodies: Transgressive Sexualities in the Caribbean Imagination*. Gainesville: University Press of Florida, 2014.

King, Wayne. "Black Commissioner of Police Overcomes Bad Start in Atlanta." *New York Times*, May 31, 1976, 9. https://www.nytimes.com/1976/05/31/archives/black-commissioner-of-police-overcomes-bad-start-in-atlanta.html.

Kruse, Kevin Michael. *White Flight: Atlanta and the Making of Modern Conservatism*. Princeton, NJ: Princeton University Press, 2005.

Lawrance, Benjamin N. *Amistad's Orphans: An Atlantic Story of Children, Slavery, and Smuggling*. New Haven, CT: Yale University Press, 2014.

Lescaze, Lee, and Saundra Saperstein. "Bethesda Author Settles 'Roots' Suit for $500,000." *Washington Post*, December 15, 1978. https://www.washingtonpost.com/archive/politics/1978/12/15/bethesda-author-settles-roots-suit-for-500000/f97b693c-5336-46b3-8ab0-1b19856e8964/.

Levenson, Eric. "Activist Erica Garner, 27, Dies after Heart Attack." *CNN*, December 31, 2017. https://www.cnn.com/2017/12/30/us/erica-garner-eric-death.

Lindsey, Payne. *Atlanta Monster*. January 4–August 22, 2018. https://atlantamonster.com.

Lingel, Jessa. "This Is Not an Archive." Tumblr, November 5, 2013. https://jessalingel.tumblr.com/post/66108958850/this-is-not-an-archive.

Lorde, Audrey. *Sister Outsider: Essays and Speeches*. Trumansburg, NY: Crossing Press, 1984.

Los Angeles Times staff. "Hear the 911 Call about Tamir Rice: Gun Is 'Probably Fake,' Caller Says." *Los Angeles Times*, November 26, 2014. https://www.latimes.com/nation/nationnow/la-na-nn-tamir-rice-911-call-20141126-htmlstory.html.

Lozano-Hemmer, Rafael, et al. "Alien Relationships from Public Space." In *Transurbanism*, edited by Joke Brouwer and Arjen Mulder, 139–60. Rotterdam, Netherlands: V2 Publishers/NAi Publishers, 2002.

MacArthur Foundation. "Saidiya Hartman, Literary Scholar and Cultural Historian | 2019 MacArthur Fellow." YouTube video, September 25, 2019. https://www.youtube.com/watch?v=bG5Y8NDdGtY.

Manoff, Marlene. "Theories of the Archive from across the Disciplines." *Portal: Libraries and the Academy* 4, no. 1 (2004): 9–25.

Marmon, William. "Why 'Roots' Hit Home." *TIME* 109, no. 7 (1977): 69–71.

Marriott, D. S. *Haunted Life: Visual Culture and Black Modernity*. New Brunswick, NJ: Rutgers University Press, 2007.

Maynor, Ashley. "Response to the Unthinkable: Collecting and Archiving Condolence and Temporary Memorial Materials Following Public Tragedies." In *Handbook of Research on Disaster Management and Contingency Planning in Modern Libraries*, edited by Emy Nelson Decker and Jennifer A. Townes, 582–624. Hershey, PA: IGI Global, 2016.

McClain, Dani. "The Murder of Black Youth Is a Reproductive Justice Issue." *The Nation*, August 13, 2014. https://www.thenation.com/article/archive/murder-black-youth-reproductive-justice-issue/.

McFadden, Robert D. "Novelist's Suit Charges 'Roots' Copied Parts of Her 1966 Book." *New York Times*, April 23, 1977, 1.

McKenzie, Lindsay. "Racism and the American Library Association." *Inside Higher Ed*, January 31, 2019. https://www.insidehighered.com/news/2019/02/01/american-library-association-criticized-response-racism-complaint.

McKittrick, Katherine. *Demonic Grounds: Black Women and the Cartographies of Struggle*. Minneapolis: University of Minnesota Press, 2006.

McKittrick, Katherine, and Clyde Adrian Woods. *Black Geographies and the Politics of Race*. Toronto, ON: South End Press, 2007.

Mercer, Kobena. "Art History and the Dialogics of Diaspora." *Small Axe* 16, no. 2 (2012): 213–27. https://doi.org/10.1215/07990537-1665632.

Mercer, Kobena. *Travel and See: Black Diaspora Art Practices Since the 1980s*. Durham, NC: Duke University Press, 2016.

Minnesota Historical Society. "Duluth Lynchings." Accessed June 11, 2020. https://www.mnhs.org/duluthlynchings.

Mitchell, Koritha. *Living with Lynching: African American Lynching Plays, Performance, and Citizenship, 1890–1930*. Urbana: University of Illinois Press, 2011.

Morehouse School of Medicine. "Two Year Study Finds Black Children with Covid-19 Had Twice as Many Deaths as White Children with the Virus." March 13, 2023. https://www.msm.edu/RSSFeedArticles/2023/March/2022BCAC_Report.php.

Morgan, Jennifer L. *Laboring Women: Reproduction and Gender in New World Slavery*. Philadelphia: University of Pennsylvania Press, 2004.

Morgan, Jennifer L. "Partus Sequitur Ventrem." *Small Axe* 22, no. 1 (2018): 1–17. https://doi.org/10.1215/07990537-4378888.

Morrison, Toni. *Beloved*. New York: Random House, 1987.

Morrison, Toni. *Song of Solomon*. New York: Vintage International, 2004.

Morrison, Toni. *Toni Morrison: What Moves at the Margin: Selected Nonfiction*. Edited by Carolyn C. Denard. Jackson: University Press of Mississippi, 2008.

Morrison, Toni, and Danielle Kathleen Taylor-Guthrie. *Conversations with Toni Morrison*. Jackson: University Press of Mississippi, 1994.

Moss, Jada L. "The Forgotten Victims of Missing White Woman Syndrome: An Examination of Legal Measures That Contribute to the Lack of Search and Recovery of Missing Black Girls and Women." *William and Mary Journal of Race, Gender, and Social Justice* 25, no. 3 (2019): 737–62.

Musgrove, George Derek. *Rumor, Repression, and Racial Politics: How the Harassment of Black Elected Officials Shaped Post–Civil Rights America*. Athens: University of Georgia Press, 2012.

Mwangi, Wambui. "Silence Is a Woman." *New Inquiry*, June 4, 2013. https://thenewinquiry.com/silence-is-a-woman/.

Nash, Jennifer C. *Black Feminism Reimagined: After Intersectionality*. Durham, NC: Duke University Press, 2019.

Nash, Jennifer C. "'Home Truths' on Intersectionality." *Yale Journal of Law and Feminism* 23, no. 2 (2011): 445–70.

Neely, Chanda. "Tamir Rice Gazebo Demolition Stirs Emotions in Cleveland's Cudell Neighborhood." *Cleveland.com*, April 29, 2016. https://www.cleveland.com/metro/2016/04/tamir_rice_gazebo_demolition_s.html.

Nixon, Rob. *Slow Violence and the Environmentalism of the Poor*. Cambridge, MA: Harvard University Press, 2011.

Noble, Safiya Umoja. "Teaching Trayvon: Race, Media, and the Politics of Spectacle." *Black Scholar* 44, no. 1 (2014): 12–29. https://doi.org/10.1080/00064246.2014.11641209.

NPR staff. "Emmett Till's Father Was Also Hanged: A New Book Tells His Story." NPR, November 12, 2016. https://www.npr.org/2016/11/12/501622050/emmett-tills-father-was-also-hanged-a-new-book-tells-his-story.

Ortega, Kirsten Bartholomew. "The Black *Flâneuse*: Gwendolyn Brooks's 'In the Mecca.'" *Journal of Modern Literature* 30, no. 4 (2007): 139–55.

Pacific College. "Emotions and Traditional Chinese Medicine." September 5, 2014. https://www.pacificcollege.edu/news/blog/2014/09/05/emotions-and-traditional-chinese-medicine.

Patterson, Orlando. *Slavery and Social Death: A Comparative Study*. Cambridge, MA: Harvard University Press, 1982.

Pelly, Jenn. "An Artist Who Paints in Cryptic Pastel Symbols." *New York Times*, November 16, 2020, sec. T Magazine. https://www.nytimes.com/2020/11/16/t-magazine/caroline-kent.html.

The People's Paper Co-Op. "The People's Paper Co-Op." Accessed June 5, 2020. http://peoplespaperco-op.weebly.com/.

Perry, Keisha-Khan Y. *Black Women against the Land Grab: The Fight for Racial Justice in Brazil*. Minneapolis: University of Minnesota Press, 2013.

Philip, M. NourbeSe. *She Tries Her Tongue, Her Silence Softly Breaks*. Middletown, CT: Wesleyan University Press, 2014.

Philip, M. NourbeSe, and Evie Shockley. *Zong!* Middletown, CT: Wesleyan University Press, 2008.

Plantz, Scott H. "Coral Cuts." EMedicineHealth. https://www.emedicinehealth.com/wilderness_coral_cuts/article_em.htm.

Polanco, Gerardo. "Ringing Inside the Open Spaces of My Lungs, and: Neruda, Please Explain a Few Things." *Callaloo* 39, no. 3 (2016): 623–25. https://doi.org/10.1353/cal.2016.0098.

Powell, Chaitra, et al. "This [Black] Woman's Work: Exploring Archival Projects That Embrace the Identity of the Memory Worker." *KULA* 2, no. 1 (2018): Article 5. https://doi.org/10.5334/kula.25.

Prescod, Paul. "When the Black Political Class Betrayed Black Workers." *Jacobin,* April 1, 2020. https://jacobinmag.com/2020/04/atlanta-sanitation-workers-strike-maynard-jackson.

Quashie, Kevin. *The Sovereignty of Quiet: Beyond Resistance in Black Culture.* New Brunswick, NJ: Rutgers University Press, 2012.

Ramirez, Mario H. "Being Assumed Not to Be: A Critique of Whiteness as an Archival Imperative." *American Archivist* 78, no. 2 (2015): 339–56. https://doi.org/10.17723/0360-9081.78.2.339.

Ramos, Manny. "2 Mothers Killed in Drive-by Shooting Had Worked to Stop Gun Violence in Their Neighborhood." *Chicago Sun-Times,* July 29, 2019. https://chicago.suntimes.com/news/2019/7/29/8937962/two-women-killed-mothers-against-senseless-killings-gresham-chicago-gun-violence.

Rankine, Claudia. "'The Condition of Black Life Is One of Mourning,'" *New York Times Magazine,* June 22, 2015. https://www.nytimes.com/2015/06/22/magazine/the-condition-of-black-life-is-one-of-mourning.html.

Rebuild Foundation. "Objects of Care: Material Memorial for Tamir Rice." November 12, 2017. https://www.rebuild-foundation.org/objects-of-care/. Site discontinued.

"Reps. Adams, Underwood and Sen. Booker Introduce Black Maternal Health Week Resolutions." Press release, US Congresswoman Alma Adams, April 13, 2023. https://adams.house.gov/media-center/press-releases/reps-adams-underwood-sen-booker-introduce-black-maternal-health-week-1.

Revilla, Anita Tijerina. "Attempted Spirit Murder: Who Are Your Spirit Protectors and Your Spirit Restorers?" *Educational Foundations* 34, no. 1 (2021): 31–46.

Rice, Bradley R. "Maynard Jackson (1938–2003)." *New Georgia Encyclopedia.* Last updated August 1, 2020. https://www.georgiaencyclopedia.org/articles/government-politics/maynard-jackson-1938-2003.

Rice, Samaria, and Theaster Gates. *Samaria Rice: A Mother Speaks (Excerpt).* SoundCloud. Accessed June 11, 2020. https://soundcloud.com/user-803138657/samaria-rice-a-mother-speaks-excerpt.

Richardson, Matt. *The Queer Limit of Memory: Black Lesbian Literature and Irresolution.* Columbus: The Ohio State University Press, 2013.

Roberts, Dorothy E. *Killing the Black Body: Race, Reproduction, and the Meaning of Liberty.* New York: Pantheon Books, 1997.

Rocío, Aranda-Alvarado. "Bodies of Color: Images of Women in the Works of Firelei Báez and Rachelle Mozman." *Small Axe* 21, no. 1 (2017): 58–70.

Ross, Loretta J. "Loretta J. Ross: Biographical Note." Accessed January 19, 2021. https://lorettajross.com.

Ross, Loretta, and Ricki Solinger. *Reproductive Justice: An Introduction.* Oakland: University of California Press, 2017.

Rouse, Karen. "Family and Faith Guide Eric Garner's Mother after His Death." *WNYC,* July 17, 2015. https://www.wnyc.org/story/family-and-faith-guide-eric-garners-mother-after-his-death/.

Sakho, Jacqueline Roebuck. "Black Activist Mothering: Teach Me about What Teaches You." *Western Journal of Black Studies* 41, no. 1–2 (2017): 6–19.

Saunders, Patricia. "Defending the Dead, Confronting the Archive: A Conversation with M. NourbeSe Philip." *Small Axe* 12, no. 2 (2008): 63–79.

Sawyer, Lena, and Nana Osei-Kofi. "'Listening' with Gothenburg's Iron Well: Engaging the Imperial Archive through Black Feminist Methodologies and Arts-Based Research." *Feminist Review* 125, no. 1 (2020): 54–61.

Schwartz, Marie Jenkins. *Birthing a Slave: Motherhood and Medicine in the Antebellum South.* Cambridge, MA: Harvard University Press, 2006.

Schwartz, Marie Jenkins. "The WPA Narratives as Historical Sources." In *The Oxford Handbook of the African American Slave Narrative*, edited by John Ernest, 89–100. Oxford University Press, 2014. https://doi.org/10.1093/oxfordhb/9780199731480.013.007.

Scott, David. "Introduction: On the Archaeologies of Black Memory." *Small Axe* 12, no. 2 (2008): v–xvi.

Sexton, Jared. *Black Men, Black Feminism: Lucifer's Nocturne.* London: Palgrave McMillan. 2018.

Sexton, Jared. "Unbearable Blackness." *Cultural Critique* 90 (2015): 159–78.

Sharpe, Christina Elizabeth. *In the Wake: On Blackness and Being.* Durham, NC: Duke University Press, 2016.

Shockley, Evie. "Going Overboard: African American Poetic Innovation and the Middle Passage." *Contemporary Literature* 52, no. 4 (2011): 791–817. https://doi.org/10.1353/cli.2011.0051.

Siemaszko, Corky. "City of Cleveland Settles Lawsuit over Tamir Rice Shooting for $6M." *NBC News*, April 25, 2016. https://www.nbcnews.com/news/us-news/city-cleveland-settles-tamir-rice-lawsuit-6-million-n561671.

Singh, Gurcharan, and G. Archana. "Unraveling the Mystery of Vernix Caseosa." *Indian Journal of Dermatology* 53, no. 2 (2008): 54–60. https://doi.org/10.4103/0019-5154.41645.

Singh, Julietta. *No Archive Will Restore You.* Santa Barbara, CA: Punctum Books, 2018.

Singh, Rachel. "Atlanta Streets: When Roads Become Walls." Atlanta History Center. March 11, 2022. https://www.atlantahistorycenter.com/blog/atlanta-street-names-when-roads-become-walls/.

Sirvent, Roberto. "BAR Book Forum: Alys Eve Weinbaum's 'The Afterlife of Reproductive Slavery.'" *Black Agenda Report*, March 13, 2019. https://www.blackagendareport.com/bar-book-forum-alys-eve-weinbaums-afterlife-reproductive-slavery.

Skakur, Assata. *Assata: An Autobiography.* Chicago: Lawrence Hill Books, 1978.

Skinner, Makala, and Ioana Hulbert. "A*CENSUS II All Archivists Survey Report." *Ithaka S+R*, August 22, 2022. https://doi.org/10.18665/sr.317224.

Smith, Barbara. *Toward a Black Feminist Criticism.* Brooklyn, NY: Out & Out Books, 1980.

Smith, Christen A. "Slow Death: Is the Trauma of Police Violence Killing Black Women?" *The Conversation*, July 11, 2016. http://theconversation.com/slow-death-is-the-trauma-of-police-violence-killing-Black-women-62264.

Smith, Christen A. "Sorrow as Artifact: Radical Black Mothering in Times of Terror—a Prologue." *Transforming Anthropology* 24, no. 1 (2016): 5–7. https://doi.org/10.1111/traa.12061.

Smith, Mitch. "Tamir Rice's Family to Receive $6 Million from Cleveland." *New York Times*, April 26, 2016. https://www.nytimes.com/2016/04/26/us/tamir-rice-family-cleveland-settlement.html.

Smith, TK. "Embracing the Infinite Mother." *We No Longer Consider Them Damaged* exhibition essay, Flaten Art Museum, October 1, 2020.

Smithsonian Institution. "Bill of Sale for Charlotte and Her Daughter Kate to John Rouzee." Object 2011.104.4. Collection of the Smithsonian National Museum of African American History and Culture, Gift from the Liljenquist Family Collection. https://collections.si.edu/search/record/ark:/65665/fd51f7cdac4578a48608e13e780debbc6d6.

Snorton, C. Riley. "What More Can I Say? (A Prose-Poem on Antiblackness)." *Feminist Wire*, September 3, 2014, https://thefeministwire.com/2014/09/can-say-prose-poem-antiblackness/.

Society of American Archivists. "Appraisal." Dictionary of Archives Terminology. Accessed June 17, 2020. https://dictionary.archivists.org/entry/appraisal.html.

Society of American Archivists. "Document." Dictionary of Archives Terminology. Accessed January 29, 2020. https://dictionary.archivists.org/entry/document.html.

Southworth, B. (contributor 47206904). "Memorial Page for Eric Antonio Middlebrooks (1966–19 May 1980)." Find a Grave Memorial ID 7874183, citing Kennedy Memorial Gardens, Cedar Grove, DeKalb County, Georgia, USA. https://www.findagrave.com/memorial/7874183/eric-antonio-middlebrooks.

Spencer, Robyn C. *The Revolution Has Come: Black Power, Gender, and the Black Panther Party in Oakland*. Durham, NC: Duke University Press, 2016.

Spillers, Hortense J. "Mama's Baby, Papa's Maybe: An American Grammar Book." *Diacritics* 17, no. 2 (1987): 65–81.

Springer, Kimberly. *Living for the Revolution: Black Feminist Organizations, 1968–1980*. Durham, NC: Duke University Press, 2005.

Steinhauer, Jillian. "An Artist Honors Tamir Rice, One Orange Object at a Time." *New York Times*, July 29, 2018. https://www.nytimes.com/2018/07/29/arts/design/tamir-rice-cleveland-triennial-orange-rakowitz.html.

Stewart, Elizabeth A., et al. "The Burden of Uterine Fibroids for African-American Women: Results of a National Survey." *Journal of Women's Health* 22, no. 10 (2013): 807–16. https://doi.org/10.1089/jwh.2013.4334.

Stoler, Ann Laura. *Along the Archival Grain: Epistemic Anxieties and Colonial Common Sense*. Princeton, NJ: Princeton University Press, 2010.

Story, Kaila Adia, ed. *Patricia Hill Collins: Reconceiving Motherhood*. Bradford, ON: Demeter Press, 2014.

Suggs, Ernie. "From 2003: Maynard Jackson, 1938–2003: 'A Lion of a Man.'" *Atlanta Journal-Constitution*, August 19, 2019. https://www.ajc.com/news/atlanta-news/maynard-jackson-1938-2003-atlantas-first-black-mayor/BVCYTP3YELVSS3Y2LAJBB6ROGI/.

Suggs, Ernie. "From 2005: Atlanta Child Murders: Parents Never Gave Up Vigil for Missing Children." *Atlanta Journal and Constitution*, August 19, 2019. https://www.ajc.com/news/crime--law/atlanta-child-murders-parents-never-gave-vigil-for-missing-children/vktuFnWGSl3DkisN8dHi7H/.

Summers, Brandi Thompson. "*La Douleur Exquise*: Neoliberalism, Race, and the Un/Making of Blackness in the 21st Century." PhD diss., University of California Santa Cruz, 2014. https://escholarship.org/uc/item/0cm3k0c7.

Sutherland, Tonia. "Reading Gesture: Katherine Dunham, the Dunham Technique, and the Vocabulary of Dance as Decolonizing Archival Praxis." *Archival Science* 19, no. 2 (2019): 167–83. https://doi.org/10.1007/s10502-019-09308-w.

Swaby, Nydia A., and Chandra Frank. "Archival Experiments, Notes and (Dis)Orientations." *Feminist Review* 125, no. 1 (2020): 4–16.

Taylor, Diana. *The Archive and the Repertoire: Performing Cultural Memory in the Americas*. Durham, NC: Duke University Press, 2003.

Thompson, Krista. *Shine: The Visual Economy of Light in African Diasporic Aesthetic Practice.* Durham, NC: Duke University Press, 2015.

Tinsley, Omise'eke N. "Black Atlantic, Queer Atlantic: Queer Imaginings of the Middle Passage." *GLQ: A Journal of Lesbian and Gay Studies* 14 (2008): 191–215.

Trivedi, Somil. "The Family Separation Crisis Exposes America's Addiction to Incarceration." *TheHill.com,* June 30, 2018. https://thehill.com/opinion/criminal-justice/394197-the-family-separation-crisis-exposes-Americas-addiction-to-incarceration.

Trouillot, Michel-Rolph. *Silencing the Past: Power and the Production of History.* Boston: Beacon, 1995.

Tucker, Susan, Patricia Buckler, and Katherine Ott, eds. "An Introduction to the History of Scrapbooks." In *The Scrapbook in American Life,* edited by Tucker, Buckler, and Ott, 1–21. Philadelphia: Temple University Press, 2006.

Turner, Sasha. *Contested Bodies: Pregnancy, Childrearing, and Slavery in Jamaica.* Philadelphia: University of Pennsylvania Press, 2017.

Tynes, Brendane. "What the Reimagination of Breonna Taylor's (After)Life Reveals." *Feminist Media Studies* 21, no. 5 (2021): 864–67. https://doi.org/10.1080/14680777.2021.1944892.

Urban Dictionary. "Can I Live." Accessed June 16, 2020. https://www.urbandictionary.com/define.php?term=can%20i%20live.

US Copyright Office. "Definitions." Copyright.gov. https://www.copyright.gov/help/faq/faq-definitions.html.

US Department of Labor and Office of Policy Planning Research. *The Negro Family: The Case for National Action.* Michigan, 1965, 1982.

VanDiver, Rebecca K. "Off the Wall, into the Archive: Black Feminist Curatorial Practices of the 1970s." *Archives of American Art Journal* 55, no. 2 (2016): 26–45. https://doi.org/10.1086/689714.

Walcott, Rinaldo. "Outside in Black Studies: Reading from a Queer Place in the Diaspora." In *Black Queer Studies: A Critical Anthology,* edited by Mae Henderson and E. Patrick Johnson, 90–105. Durham, NC: Duke University Press, 2005.

Walker, Alice. *The Color Purple.* New York: Harcourt Brace Jovanovich, 1970.

Walker, Alice. *In Search of Our Mothers' Gardens: Womanist Prose.* A Harvest Book. San Diego, CA: Harcourt Brace Jovanovich, 1983.

Walker, Margaret. *How I Wrote Jubilee and Other Essays on Life and Literature.* Old Westbury, NY: Feminist Press, 1990.

Walker, Margaret. *Jubilee.* Boston: Houghton Mifflin, 1966.

Walker, Margaret. *On Being Female, Black, and Free: Essays by Margaret Walker, 1932–1992.* Edited by Maryemma Graham. Knoxville: University of Tennessee Press, 1997.

Walker, Margaret. "We Have Been Believers." *Poetry* 53, no. 6 (1939): 302–3.

Walker, Margaret, and Claudia Tate. "Interview with Margaret Walker." In *Black Women Writers at Work,* edited by Claudia Tate, foreword by Tillie Olsen. Chicago: Haymarket Books, 2023.

Wallace, Michele. *Black Macho and the Myth of the Superwoman.* New York: Dial Press, 1979.

Ward, Jesmyn. *Men We Reaped: A Memoir.* New York: Bloomsbury, 2013.

Washington, Isaiah. "Our Black Ophelias and Poseidons: Forming a Black Aquatic Heritage in Film and Literature When Swimming Inability Is a Family Heirloom." Senior thesis prospectus, American University, 2022.

Weber, Jasmine. "Samaria Rice, Mother of Tamir Rice, Speaks Out about Art Depicting Her Son after Canceled Exhibition in Cleveland." *Hyperallergic,* July 8, 2020. https://hyperallergic.com/573053/moca-cleveland-the-breath-of-empty-space/.

Weinbaum, Alys Eve. *The Afterlife of Reproductive Slavery: Biocapitalism and Black Feminism's Philosophy of History.* Durham, NC: Duke University Press, 2019.

Wilderson, Frank B. Verfasser. *Incognegro: A Memoir of Exile and Apartheid.* Durham, NC: Duke University Press, 2008.

Wilderson, Frank B. *Red, White and Black: Cinema and the Structure of U.S. Antagonisms.* Durham, NC: Duke University Press, 2010.

Williams, Rhaisa Kameela. "Toward a Theorization of Black Maternal Grief as Analytic." *TRAA Transforming Anthropology* 24, no. 1 (2016): 17–30.

Williams-Forson, Psyche. *Building Houses out of Chicken Legs: Black Women, Food, and Power.* Chapel Hill: University of North Carolina Press, 2016.

Woodard, Vincent. *The Delectable Negro: Human Consumption and Homoeroticism within US Slave Culture.* New York: NYU Press, 2014.

Yates-Richard, Meina. "'What Is Your Mother's Name?': Maternal Disavowal and the Reverberating Aesthetic of Black Women's Pain in Black Nationalist Literature." *American Literature* 88, no. 3 (2016): 477–507. https://doi.org/10.1215/00029831-3650211.

Yehuda, Rachel, and Amy Lehrner. "Intergenerational Transmission of Trauma Effects: Putative Role of Epigenetic Mechanisms." *World Psychiatry* 17, no. 3 (2018): 243–57. https://doi.org/10.1002/wps.20568.

INDEX

abstraction, 21–22
activism, 136–40
Alexander, M. Jacqui, 9
Anthony, Susan B., 13
anti-Blackness, 45, 83–84, 132
appraisal, standpoint, 127–30
archival labor, 6, 20, 112, 118, 133. *See also* Black maternal archival praxis
archival misrepresentation, 16–19
Arnheim, Rudolph, 21
arterial imagery, 101–2, 105, 121
arts production, 23–24
Atlanta: Bowen Homes day care explosion, 43, 49; as "The City Too Busy to Hate," 30, 42n47; criminal neglect, 46; Maynard Jackson as mayor, 30–32, 39–44; during midcentury, 38–44; missing cases in, 25, 43–44; and Reagan administration, 46–47. *See also Those Bones Are Not My Child*
Atlanta Child Murders, 25, 29–31, 41, 44–45, 49, 53–54, 56–57
Autobiography of My Mother, The (Kincaid), 93, 94

Avilez, GerShun, 48
Awgeman, Yaw, 113–14

Báez, Firelei, 26, 91, 101
Bailey, Jefferson, 131
Baldwin, James, 48–49
Bambara, Toni Cade, 3, 25, 144. *See also Those Bones Are Not My Child*
Belle, La Vaughn, 26, 106
Beloved (Morrison), 9
bill of sale, 16–18, 17 fig. 1
Birmingham Church attack, 49n75
black belief, 22, 89
Black death, 30, 110–11, 116–17, 119, 127, 129
Black feminists, 70, 118–19, 131; activism, 14–16, 133, 136–38, 144; standpoint appraisal, 127–30; truth and history, 75–79
Black futurity, 137, 138
Black Girl's Window (Saar), 125
Black light / Black life, 53
Black Lives Matter movement, 15, 25, 110, 116, 148

Black Macho and the Myth of the Superwoman (1979), 143

Black maternal archival praxis, 3, 110–16; exclusion and, 131–34; gazebo within histories, 124–27; in historical space(s), 116–24; practice of refusal, 122–24; standpoint appraisal, 127–30

Black maternal superbody, 136–37, 140, 145–46

Black memorial, 111

Black motherhood, 2, 6–8, 15–16, 21–24, 143; bad, 48–52; in discordant archive, 23; historicizing, 10–14; origins of, 24n75

Black mourning, 123, 139

Black Panthers, 69, 142

Black visuality, 112, 119, 124

Blake, Felice, 90

body and separation, 90–93; lung (grief), 107–9; mother tongue, 93–104; womb (displacement), 104–7

Bonaparte, Alicia D., 12n39

Bontemps, Arna, 62, 64, 65

Booker, Chaikaia, 125

Bowen Homes day care, 43, 49

Brand, Dionne, 26, 91, 92, 93

Breath, Eyes, Memory (Danticat), 91, 93, 95, 103

Brooks, Gwendolyn, 42

Brother, I'm Dying (Danticat), 91, 93, 103

Brown, Elaine, 69

Brown, Kimberly Juanita, 139

Butler, Octavia, 21, 68

Campt, Tina, 19n58, 122, 130, 137, 138

captivity, 105, 106, 107

Caribbean islands, 93

Caswell, Michelle, 128, 133

Catlett, Elizabeth, 22, 23, 62, 64–65

chattel slavery, 2, 11, 12, 144

Christian, Barbara, 23

cisgendered women, 8, 10–11

civil rights movement, 38, 42n47, 49n75, 68

Cleveland, 113

Clifton, Lucille, 20

Clitandre, Nadège, 102

Cooks, Bridget R., 117

Cooper, Anna Julia, 13

Cooper Owens, Deirdre, 135–36

copyright infringement, 60, 73

corals, 106–7

corporality, 91, 109, 139

Courlander, Harold, 74

criminal neglect, 46

cultural production, 16, 22, 26, 49n73; as archival labor, 118; as history-telling, 91

cut-outs, 123

Cvetkovich, Ann, 118n26

Dalkon Shield, 15

Danticat, Edwidge, 26, 99, 108–9; *Breath, Eyes, Memory,* 91, 93, 95, 103; *Brother, I'm Dying,* 91, 93, 103

Davis, Angela, 69, 144

demographic changes, 40

diasporic Blackness, 105

disappearance, 29–35, 43, 54–55, 58

disposable subjects, 54–55

dispossession, 9–10. *See also* maternal dispossession

documentation, institutional, 16–19

Doubleday, 61, 72

Dunham, Katherine, 131

Economic Opportunity Atlanta, 53

Ellis, Nadia, 94

enslavement, 19

Enwezor, Okwui, 120

epistemic violence, 112, 121

Evidence of Things Not Seen, The (1985), 49

fact creation, 83, 139

Farmer, Ashley, 131

Fett, Sharla M., 12

filial dispossession, 8, 11, 21

forced migration, 4

Frazier, E. Franklin, 13–14

frustration, 94

fungibility, 35

Garner, Erica, 27, 138, 147–50
Gates, Theaster, 27, 112, 132–33
gazebo, 110–12, 113, 115–16, 120, 124–27, 130, 132–33
gendered violence, 12, 99n32, 117
generational traumas, 91, 95
genocidal violence, 120–21
German, Vanessa, 125
Gilger, Kristin, 88
Giovanni, Nikki, 61, 69, 71, 78
Gordon, Avery, 35
Graham, Maryemma, 67, 79, 100n34
Grant, Chantell, 137–38
Great Migration, 11, 34, 56
Gregson v. Gilbert (1783) case, 33
grief, 27, 93, 102–4, 108, 109, 111–12, 117, 122–24
Ground Cover. See *Those Bones Are Not My Child*
Gumbs, Alexis Pauline, 139–40
gun violence, 137

Haiti, 95–96, 99, 103
Haley, Alex, 25, 61, 69, 72, 78–79, 82, 86. See also *Roots*
Hartman, Saidiya, 35
Hartsfield, William B., 55
Hartsfield Airport, 40, 55
haunting, 35
health care system, 148
heterosexuality, 8
Histology of Different Classes of Uterine Tumors, The (Mutu), 104
historical mining, 130
homicides, 137–38
Horton-Stallings, LaMonda, 32–33
Huggins, Ericka, 142
Hughes, Langston, 34
Hunter, J. Muscoe G., 16

illegal immigrants, 103
imaginations, 33, 75, 80, 85, 139
In The Mecca (Brooks), 42
institutional documentation, 16–19

intergenerational trauma, 91, 96
intersectionality, 140, 144

Jackson, Maynard, 30–32, 39–44, 46, 53, 56, 58
Jefferson, Atatiana, 149
Jordan, June, 149
journaling, 64, 85
Jubilee (Walker), 25, 59–63, 69–70, 81
Judd, Bettina, 93

Kent, Caroline, 21n67
kidnappings, 48–49, 53–54
Kincaid, Jamaica, 93, 94
Kindred (Butler), 21, 68

Larsen, Nella, 34
Lawrence, Jacob, 62, 64, 65
literary arts, 33
Lorde, Audre, 143–44
loss of voice, 100
lungs, 104, 107–9
lynching, 11, 22, 34, 110

mapping, 55
marginalization, 37, 142, 145
Martin, Trayvon, 110
materiality and memorial making, 110–12; Black maternal grief (Tamir Rice), 113–16; exclusion and Black archival practice, 131–34; in historical spaces, 116–21; practice of refusal, 122–24; situating gazebo within histories, 124–27; standpoint appraisal, 127–30
maternal dispossession: definition of, 7; engaging nonrecord, 20–27; in institutional documentation, 16–19; reproductive justice violation, 10–14; schema of, 10; theory and experience, 8–10
maternal estrangement, 95–96
McClain, Dani, 143, 146
medical superbody, 135–36
memorialization, 122. See also materiality and memorial making
memory work, 4, 24, 56, 112, 119, 129

memory-keeping, 20, 26, 74–75, 83, 85; *Alexander v. Haley* case, 71–75; toward historical (un)knowability, 80–84; materialities and documentation, 84–89; reproductive labor and maternal connection, 63–68; truth, 75–79; Walker's literary importance, 60–63, 68–71
#MeToo movement, 19, 86
Middlebrooks, Eric, 56
Mining the Museum (Wilson), 117
Missing and Murdered Children crisis. *See* Atlanta Child Murders
Morgan, Jennifer, 12
Morrison, Toni, 9, 49n71, 72, 82, 83, 94
mother tongue, 93–104
mother-child dispossession. *See* maternal dispossession
motherhood, 14, 23. *See also* Black motherhood
motherlands, 92, 94–95
Mothers of the Movement, 128n67
Movement for Black Lives, 15, 110, 136
Moynihan, Daniel, 13–14
Moynihan Report, 13–14, 52
Mutu, Wangechi, 91, 104
mythmaking, 143, 145

Nash, Jennifer C., 144
natal alienation, 8–9
National Museum of African American History and Culture (NMAAHC), 16–17
Nixon, Rob, 49n73
No Language Is Neutral (Brand), 91
nuclear family, 14

Objects of Care, 111, 113–16, 127
online campaigns, 19
Outsider, The, 34
overprotective parenting, 10
Owens, Deirdre Cooper, 12

parturiency, 12
Patterson, Orlando, 8–9
Philip, M. NourbeSe, 33, 91, 94, 97–98

photography, 120
plagiarism, 71–72, 81
Polanco, Gerardo, 93, 108
police brutality, 146, 148
practice of refusal, 122–24

quantum immortality, 149
Queer Limit, 7n18

racial passing, 34
racialized mapping, 55
Rakowitz, Michael, 126
Randall, Tom, 4n6
Reagan administration, 46–47
refusal, practice of, 122–24
refused materials, 124–26
religion, 70
reproductive injustice, 74–75, 83, 86, 147
reproductive justice, 73, 136, 145–46; and Black women's activism, 14–16; framing dispossession as violation, 10–14
reproductive labor, 59, 71–72, 85; cultural production and, 26; and maternal connection, 63–68
reproductive rights, 11–12, 21, 111, 140, 142, 145
reproductive violence, xiii, 12, 20, 62
restorative justice, 10
Rice, Samaria, 27, 111, 113–16, 120–21, 125–27, 132–33
Rice, Tamir, 27, 109, 110–12, 113–16, 120, 126–27, 131
Roberts, Dorothy E., xi–xii
Robins, A. H., 15
Roots (Haley), 26, 61, 72–73, 82
Ross, Loretta, 14, 15
Rouzee, John, 16–18

Saar, Betye, 124–25
#SayHerName movement, 19
Schwartz, Marie Jenkins, 12
Scott, David, 88
scrap aesthetics, 86, 88
scrapbooks, 60, 72, 77, 85–89

scraps, 4–6, 112, 128; theorizing, 122–24; writing using, 35–38
self-care, 140
self-possession, 9
separation. *See* body and separation
Sexton, Jared, 146
sexual violence, 95–97
Shakur, Assata, 69, 124n51, 142
sharecropping, 11
Sharpe, Christina, 106, 121
She Tries Her Tongue, Her Silence Softly Breaks (Philip), 91, 94, 97–98
Silencing the Past (Trouillot), 117–18
silencing/unsilencing framework, 102
slave subjectivity, 9
slow violence, 49n73
Snorton, C. Riley, 4n8
social isolation, 104
social locations, 143
Solinger, Rickie, 14
Song of Solomon (Morrison), 94
Spillers, Hortense J., 24n75
standpoint appraisal, 127–30
Stony Island Arts Bank, 112, 117, 132
S.T.O.P. (Save Them or Perish), 32, 46n57, 50
story theft, 74
Stoudemire, Andrea, 137–38
stress, 105
structural dispossession, 35
Sutherland, Tonia, 131

Thomas, Hank Willis, 112
Those Bones Are Not My Child (Bambara), 28–32, 41–42; and Atlanta during mid-century, 38–44; dedication page, 44–48; and disappearance, 32–35; and material memorialization, 56–58; and maternal terror, 48–52; shared space of visibility, 53–56; writing using scraps, 35–38; Zala Spencer (character), 29, 38, 41, 45, 47–48, 50, 54
Till-Mobley, Mamie, xiii, 116
Tinsley, Omise'eke Natasha, 7–8, 92
transformative speech, 139

transnational feminism, 118
Trouillot, Michel-Rolph, 117–18, 139
T-shirts, 123
Turner, Sasha, 12
Twenty-First Amendment, 13
Tynes, Brendane, 99n32

uncomfortability, 130
unspeakability, 16
urban renewal, 125
urtext, 69

VanDiver, Rebecca, 125–26
vernix, 98–99
veterans' struggle, 43
Vietnam, 43
violations against Black women, 10–14
visual literacy, 131
Voice after Memory (Báez), 101

wake work, 121
Walker, Alice, 23, 68–69
Walker, Margaret, 25–26, 100n34; *Alexander v. Haley* case, 71–75; astrology practice, 66, 76; *How I Wrote Jubilee*, 80, 81n56; *Last Rites*, 87; literary importance, 61–63; philosophy of history, 68–71, 84; *This Is My Century*, 64. See also *Jubilee*
Wallace, Michele, 136, 142–43
Ward, Jesmyn, 123
water, 92, 106–7
Weinbaum, Alys Eve, 20, 75
Wells, Ida B., 13
white supremacy, 45–46, 130, 144
wholeness, 94–95, 139
Wilderson, Frank B., 24n75
Williams, Wayne, 43–44, 49
Wilson, Fred, 117
womb, 104–7
Wright, Richard, 34, 62, 63, 79

Zong, 33

www.ingramcontent.com/pod-product-compliance
Lightning Source LLC
Chambersburg PA
CBHW030139240426
43672CB00005B/189